Lucky is the Na...

by Alfred Barrows

Compiled and edited by Michael Anderton
& Pip Wright

Published by **Pawprint Publishing**
14, Polstead Close, Stowmarket, Suffolk   IP14 2PJ

Other books by Pip Wright
Lydia
Death Recorded
I Read it in the local Rag (pub. by Poppyland Publishing)
Exploring Suffolk by Bus Pass
Exploring East Anglia by Bus Pass
Thomas Slapp's Booke of Physicke
The Watery Places of Suffolk

Books by Pip & Joy Wright
**The Amazing Story of John Heigham Steggall,
'The Suffolk Gipsy'**
Newspapers in Suffolk (6 vols)
Grave Reports
Witches in and around Suffolk
Bygone Cotton
The Diary of a Poor Suffolk Woodman
(with Léonie Robinson, pub. by Poppyland Publishing)

Other books by Michael Anderton
Suffolk Town Trails
Suffolk Country Walks: volumes 1-4
R.A.F. 'Plumber'
Six Country Walks from The Case

www.pipwright.com   www.anderton.btinternet.co.uk
www.poppyland.co.uk

This is the story of a Suffolk farming family over a period of about one hundred years, and is perfectly true. (any uncertainty regarding the facts is clearly indicated) It begins with an introduction to the head of the family, Lucky Burrows. Born in humble surroundings, but by dogged determination, hard work and no outside financial help, he was able to build up a group of farms consisting of over a thousand acres, four hundred of which he owned.

The author, Alfred Burrows, was the youngest of Lucky Burrows' eleven children, and the story ends when Alf marries for the second time. All the incidents described are closely connected with the immediate members of the family and the villages in which they lived.

It is life exactly as it happened and includes excitement, ambition, disappointment, love, sorrow, joy, frustration and contentment. Involved in the narrative is murder, several suicides and the known history of two of the farms going back to before Domesday.

The author at one time lived at a farm, the land of which was once owned by Edward the Confessor's brother-in-law, who later became King Harold II. Nineteen years were spent at a second farm whose recorded history goes back to the same period, and King John and his court were entertained for a night at this farm where, at that time, stood a large manor house.

"Time like an ever rolling stream bears all its sons away." Isaac Watts

Thanks are owed to Lucky Burrows, Nan Drew,
David Bannister, Melanie Blanchard,
Christopher & Philip Turner,
Peter Davidson & Wickham Skeith History Group,
Jeremy Steventon-Barnes, Keith Baker, Ted Fenning,
Mrs. Deed, Julian Cunningham, Judy Broadway,
Mr. & Mrs. Williamson, Mr. & Mrs. Wyatt,
Mr. & Mrs. Stanford and the staff of the Suffolk Record Offices
at Bury St. Edmunds and Ipswich.

Photographs used in this book were supplied by: Peter Davidson, David Bannister,
Philip Turner & Nan Drew: also a number belonging to the editors have been used.
Pictures used in this book include those by Daniel Wright: pages 49, 146.
Sandra Canning: pages 4, 24, 35, 41, 155, 167, 253, 256, 295.
Leonard Squirrell: on page 247 (reproduced by kind permission of Annette Kenny)
Harry Becker: on pages 21, 40. G. Leon Little: on pages 18, 193.
J. Hulmes: front and back cover reproduced by kind permission of Andrew Jackson.
The artist who painted the picture on page 2 is so far unidentified.

The Burrows Family

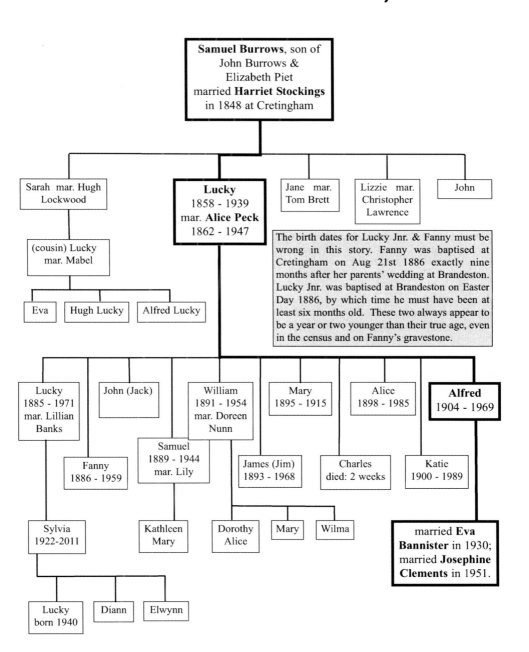

Samuel Burrows, son of John Burrows & Elizabeth Piet married **Harriet Stockings** in 1848 at Cretingham

Sarah mar. Hugh Lockwood

Lucky 1858 - 1939 mar. **Alice Peck** 1862 - 1947

Jane mar. Tom Brett

Lizzie mar. Christopher Lawrence

John

(cousin) Lucky mar. Mabel

The birth dates for Lucky Jnr. & Fanny must be wrong in this story. Fanny was baptised at Cretingham on Aug 21st 1886 exactly nine months after her parents' wedding at Brandeston. Lucky Jnr. was baptised at Brandeston on Easter Day 1886, by which time he must have been at least six months old. These two always appear to be a year or two younger than their true age, even in the census and on Fanny's gravestone.

Eva | Hugh Lucky | Alfred Lucky

Lucky 1885 - 1971 mar. Lillian Banks

John (Jack)

William 1891 - 1954 mar. Doreen Nunn

Mary 1895 - 1915

Alice 1898 - 1985

Alfred 1904 - 1969

Fanny 1886 - 1959

Samuel 1889 - 1944 mar. Lily

James (Jim) 1893 - 1968

Charles died: 2 weeks

Katie 1900 - 1989

Sylvia 1922-2011

Kathleen Mary

Dorothy Alice | Mary | Wilma

married **Eva Bannister** in 1930; married **Josephine Clements** in 1951.

Lucky born 1940 | Diann | Elwynn

Lucky is the Name

Chapter 1

Do you ever feel you have lived a century? Actually, I very much feel that I have been around for at least one hundred and fifty years.

The fact is, I was born in 1904, but the reason I can place myself so far back is because I am the youngest child of a family of ten, which means that my eldest brother is eighteen years older than I, and following everything he did took me back some fifteen years before I was born. Then again, Father being forty-six when I was born, took me back forty years before my time, and listening eagerly to tales of his father, my knowledge of life seems to have begun about 1820.

This is not a story of a national hero, inventor or discoverer, but just a span of time within the lifetime and memory of a very ordinary country family, living on isolated farms. The name of the family is 'Burrows'; my name is Alfred. I am not named after anyone. My parents had not thought of a name until the time was running out to have me registered. Father, standing at the door demands, "What shall we call it?" Mother suggests Stanley, Percy or Benjamin.
Father says, "What about Alfred?"
Mother says wearily, "Yes, that will do."

Forty-six years before my birth, when Father was born, his name was easily decided upon. A neighbour bet my father's parents half-a-crown they dare not name him Lucky. As the half-a-crown was more valuable than a name, Lucky he was called, registered and christened. So, Lucky he was by name and nature for the next eighty years.

Sam & Harriet Burrows (Alf's grandparents)

An old aunt of mine tried in her way to build a family tree. She traced the family back to my great-great-grandfather, who happened to be some kind of wanderer from no-one knew where, and settled in a village called Brandeston near Framlingham in Suffolk. Father was born in the adjoining village of Cretingham in 1858, the son of a farm-worker who brought up five children on nine shillings a week. This was an improvement on his grandfather who, at one time, got just six shillings a week. At one period, this barely paid for the flour. They had to steal turnips and swedes to exist.

However, my father, survived. His first job, as was usual in his day, was scaring rooks for the reward of twopence a day. His mother worked on the land picking stones to be used for mending the roads, and other seasonal work. At the age of nine, he left school and started work in earnest. Compulsory education after the age of ten did not begin until 1876. He started ploughing with a pair of horses before he was strong enough to lift the plough, so the men turned the horses and set the plough at the ends of the field. He did the rest. Thus he carried on with the routine of farm work for several years.

At about the age of eighteen, he went to Burton-on-Trent to work in the maltings, and he went back there for another season or two. After that, feeling he would like a change, Lucky joined one of the North Sea fishing fleets, but being such a bad sailor, he could only endure it for a fortnight.

Lucky Burrows senior - Alf's father

He then at Yarmouth joined the army; the 9th Norfolks. One morning, the parents of this would-be fisherman received a parcel of clothing, Lucky's civilian clothes, with no information enclosed as to why these garments had been sent home. As the last news that the poor old parents had received was that their son had joined the fishing fleet, they assumed he had been drowned at sea. This they believed for five years, a thing my father regretted all his life.

After being enrolled as Private Burrows, number 1914, 9th Norfolk Regiment, he was sent to Currah Camp in Ireland for a short time. Then he was sent to India for five years.

He had been in India for four years when he recognised a man from near his home in Suffolk. Private Burrows was on guard duty at the time. Deciding on the spur of the moment that he would not make himself known, he did an about-turn and marched in the opposite direction. The other Suffolk man shouted, "Hello Lucky; you should

have stood still. As soon as you walked, I knew it was you."
You see, Lucky had one leg slightly longer than the other, which made his walk quite recognisable.

This other man was soon drafted back to England. He, of course, saw Father's parents and told them that their son was alive and well, and that he had seen and spoken to him in India. For five long years they had thought their boy was drowned. On hearing this news, their feelings are better imagined than described.

During his service in India, Father was caught up in the Afghanistan War of 1879. He, with his unit, went through the Khyber Pass and on to Kabul. I have no idea about their form of transport; perhaps they marched. I wish I had shown more interest when Father used to talk about his experiences, but that is the way of life: youth looks forward and age looks back; then when youth becomes old, he regrets having become bored by the tales told by his parents.

It was during an Afghanistan War in 1838-42 in which the British were involved, that a massacre occurred in the Khyber Pass: this pass is apparently thirty-three miles long and only ten feet wide in places.

Forty years later in 1879, the Norfolks including my father, were in the fighting and skirmishes around Kabul. They finished their mission and had to leave for India. Father, however, was very ill with a fever, much too ill to travel. In fact, it was believed that he would not recover. An officer left him in the care of some natives who were very kind to him and nursed him back to health. He always spoke of them with gratitude and tenderness. When he had fully recovered, he made his way from one lot of natives to another until he reached India again and rejoined his regiment. It must have been a journey of several hundreds of miles and, owing to the fever, he lost his hair, and therefore, was bald from his early twenties.

Father did contact his parents, during the last few months he was in India, by letter. My family still possesses several letters that Father wrote to his mother. These letters are now eighty-four years old and they make pathetic reading. Apparently, Father became converted while in the army and he wrote, "May God forgive me for being such a bad son. Should He spare my life to return home, I will do better." In another letter, he said, "Tell Father not to drink too much. I have taken no intoxicating drink for five years; it is not good for the health." Later, he wrote, "I am glad Father is not troubling the 'Bell' so much." ...also, "My dog Prince will be old when I come home; you must do what you think best; perhaps you had better make away with him."

My father never drank anything stronger than home-brewed beer for the rest of his life. He was also a non-smoker and his faith never weakened to the end of his days.

From reading his letters, I gathered the reason he decided not to contact his parents for so long was because in the small world he left behind him, folks believed that a man joining the army was escaping from something, or they thought it was to evade work.

In one letter, he wrote, "I don't suppose people will speak to me when I return. I know how they look upon a soldier. If they despise me, I know One who will not." No doubt these people knew of some-one who had reason to lose himself, and so judged all soldiers by him.

Well, Father was presented with his service medals; one for good conduct and another for abstention. We, his children, looked upon him as a hero and a model of righteousness. I never once heard him swear. He was an example we could hardly hope to live up to.

After completing his seven years service, he returned home and drew a small reserve pension for a few years, in addition to working on a farm, at the same time wondering how to improve his position. Regularly, he walked to Framlingham to collect his pension, a distance of about five miles. He was then a man of about twenty-seven, small but well made, a very good chest; five feet seven and a half inches tall and hardly known to ail anything. In fact, he was tough and very strong until he was nearly eighty.

It was going on one of those journeys that the reserve soldier saw a red-headed girl standing on a river bridge. I cannot ever imagine my father being a romantic lover; he seemed too practical.

In fact, I remember hearing him say forty years after the event, he realised he wanted someone to look after him. No doubt he managed as well as those before him and the millions who came after. These two young people knew each other by sight and by name.

The young man said, "Hello Alice."

The red-head said shyly, "Hello Lucky."

He asked, "Would you care to walk to Framlingham with me?"

The young lady accepted.

I never did hear any more details of the courtship: anyway, they walked down to the altar and Alice Peck became Alice Burrows. Whether there was a reception or honeymoon I cannot say. At least their celebrations could not have been less than one of the bride's older sisters, whose bride-groom could not afford time off to marry. They arranged their marriage when the bridegroom was working in a field close to the church. He tied his horses to the hedge, met his bride in the church, had the ceremony and then returned to work in the field.

Alice Burrows Snr.

Lucky and Alice are now to start their new life together.

Chapter 2

The newly-weds are now established in their cottage and father is working for a farmer. A year passes and their first son arrives. He of course has to be named 'Lucky.' Eighteen months pass: they have a daughter and call her Fanny. Thirty years later, when revisiting Cretingham to see relations, on passing a wood Father would say, "That used to be a meadow. I was mowing grass with a scythe there the day Fanny was born."

Within a year of Fanny's arrival, Father hired a smallholding of twenty-six acres in Stowupland, a village adjoining the small market town of Stowmarket. Here he kept pigs which increased rapidly by breeding. Father and Mother continued breeding children as quickly as possible. I would imagine it was a struggle of survival between pigs and kids. They now had Lucky, Fanny, John, Samuel, William, James, Mary and Alice. Between Mary and Alice was Charles: but he died at two weeks old.

Just about in the middle of the time when Father and Mother were producing their first eight children, paternal grandfather needed a home. Evidently it was not convenient for his daughters to have him as they had not the room. Father kindly said he could have a home with him; it did not actually make much difference to Father; it was Mother who bore the brunt of it all. Old people can get a bit irritable with small children and it upsets the harmony a little. Anyway, they managed somehow and grandfather stayed six years to finish his days.

Another twenty or so acres were added to the holding during the increase of pig and people population. The family still possess a photograph of Father, Mother and the eight children. Mother had every reason to be proud of the picture because, apart from Father's suit, she made all the clothes they wore. These were her own and the

13

girls' dresses, Father's and the boys' shirts, and even all the boys' suits. Mother was exceptional at needlework, a gift she inherited from her mother, aided by her teaching and her own experience. The feeding, clothing, nursing and the general demands of a family of eight just about taxed Mother's nerves and strength to the limit.

It would appear that after reaching eight in a family, each one that follows is less trouble to bring up. Because young Lucky was now twelve years old and had left school, he could help his father and save Mother many steps by doing errands and getting fire-fuel in. Fanny at eleven was beginning to become a second mother, so on my assumption, the older ones grew capable quicker than the younger ones arrived.

On the same principal, taking a second farm is less strain than the first, and the third even less, and so on. This brings me to the point that ten children do not create ten times more effort on their parents than one child.

The family kept growing up: young Lucky now thirteen and little Alice was one year old, with the other six in between. Father hired a farm of one hundred and thirty acres at Wickham Skeith, situated nine miles north of Stowmarket. This was called Oak Farm, the year was 1899 and the date to take possession was October 11th. The tribe of Lucky was all keyed up for the great move and the leader carefully planned the most economical method of doing so. Mother was flustered and worried; the children were so excited and making things more hectic. Each part of the plan had to coincide with the last night spent at Town Farm, Stowupland, followed by a breakfast. The next meal would be at Oak Farm, Wickham Skeith.

Between the two meals, all beds had to be taken down and loaded on the waggons with the essential last-used utensils. When the loading-up was completed, the horses were harnessed: Mother and the younger children on the first waggon with Father in charge. Young Lucky took charge of the second waggon, and with him some of the older children. Of course, Mother and some of the children had to find nooks and spaces amongst the bedsteads, bedding, pots and pans, carpets, meat-safes and 'wotnots' to travel in. The great exodus moved off. The seven and a half mile journey would take two and a half hours. They must have felt like the Israelites going to the promised land.

I know Mother would have had a snack meal prepared beforehand to eat before they began to unload. The horses would have been unharnessed, fed and watered, and Father would then have helped to get some of the things in place. I am sure Mother could not have done the rest alone; perhaps Mary Scarlett helped. I remember hearing she was a good neighbour.

Oak Farm, Wickham Skeith - compare with the picture on page 111

There were many more things to fetch from Stowupland; everything that could not walk had to be moved by horse transport. It would take several days. Next day, October 12th 1899, Father set off with horse and waggon, taking the five boys. He had a job for them.

This also was the day the the South African Boer War started, not that it made much difference to this family. After all, war in a distant country isn't of much consequence compared to moving a farm. They did just realise something was going on because Father's sister's son, our cousin Lucky (he had to have the family name) was soldiering as a career and was already in South Africa.

In the upheaval of their changing lives, Father and the boys had to get on with the moving and leave the South African job for someone else to deal with. No doubt they talked about it as they jogged along back to Stowupland.

When they arrived, and whilst having some food, the boys received further instructions about their respective jobs. Lucky and John were to drive the sows, an unenviable job you can imagine. These rather awkward creatures would want to turn into everybody's garden gate. They would have to be guided past the farms en-route. So off went these two boys aged thirteen and eleven, in charge of a herd of sows and responsible for getting them all the way to the new farm.

In my opinion, the other three boys had a very much worse task. They were detailed to drive the turkeys. Can anyone think of a more ridiculous problem than a flock of these birds being driven seven and a half miles on public roads by three small boys: Samuel aged ten, William eight and James only six. The story of this journey has been related to me several times in later years by Jim, as we now call him. One comfort at least was that there would be no possibility of encountering any self-propelled vehicles: it would have been rather unusual to see a bicycle, so it was just pedestrians or farm carts.

These boys had such difficulty in keeping the turkeys from flying over the field gates. When they saw a farm cart approaching, they had to manoeuvre the birds into a close pack near the hedge until the road was clear again. The last mile or so was the most difficult; the boys were tired, twilight was falling and the turkeys were instinctively flying onto gates, hoping to roost for the night.

Going back to Father, he had got the two older boys and the herd of swine onto the road and going well. He then went back to get the turkey drovers started. Returning again, he loaded all he could on the waggon and commenced his journey to Oak Farm. When he caught up with the turkey men, they had completed about one third of their journey, so with a few words of encouragement and more advice, he continued on his way. About one mile further on, he contacted the herdsmen with the sows; they were progressing very well. A few words to them, and Father finished his journey, attended to the horses and generally viewed the situation at the new farm. Then, it was indoors to see if the rest of the family were alright. After he had had some food, he walked back to meet the two lads and, getting the pigs safely installed, he went back to meet the turkey flock.

The last mile was a fairly straight, narrow piece of road known locally as Chantry Lane; grass was growing between the horse tracks and wheel tracks. It is tarred now. It finished at a triangular piece of grass known as 'Ox's Knoll'. Here the road divided. The right led to the village of Wickham Skeith, the left to Oak Farm and beyond this to another farm which was approached by a mile-long drive through meadows. So, we picture these three little lads, their father and a bunch of turkeys coming over Ox's Knoll, up the lane, through the farm gate and into the yard. Mother would surely have been there to meet the pathetic little band of settlers. Allowing for going from one side of the road to the other and back a few yards to keep up the stragglers, those boys must have walked at least fifteen miles. How her heart must have ached for them.

But when Father wanted a job done, it just had to be done. He never appeared to command anyone; never shouted at the children, but always kept a little apart from them, creating in them a sense of respect and fear. He was considerate, but beyond that displayed no pity and never admitted that he had given more to do than was possible.

If we did not complete his requests, he just looked straight at us with those very deep set eyes and would quietly say, "You did not do as I asked," or perhaps, "I see you did not quite finish your job." You would feel so guilty, you thought you were being looked upon as a shirker. Inside, you felt so bad that in time you found out that it was more pleasant to do the job than try to avoid it.

We dared not answer back; it was ridiculous to make excuses because he was always right. I think that during the time we were working for our father, each one of us went through frustration, worked ourselves into such a state of self-pity; inwardly we rebelled against him to an extent beyond reason, that it became beyond control. Each of us at some time, some of us more than others according to our sensitivity, turned on our father and told him it was impossible to satisfy him; that he was always finding fault, we could never do enough for him - and even if we did, there was no praise - and so on. On these occasions, his face would turn white and looking like marble; he would address us by our full name. In the case of myself who always went as Alfie in the family, it would be, "Alfred, if you are not satisfied, you can go. If you can better yourself anywhere else, you go. Never let it be said I stood in your way..." And of course he meant it. Had I packed my bags, he would in no way have tried to make me change my mind. If I had asked him to drive me to the station, he would have done so. In fact, two of my brothers did leave home. One of them left early one morning for Canada without a word to anyone. Father never asked either of them to come back.

To return to the story, it was a struggle of course. Father had more than doubled his acres; Mother had her brood of eight to attend to and a larger house to manage.

The moving completed, Father engaged a full-time horseman and a labourer. The farm began to settle to a pattern. The seasons brought their different demands and problems.

Chapter 3

It is now December 1900. Fanny, having left school about a year, is now thirteen years old and a full-time home help for Mother. John will leave school this Christmas, now he is twelve. All my brothers left school at that age.

December 23rd, and another baby girl arrives. She is given the name of Katie. Had she waited another nine days, she would have been a twentieth-century model, but Katie, not being conversant with dates at that period of her life, left me the honour of being the only one in the family to be born in this century. But Katie could possibly have the last laugh because, should she live to be a hundred years and nine days old, to her would go the glory of living in three centuries. Should this occur, I do not expect any of the family will be there to hear the laughter or join in the celebrations.

Oh I wonder how that little old war is going on in South Africa just at this time. Cousin Lucky is there, so it cannot possibly last long. Just to make sure, I will have a look in my encyclopaedia: but no cousin Lucky is mentioned. It says, 'In January 1900, Lord Roberts and Kitchener took command and the tide began to turn in the favour of Britain.' Oh well, they are older, I expect. Cousin Lucky Lockwood would only be twenty. He is a saddler in the Royal Field Artillery, so he cannot do much.

I am not due to be born for another four years. Then for sixteen years, Oak Farm will be my home and, as mentioned before, my world. The formative years of a person's life are the years when a character is moulded: there have been many times since when I have wondered if I dropped out of the mould before I was properly set.

The farmhouse was an L-shaped dwelling with four bedrooms in one length and landing for access to rooms; on the other angle there were three more bedrooms. These were used in bygone days for farm-workers and servants who 'lived in.' Not having been used as bedrooms for some years, they were sealed off from the other four bedrooms. A hatch, about four feet from the floor and about a foot square with a small door remained. Through this aperture could be seen the ghostly unoccupied rooms, which were joined to a corn granary. Under the granary were stables for two horses, a harness house and gig house.

Beneath the bedrooms, starting from the end farthest from the stables etc., we had the parlour, dining room, large pantry, cellar (on the same level) full of casks for home-brewed beer & bottles of home-made wine, two old kitchens with coppers for heating water, other coppers for brewing beer and for pig-killing days. There was a big 'old-time' brick oven and open fireplaces. Another sort of scullery-cum-workshop completed the compartments. So we had granary, stables, gighouse and living quarters all contained in one building.

I should add that the bedrooms once used by the servants now formed a storage for apples, so the boy's bedroom where four of my brothers slept (none of them yet thirteen years old) joined the apple room. This was too much for them. One brother was selected to scramble through the hatch and pass the apples back. This had to be William as he was the only one skinny enough to get through the hole in the wall. Well stocked up, they had an apple feast, shying the cores through the window or at each other, according to their mood. Sometimes when William was getting the apples, the others would make weird sounds through the hatch and scare the life out of him: he was only nine at the time.

This was the house Mother had to cope with, where she fed and sheltered her brood. Fanny of course helped and grew more efficient every year, but it was hard going. If the men thought they worked hard, the women's lot was even worse. Electricity and gas were unheard of in the villages. For water, we actually had a pump over the sink: lots of farm families had to wind their water up from a well, many of them eighty feet deep. In the village, one pump served a community of about thirty houses covering an area about half a mile wide.

I am using Oak Farm and my family as an illustration of this period and by no means were we outstanding in any way. You might call at any farm and discover the procedure would be much the same, and a family of eight or more seemed to be the rule rather than the exception.

Here would be some of Mother's responsibilities in the year 1900... There were Father, Mother and nine children to feed and the oldest was fourteen, so Friday was baking day, a long hard day's work. All the baking was done in the brick oven and everything eaten was home-made. The cavity to form the oven was exactly in shape like an electric light-bulb, cut in half lengthways, with a dome-shaped top, the small end having the access and cast-iron door. The brick work round the cavity was about two feet thick for the purpose of holding the heat long enough after the embers were taken out to bake the goods. In size, it was between five and six feet in length. At the widest part (in the centre) it was about three feet wide, and about two and a half feet at the highest point. The fuel, being hedgerow wood, was cut during the winter months and made into faggots. The faggots were bundles about seven feet long and forty or fifty inches around. They contained sticks up to about the size of a garden fork handle and weighed about four stones in the green state. They needed a year to dry out before use.

'Tending the oven' by Harry Becker

"Don't forget to get my oven wood ready," Mother would say to Father. "This is baking day."

For Father, getting oven wood ready meant bringing two faggots from the wood yard (which was in a corner of the orchard) near to the back door. Here, he had a long heavy log, and laying across this he placed a

21

faggot. Then, with an axe, he halved the faggot. Taking the two halves, he would put them on the floor near the oven in the kitchen. The other faggot was halved and left outside where Mother could help herself if she needed it. Usually a faggot and a half made the necessary heat. With the materials ready, it was in the hands of the women-folk to accomplish something. As the only thing I can cook is an egg, I cannot hope to say in what order each job was done.

I know a large lump of dough was prepared and kneaded, placed in a galvanised bath kept for this purpose and placed near the fire to rise.

The oven was laid by first putting a layer of dry, clean straw, then a layer of the top half of the faggot, being the small sticks, and finally the bigger pieces. All of these of course were in the same compartment that would later receive the stuff to be cooked. Soon after, the straw was lit and the whole lot would be ablaze and begin to sink; then Mother would add some more fuel. She knew exactly how much it needed. When feeding the oven, all the heat, flames and smoke were coming straight at you, there being only one aperture. But when the smoke and flames reached the oven door, they were carried upwards by the draught into the flue. It was a terribly hot job, stooking up. I can picture poor old Mother now, a few tendrils of hair slipping down, to be pushed back with smoky hands leaving a dark smear across her face. I ought to mention that the wood often used was the thorn type with long sharp spikes, as it was considered more heat producing.

When the fire had almost died down, the large and smoky pieces were taken out by means of a flat shovel on a long handle, called a peel. These unwanted ashes were put in a space provided for that purpose on the ground level. Usually, large potatoes in their jackets went into those ashes, timed to come out cooked and ready for their midday dinner. The hot oven, with a few red embers was ready to receive all the prepared food in the order according to how long it took to bake.

Years later, Mother was still using this system. I used to love watching her take out the finished articles. It was all done with the peel, an awkward looking utensil, weighing perhaps eight pounds.

With this tool, she could move and turn the things about to different parts of the oven as deftly as a musician with his little hammer on a xylophone. Cooking by this method is reputed to be the most appetising, but I am of the opinion that time and memory add flavour to most things.

Friday baking day ended with a general kitchen clean-up, and with a week's supply of food, giving Mother a contented look.

Saturday was the day to prepare for Sunday. That meant an extra clean-up right through the house, outside paths to be washed down, all shoes and boots cleaned, kindling for fires to be ready for Sunday, cutlery cleaned, and so on. Nothing but the bare necessities must be done on the Sabbath Day; a cold joint of meat, leaving just the vegetables to cook. All the children, down to about five years old had to go to Sunday School, and there was to be no playing about when they arrived home as their clothes had to be kept tidy. After dinner, the entire family went to worship at the Methodist Chapel, returning home about four o'clock. Then, Father and the older boys fed the stock, and milked the cows kept for the house. Getting back into their Sunday clothes, they all had tea. At six o'clock, Father and the older children would start off for the evening service. Mother stayed at home to get the younger ones to bed.

The great weekly wash was Monday's job. On Tuesday, the dairy appliances were brought out for butter making. I do not believe the family had a separator in those days for dividing the cream from the milk The milk would have been put into shallow pans and the cream skimmed off every day. On Tuesday, it was churned into butter. The butter not needed for the house was sold to the local shop, or at the door. Wednesday was filled up with odd jobs and a bit of gardening.

To complete the week's routine, Thursday was market day. Father drove to Stowmarket with horse and trap, taking Mother; he to do his business, she to stock up for another week. This went on week after week, year after year, with little variation.

Mother fitted in her sewing and was, as usual, making and mending for the whole family.

The farm buildings were made mainly of clay lump walls with thatched or tiled roofs; they were designed to meet the requirements of farming those 130 acres.

There was a stable for five cart-horses with yard and shelter to sleep in, a cow shed for milking and yard attached, pig-sties, cattle yards, sheds to house the carts, waggons etc., and a large barn that I would estimate was erected in the sixteenth century.

Originally, the farm was called 'Wizard's Farm,' but the name was changed to Oak Farm owing to the presence of a famous oak tree growing there. It was cut down in the year 1898 because it was unsafe and hollow. The size was so immense, a bullock could stand in the hollow part. Although it was hollow, the weight was such as to require two steam engines to cart it away. In later years, I met one of the men who drove the engines. The scar left where the tree had stood

was visible twenty years later and the tracks left by the engines lasted at least half as long.

In Kelly's Directory of Suffolk 1933, with reference to Wickham Skeith, are written the following words, and I quote... "Under an ancient oak on Wizard's Farm many Saxon coins of Harold and Edward the Confessor have been found and deposited in the British Museum."

Moving on to 1902: Queen Victoria had died and was returned to earth. Cousin Lucky had returned from the Boer War. Even my brother Jim could not remember much of Cousin Lucky's experiences, but this is understandable as he would be looking back sixty-five years, and he was only nine when Lucky returned from South Africa.

Since then, Jim has also had his taste of war. He too was in the Royal Field Artillery as a signalman during the First World War, so his faint memories of the Boer War faded into the reality of the war in which he was involved. His own experiences quickly joined the past as he struggled through the years of depression in which every one of that age was involved. And so on to the rumblings of another war.

My sister Alice has uncovered an article from a local Suffolk newspaper dated Feb. 1950. Cousin Lucky, in company with other survivors of Ladysmith was invited by his former enemies to be their guests at the Fiftieth Anniversary of the event. He recalled how, at the age of nineteen, in 1899, he had arrived in South Africa just in time for the war and was in the 117 days siege of Ladysmith.

The Boers had systematically poisoned the water supply and there was not even any water for washing. Very soon, 2000 of the 7000 officers and men were in hospital, suffering from

Chronicle & Mercury, Friday, February 3, 1950   Page Five

Lucky Lockwood of Ladysmith

Boer War Veteran Sailing to S. Africa

FIFTY years ago the 117-day Siege of Ladysmith was in full swing. One of the members of the garrison was 19-year-old Gunner Lucky Lockwood. Now aged 69, Mr. Lockwood, who lives at Ashburnham, Victoria Road, Felixstowe, this week reviews some of his memories of those terrible and heroic days.

Lucky by name and lucky by nature might be Mr. Lockwood's motto for, after a lifetime of fighting and adventure, he still remains in one piece. Also, it takes something more than luck to rise from corporal to captain in the space of five brief months.

On Thursday next, in company with other survivors of Ladysmith, Lucky Lockwood will sail for South Africa as the guest of his former enemies. The thoughts of those other Boer War veterans who are still scattered throughout the breadth of Suffolk will go with Lucky as, half a century later, he returns to the scene of their former exploits.

BORN on the 9th of May, 1880, at Bedingfield, 69-year-old Captain Lucky Lockwood, M.C., sets sail together with four other Boer War veterans, from Southampton on February 9th in the Union Castle liner Warwick Castle. Their destination is South Africa, where they are to be received as guests of the Durban Tin Hat Club and the Corporation of Ladysmith.

Captain Lockwood or Lucky (it is his Christian name) as he is known to his many friends, is a veteran of the battlefield. A survivor from the Siege of Ladysmith, he was later taken prisoner at the famous Blood River engagement. Wounded in the campaign, he was awarded the South African Medal with six bars. He served in France, where he witnessed the first German gas attacks, and—at the second battle of Ypres—was complimented by the general of his division for conspicuous bravery. Rising from corporal to captain in five months, Lucky then commanded, and went into action with, a battery at

25

one of a number of diseases. Their rations were barely enough to sustain life. They were relieved by General Buller, only to be taken prisoner. Twenty men were put into a barn; one man escaped during the night and walked fourteen miles to get in touch with Kitchener. Consequently, the rest of the men were stripped to their underclothes. They had to cut pieces from a slaughtered ox and toast it on sticks for food. As there was nothing more for food, the Boers freed them. In their underclothes and with nothing on their feet, the men including Cousin Lucky, marched seventeen miles to get back to their comrades.

After the Boer War, our cousin returned home to England for a time, before being sent to serve in India. We always included Lucky as part of our family, mainly because he spent all his holidays and leaves with us. After he married, his wife and children spent nearly all their school holidays at the farm. It had been through my father that cousin Lucky had been inspired and influenced to join the army.

I know many other families gave more to their country; many members of families gave their lives, their all. I am merely recording the day-to-day events in my small world.

The next event at Oak Farm was alterations to the house. All the unused bedrooms and rooms below them were demolished and replaced by (according to the standards of the day) one modern kitchen. A brick oven was built in; there were two coppers, one for everyday use, the other for making the home-brewed beer and to use for scalding the pigs. These coppers were used for this purpose as my people had two pigs killed for the house each year, and they brewed beer there until about 1916.

With a family of this size, each day would bring its complement of accidents, illnesses, excitements and disappoint-ments; each in itself a milestone in the life of the one it concerns. The farm was getting firmly established under the management of Father, whose regular steady daily toil must have been driven by some kind of ambition. Mother had little choice other than to be carried along by the daily demands of the family. The year 1903 had begun to wear away and over two years had passed without Mother conceiving, the first time this had happened in her eighteen years of married life. I have reason to believe that her mind had started to turn towards making the home more attractive, as she told a friend of hers that she was planning to get a nice sideboard. Her mind was set on it. However, poor Mother's new-found interest began to fade as she again had warnings that another child was on the way; the eleventh time she was to face this ordeal.

The year wore away to a finish, and this poor woman and her duties became heavier. A new year started, not with the promise of Spring for Mother; she was tired and the time of year would mean nothing. Life was a drag and she was weary of child-bearing, but a young life started cannot easily be stopped.

Sister Fan, now seventeen, had never known a light-hearted childhood. Her life had been fully devoted to bringing up her younger brothers and sisters. If she had viewed the forthcoming event with disgust, my sympathies would have been with her entirely. She told me in after years that she was fed up at this time with bringing up children, and the last thing she wanted was to bring up another.

Fanny, Mary and friend

January spent itself and gave way to February. A touch of Spring was in the air and Mother's time to deliver the child was near. The days were definitely lengthening, and the routine was well understood. Mother was upstairs; she could hear the children playing and shouting in the meadow as twilight began to fall.

At seven o'clock in the evening of Sunday 7th February 1904, the law of nature for the survival of the species had its way and another human being, in the shape of myself was cast into the world. Mother still could not forget that sideboard she had set her heart upon, but she accepted me as a substitute. When writing to a friend to tell her I had arrived, she wrote, "I have my sideboard and it has a mahogany top." This was because I was born with a head of thick auburn hair.

Chapter 4

After three score years, I still cannot see that the world has been much enriched by my presence. Any niche I may have filled could easily have been occupied by someone else, had I never been born. Yet, born I was; to begin with, crying in the crib or bubbling at the bottle. Mother said I did not cry much, but when I did, I properly 'let it rip.' Anyway, I grew enough to qualify for a name. As I mentioned previously, my family had not thought of a name until the last minute. They settled for Alfred. 'A rose by any other name would have smelt just as sweet.' I mean, one name is as good as another. My people accepted me into the family with love and tenderness. I suppose one more or less did not make much difference. Fan said later, "I got fond of the little ol' thing and wouldn't have parted with it." She had a velvet bow on the shoulder of her dress and when she carried me, I loved to stroke it. For some time I had to have the bow to soothe myself to sleep.

One day, my sister Alice took me out in the pram. She would have been about six years old. She was running with the pram when she stumbled and fell. She kept a firm grip on the handle and consequently, the pram tipped over, throwing me out. Poor Alice thought she had killed me, but the only damage was to her two grazed thumbs. Mother had tried for a long while to stop Alice from sucking her thumbs and this cured her.

We have now reached the year 1906, and I suppose I was observing things and people but, being only two, my memory had not yet begun to function. At about this time, Mother became pregnant again for the twelfth time. I did not learn of this until I was over fifty. In my family, such things were not freely spoken of. Unfortunately or fortunately, this pregnancy ended in a miscarriage.

At an early age, an ordinary thing impressed itself on my memory. It was a pair of brother Lucky's trousers lying on his tin trunk. I can remember a yellow stripe running down the leg; it was part of his Suffolk Yeomanry uniform. I understand that he belonged at that time to a kind of voluntary Territorial Cavalry unit, where they supplied their own horses. He was never called upon to do a 'Charge of the Light Brigade.' The only charge I heard of was when Lucky was in the lavatory and the bugle sounded for 'Fall In.' He rushed out to get his horse and couldn't find it. He looked towards the line of mounted men and saw that his horse had obeyed the order and had lined up, minus himself. He had to put up with a lot of leg-pulling, so decided to get his own back on at least one man. My brother and others conspired to play a trick on a chap who was not too bright.

Just before the 'Fall In', one man occupied his attention while others whitewashed two or three of the fetlocks of his horse and painted a large blaze on its nose. When the unfortunate chap rushed to get his mount, he could not find it. He was searching for a black horse. He was reprimanded for his slackness. The main thing was, it made Lucky feel better. The man himself told me that story thirty years after the event.

The Burrows family: (rear l. to r.) Mary, Fanny, Lucky & Alice (Snr.), Alf, Lucky (Jnr.) (front l. to r.) Will, Sam, Alice (Jnr.), Katie, Jack, Jim.

Chapter 5

I do not remember Lucky living at home, apart from the stripe down his trousers because when he was twenty-one and I was three, Father hired another farm of 130 acres: Honey Pots Farm, Worlingworth, and Lucky went there to manage it. William helped with the work and Fanny went as their housekeeper. Their ages would have been twenty-one, twenty and sixteen, and the family was quickly reduced by three. Mother did not really want them to go as she loved having them all around her. Father's idea was that if Lucky proved himself well, he could take the farm over.

The family in the orchard at Oak Farm   (rear l to r) Sam, Mary, Lucky Snr., Alice Jnr., Jim, Alice Snr., Katie, Lucky Jnr., Fan.   (front l to r) Alf, Jack, Will.

It was eight years since the family had moved into Oak Farm and Father had doubled his acreage. Some of the cart-horses had been bred and the colts were old enough to work, so they supplied the 'horse-power' for Honey Pots. No doubt, the seed corn was grown at Oak Farm. I suppose the new project at that time would only have cost ten to twelve hundred pounds. Now in the 1960s, it would cost at least ten times as much to hire the same farm.

Being only three, I was not conscious of what was going on and cannot remember Lucky, William and Fan moving out. The following year, the landlord of Honey Pots Farm had a new farmhouse built and the old one was pulled down. I can especially remember that as Uncle Hugh contracted to build it. He was cousin Lucky's father.

I used to go to Worlingworth to stay, and was happy to do so as Fanny was almost mother to me. One one occasion, my sister and two brothers seemed very upset and Lucky was saying, "Who's got it then?" "I don't know," said Fan. "I left it on the corner of the table and went out, and when I came back it was gone. I only went out for five minutes." Something clicked in my small brain.
"Oh," I said, "Do you mean that little brownie?"
"What brownie?"
"Come with me," I said.
Fanny fetched the lantern as it was dark.
"Go on," she said; "I'll be close behind you."
I led the way out of the back door, through the garden, into the orchard, where I chose a particular tree with a little hollow niche and pointed. "In there."
Fan held up the lantern and peered in. There she saw a golden sovereign, the object of all the worry. They had not suspected the little human magpie. Gold coins were thereafter called 'brownies.'

Father frequently went over to Honey Pots Farm to see how it was shaping. Mother would go with him loaded with all sorts of things such as a few stones of potatoes, cauliflowers, apple-pies, fruit-cakes, a poker, shovel and fender that might come in handy for one of the fireplaces, a pair of thick socks and an old mackintosh that Fan had left behind. They often used to leave me there for a few days; this farm was ten miles from Oak Farm.

At the home farm, I spent hours following my brothers about. I was more like a four-month old spaniel puppy. Their forms and voices were familiar so I just hung on to them for safety and out of curiosity.

There used to be a heavy ladder - well, it was more like a moveable staircase; the thing weighed about two hundredweight. It was used to take chaff for the horses up to the loft. My second eldest brother Jack was moving these steps one day. I got in his way, which upset his balance and caused him to drop the thing on top of me. He heaved it up to release me, but the urgency of the situation made him panic; his knees were shaking and he dropped it a second time. I could not have suffered much injury and would not have remembered the occasion if Jack had not told me.

Jack and Sam were acting as horsemen at this time and Jim was stockman. When the horsemen were working in the fields, I followed Jim round and I expect I nearly crazed him by saying again and again, "What are you going to do next?" He used to take food to the bullocks in a bushel hod and bring me back in it, carrying me on his shoulders. Wet days and cold days I could not go out, so I followed my mother and sisters about the house. I could not join my brothers in games and sport as I was eleven years younger. I grew up, more or less, in a female world, there being three girls between myself and the next boy.

Mother would let me turn the handle when she was using the sewing-machine. I loved the bobbins to finish, as I could have the job of re-winding them, which I could manage on my own. On baking days, I was allowed a piece of dough to make anything I might choose. This was usually a man, using currants for his eyes, a raisin for his mouth and currants for jacket buttons. Mostly, after he was baked, he was too hard to eat; more like a dog's biscuit. But I thought it was delicious.

Katie was my playmate, being nearest my age. We did not play 'mothers and fathers'; just mothers. As the perambulator and push-cart would not be needed again for the purpose intended, she had the pram and I had the push-cart, which was a three-wheeled contraption. The seat and foot compartment was made of raw wood and according to my memory, it looked as if it had been made by a raw carpenter. It had a small wheel in front. My scarf frequently became tangled in the axle, so the further I went, the nearer my nose was to the wheel rim. It was like playing 'with your nose to the grindstone.' Katie had some dolls in her pram; in mine was a rag doll which Mother had made. It is my honest opinion that the total money spent on toys for all the ten children was less than five pounds, and perhaps nearer to one pound.

We used empty cotton-reels on a string, and imagined we had dogs on a lead; we were very happy. The value of our playthings was in the eye of the beholder (or the owner, might be more apt).

We were happy with what we had, but somehow Katie and I could not agree and we were always quarrelling. We were generally referred to as 'them two': such as 'shut up you two' or 'it's them two again.'

While I was still four, a wonderful and unusual adventure was arranged for the three eldest girls, Fanny (21), Mary (13) and Alice (11). It was to be a day in Yarmouth, which was fifty miles away. Jim would drive them to Finningham Station, where they would take the train to change at Norwich for Yarmouth. The whole thing was a mystery to me; nothing could ever have happened like this before or since - Amy Johnson flying to Australia, or Sir Francis Chichester sailing around the world single-handed was no comparison.
"Can I come to the station?" I pleaded.
"I suppose so," said Jim. "You'll have to sit on the floor of the cart, and Allie on Fan's lap." I was so excited.

Now, the cart was known as a dealer's cart as it would take pigs, calves or people. The sides and back were of lattice-work to let the air get through to the animals. At the top of each side was a ridge for the seat to rest upon and along these ridges, holes were drilled. The seat had two spikes at each end pointing downwards, which fitted into holes. This kept the seat from slipping backwards and forwards and could be set in a position to make the cart balance.

Well Jim, who was only fifteen, left me in the cart in the station yard while he went with the girls to the platform. From where I was sitting, I could see the girls walking over the footbridge.

To get a better view, I stood on the seat which was six feet above ground level, making my head about nine feet from the ground.

I was able to get a wonderful view until I leaned on the rest at the back of the seat. This caused the spikes to slide from the holes. The seat pitched over and I was thrown onto the granite ground. I was dazed, but luckily no bones were broken. Poor Jim had a telling-off from the station porter for leaving me alone. He took me home and Mother put me on the sofa. I was bruised quite a bit. The girls enjoyed their day as they didn't know what had happened. The three sisters were not likely to have any more days out for another year. So, it was back to normal, and Fanny returned to her house-keeping at Honey Pots Farm.

The builders were progressing with the new farmhouse. Brother Lucky was taking his farming quite seriously. He had met a young lady before moving to Honey Pots and like most girls, she was pretty. Her home was in London, but she was keeping house for an uncle who lived three miles from Oak farm. Her Uncle Bob had a small farm in the village of Westhorpe.

So, Lucky and Lillian Banks took to courting in earnest, and by the time the budding farmer was twenty-three, his new house was ready for occupation. It was rather awkward for Fanny and the boys living in the old house, or part of it, as some of it had to be pulled down to make room for the new one.

Fanny had a terrible fright one night in the old house. She was

awakened by the strange sound of cracking noises coming from one of the empty bedrooms. She sat up in bed and heard a tremendous thud. In an empty room and at the dead of night, the sound would be greatly amplified. When the strength returned to her legs, she crept into the room where her two brothers were sleeping and having woken them, told them her tale. "Go on," they said, "There's nothing there or one of us would have heard it." So they argued and Fan pleaded with them to look, but they wouldn't budge to investigate. Whether they were scared or just lazy, I know not. Poor Fanny was afraid to return to her room, so she fetched a dressing gown, wrapped it around herself and spent the rest of the night sitting in a chair in the boys' room. She discovered the next day, that a great lump of plaster had broken away from the ceiling and crashed to the floor.

The days passed by; Lucky and Lily arranged their wedding for a day in December 1908. I have calculated this to be the date as someone told me I was four years old. The reception was held at Oak Farm as it was more convenient for Lily's people to come than for Lucky's family to travel up to London. You just cannot leave farms with animals; not even for a wedding.

All I can remember about this event was that some of the women were wearing white, which seemed rather unusual. The people wearing normal colours I soon forgot about. I can recall some horse-drawn cabs and carriages pulling up at the house. One coachman was sitting up so high I couldn't fathom how he got up there as there were no ladders about.

Somehow, I was bundled into one of the cabs. I expect my older sisters were bridesmaids; my brothers would not want me on this occasion, so no doubt I hung onto my mother. I have a faint recollection of going into church, but not of returning. Whether or not I grew up with a subconscious feeling of being left there, I would not know. What I do know is that all through my life I have had a strong fascination for churchyards. Perhaps I go back to look for myself.

Lucky was happily settled and William stayed on to help with the work, but Fanny returned to Oak Farm. No doubt Mother was glad of her help as the second-eldest sister was only about fourteen years old.

A rather ridiculous incident occurred a few months after the wedding which provided me with a bit of material for bragging in later years. There are two periods in a man's life when they talk plain daft. One is when they are entering manhood at around twenty; the other, when they are leaving the prime of life, at about the age of fifty-five.

They are comparable to a March hare, who at that time of year does the most stupid things. I have seen a hare running after a dog. My dog once chased a hare over a fifteen-acre field. The hare just kept a tantalising distance in front of Pip and jumped the ditch. Pip gave up and returned, but when about halfway back, he turned to look round and saw the hare following. I could almost hear my dog swearing under his breath. He turned round in a temper, probably thinking, 'I'll get you this time,' and with an extra spurt Pip gave chase. Exactly the same thing happened again, Pip coming back, followed by the hare. The poor old dog slunk off in disgust. I think my face went red on his behalf.

Now, these frustrated men, lacking the opportunity or daring to give way to their feelings, take to boasting of their conquests with girls and of all the hearts they have broken etc. The old Romeos feel they are losing their zest, so they brag about what they have done in the past. On these occasions, I can casually say, "I'll tell you what chaps; I once slept with my brother's wife. She was twenty-three and a bride of only three months." Of course, no-one believes me until I add, "I was only five years old at the time."

These kind of things did not happen too often, so I would keep up my routine of following somebody around. This I did from morning till night. Mother would dress me up when the weather was cold, buttoning up my coat, then putting on a scarf, crossing it over my chest, under my arms and fixing it with a large safety-pin at the back. "There, off you go," she would say.

I knew Jim would be in the barn. I had to go through a yard full of bullocks to get there, so when I reached the gate and shouted, Jim would take me past the cattle. There we spent a lot of time cleaning cattle-beet. I used to put them in the mincer while he turned the handle; they came out looking like potato chips. These were mixed with chaff and meal as food for the bullocks. We always called the mixture 'bullock-bait'. The shoots, roots and dirt which were cleaned off the beet, we called chates. These were given to the sows as it is natural for pigs to chew dirt. They, of course, also had meal. All the cattle and pig-sheds and yards had to be littered down with straw so that they could lay comfortably.

Father or one of the older brothers had to help to do this as it was carted with a horse and tumbril. One loaded the straw on the tumbril while the other pitched it to him. Then it was taken to the yards. The loaders got down and the cart was tipped by means of a spring in front, emptying all the contents. One day, two of my brothers were doing this job and they had a large load of straw. Sam drew it into the bullock yard and for mischief, tipped the cart before Jack could get down. Sam ran to the back of the cart grinning, hoping to enjoy his practical joke, but alas, there was no Jack there. He became very alarmed and frantically began moving all the straw. Worried, and wiping the sweat from his face, he heard Jack say, "Have you enjoyed yourself?" Jack had calmly come down with the straw, stepped behind a wall and watched Sam's dilemma.

My brothers were always playing jokes on each other, teasing our sisters or fighting one another. I, being so much younger, was treated with a protective respect. We were always well behaved (or tried to be) when Father was around. The sound of his footsteps was enough to stop all the nonsense.

And now the spring of 1909 is here. The fields have laid in their ploughed state for most of the winter. The rain, snow, frost and wind have slowly done their work of pulverising the soil. Throughout the winter, the only occupants of the fields have been the birds. Lapwings always appear in large numbers at this time of the year and the seagulls come inland when the weather is rough. The rooks, who are more or less local birds, settle in search of food. Often a field appears to be covered with bird life, perhaps one hundred to the acre. But even the birds like to leave our mid-Suffolk heavy land in wet weather and use the pastures where they can walk in comfort with clean feet. Then the ploughed fields are forsaken and left cold and empty; perhaps just some men cutting hedges around the fields and making faggots as fuel for the brick ovens and other fires. These men will be glad when the day has ended so that they can get home to a hot meal and a warm room.

Chapter 6

Now spring is in the air; the land is drying out. We are all round the table having tea, ten of us including the parents; three each side and two at each end. Before Lucky and William left, Katie and I had a small table to ourselves near to Mother so that she could keep an eye on us. Father is talking. When the grown-ups are talking during meals, I am rather busy trying to manipulate my eating tools, so that voices sound like a distant rumble.

He is saying, "If this weather holds, we can start pulling down in a day or two. I want to get Oak Field in with oats."

Oak Field joined Oak Meadow where the big oak tree once stood. "Sheeps Close will be for spring beans, so Jack, tomorrow get one of the horses in the tumbril and take one gang of harrows to Oak Field and lay them out ready for using. Take another gang to Sheeps Close and do the same; then take Tinker and Scott to the blacksmith's to be shod. We don't want to stop for that when we get drilling. Sam and I will get the drill ready. Oh yes, it was last used for wheat seeding, so we'll take some of the coulters out, as I want the rows of beans one foot apart to have room to get the horse-shoes through them. The seed barrel will have to be reversed to use the big cups. After we have drilled the beans, we can put the coulters back to eight inches apart for the oats and barley. The cogwheel to use for rate of sowing is written on the drill lid for different types of seed and corn, so we can sort that out tomorrow."

This how the conversations used to run, talking of what had been done and discussing what was to be done the following day.

Mother chips in, looking at Father: "Another cup of tea?"

"Yes please," he answers.

To those sitting between him and her, she says, "Pass yer father's cup."

My parents never addressed each other by any term of endearment. Never did I hear them call each other Mummy, Daddy,

Dear, Darling or anything vulgar. The contact was through a third person if possible, such as: "Tell yermother I want her," when he could easily have made her hear himself. If they were close enough to each other and one wanted to draw the other's attention, they would not say, "Darling, look at those children," but one would tap the other on the arm and say, "Look at them." When there was no third person with whom to make contact and they were out of tapping distance, it was "Hi" or "Hi there." Occasionally they would be too close for "Hi" and not near enough to tap; then Father would use a name which I took to be Hindu. It sounded like "Terramarney."

Years later, when looking back on the relationship and considering the size of the family, I came to the conclusion my parents must have had some secret code of direct contact. Not for one moment can I imagine "Hi, hi there, Terramarney," or arm tapping to be a sucessful approach for romance and I am quite confident it was not done through a third person.

During the teatime conversations, which to me sounded like a distant mumble, and in spite of my concentrations of conveying food from plate to mouth, I detected the possibility of a ride when hearing the word 'tumbril.' So next day I followed Jack and got a ride in the tumbril with the harrows. Like all children, I loved to ride, even if it might have been more comfortable to walk. A day or two later, Sheeps Close was ready for drilling and I had another ride to the field with

the seed beans. I expect I followed the drill up and down the field a few times, but that would be tiring, so I would wander back to Mother for a glass of milk and a bun. This kind of procedure would go on until the spring seeding was finished.

The fields had laid so cold and desolate that even the birds forsook them, and life beneath the soil such as worms and grubs were deep down and dormant. With the spring, the fields and their connections suddenly sprang into life. But anybody that was closely connected with this annual movement of life would hardly notice: they were too busy. It was only the observant dreamer, pausing as he passed by, or the horseman with the harrows, resting his horses for a few minutes near the hedge, who would be caught up in the peaceful excitement and activity of it all.

There was the music of the connecting chains of the other gang of harrows, covering up the seeds behind the drill as they toppled over the clods; the gentle creaking of the horse collars as the seals and chains chafed them; the little squeaks of wipple-trees and chains as metal rubbed against metal; the voices of the horsemen talking to their horses; all these adding to the early signs of a new spring. Then, at the end of the field, horsemen, horses and drills would stop; coulters were wound up by a man at the back and let down with a rattle and a clank; the birds were chirping in the hedges, and always the lark was soaring overhead. You could hear individual sounds distinctly, and at the same time hear them all as a gentle and harmonious orchestra. It calmed the nerves and lifted the spirits and usually at least one man could not resist joining in, by either whistling or singing. Whatever key he used, it was never a discord.

This way of life, this mode of farming had been going on for hundreds of years with little change, and continued very much the same until just before the second World War. Slow perhaps, but very peaceful.

Over fifty years have passed since this particular spring. Through the inventions of man and the so-called progress of civilisation, I am afraid this quiet contented way of living is gone forever. But change has its advantages of course; it was necessary and unavoidable to cope with the ever increasing population.

Even if some individual wished to farm in the old way, it would be impossible, for where would he find the blacksmiths, harness-makers, wheelwrights and such like? So the horse age has to give way to the machine age. The dreamy melodies of the countryside are smothered by the bark of tractors. The operators of these machines must concentrate all the time, leaving no room for poetical thoughts. So men have grown to be part of a machine rather than part of nature.

Chapter 7

Haysel came, and to me it brought more happy discoveries. The different seasonal work gave me great excitement as life opened up new things to my mind.

July arrived, and with it a little slackness in the farming operations. The haystacks had been thatched so, until the rush of harvest came, the men mowed the grass borders round the fields, trimmed the roadside hedges and generally tidied up. Nothing was really pressing.

Aunt Jane

Mother decided she could be spared, so she arranged to have a week in London. Father agreed it would be nice for her to visit his sister, and settled that I should go too. One day, Mother said to me, "How would you like to come to London with me and see Aunt Jane?"

I wasn't particularly thrilled. I had been with my parents in the horse and trap several times to see Aunt Carrie and Uncle Abraham at Brandeston, and Aunt Harriet in the adjoining village, and married cousins nearby. All their houses to me seemed dark and low with high mantlepieces crammed full of ornaments. There were china dogs, cats, women with baskets of fruit and every other nick-nack one could think of. I used to sit amongst all this, not daring to move in case I knocked something down.

Then I recall Father, Mother, aunts, uncles and older cousins all talking at once until their voices sounded like a distant drone which made me feel drowsy. The last thing I could remember hearing before falling asleep was the loud tick of a cheap clock on the mantlepiece. This was the picture I associated with visiting aunts.

"But," said Mother, "You'll have a long train ride."

I felt a bit more interested. I had been to Ipswich by train, which was eighteen miles. I imagined Aunt Jane lived in a village called London just through Ipswich.

In 1909, at the age of five, I was introduced to London. At that age one remembers the things one would least expect and forgets the important things. I have no recollection of the train journey or the mass of streets. One thing I always remembered was riding in a bus drawn by two horses, because one of the horses fell down. This was indeed a tragedy to me. There was a slight delay while the horse got to its feet and the harness was checked before starting again. I expect the horse slipped on the greasy street. I suppose nearly all the buses were horse-drawn at this time.

Aunt Jane lived in Battersea; her husband, Uncle Tom Brett was a cabinet maker. I have no knowledge of which street they lived in, but there was a railway arch before reaching the house, and the trains ran close enough to deposit soot and smuts onto the dwelling. It was very intriguing to me to stand at their window and watch the old lamp-lighter coming up the street to light the lamps. If my facts are not technically correct, I am writing only of my impressions and the way they acted on my memory. The street lighting was by gas, the lamp-posts being about ten feet high. The lamp compartment was open at the bottom and two short chains hung through the opening, one slightly longer than the other. Obviously by pulling one, the gas jet was opened and was closed by pulling the other. The lamp-lighter had a long pole with a hook at the end for this job; also at the end of the pole was a flame for igniting the gas when the jet was opened. I never did enquire what fuel was used to make the flame on the pole.

There were two more things that actually remained in my memory, Aunt Jane's parrot and her Irish Terrier dog; so to me at the age of five, this was Aunt Jane's London - not so very different from Aunt Carrie's Brandeston in Suffolk.

Aunt Jane and Uncle Tom had one son, but sad to say he died in his early twenties. In spite of his few years on this earth, he left his mark behind in our family. His name was Percy; he was a good violinist and played in one of the London orchestras. I never heard the family say what he did for a living; I do know that his main hobby was photography and he left us with many family photographs that were taken before 1906. Aunt Jane treasured his possessions very much and I felt very honoured when, at the age of fifteen, I received from her all Percy's photographic equipment. There were three cameras. One was a very large one on a tripod, as used by photographers in that day. Then there was a box camera, and the third was a small folding type. I don't imagine films were used then, as glass plates were the actual negatives. Included with the cameras was the full equipment for developing and printing. At fifteen, I made use of everything with the exception of the very large camera and, if I may be permitted to say so, produced some fairly good pictures.

The violins were given to my brother Jack as he showed the most talent for using them.

My relations on Father's side seemed ambitious and keen, and all left their native village. Father's one brother, John, did several

Uncle John, Aunt Lizzie, Aunt Sarah

45

years in the army and later settled in London, as did Aunt Jane. Aunt Lizzie went into domestic service, eventually to become a cook. Seventy years ago, this was considered a good position. She later married the butler, Christopher Lawrence, and settled in Biggleswade, Bedfordshire. The third sister was Aunt Sarah, cousin Lucky's mother, who made her home in Ipswich. Her husband, Uncle Hugh, built Honey Pots farmhouse.

Mother's people all remained in the villages close to where they were born, near Framlingham in Suffolk. They were typically country people, quiet-speaking, contented and not bothering to converse very much. They seemed to be happy alone with their thoughts.

My parents and all my aunts and uncles were all born over one hundred years before I began writing this story.

Chapter 8

Having followed Aunt Jane and Mother about London, it was really lovely to be back at Oak Farm so that I could follow my brothers about again. About two weeks after returning from London, it was time for harvest and to me, this was far more exciting than sightseeing in London.

On the 130 acres at Oak Farm, Father used to grow about eighty acres of corn, ten acres of clover, ten acres of roots for the cattle, and the remaining thirty acres were permanent pastures. With the method of the day, it needed a gang of eight men to get the harvest in. The only mechanical reaper we had was the same as the one used for cutting grass for hay. For cutting corn, a rack was fitted behind the cutter bar. This was held at about forty-five degrees by a man with his foot, sitting on the machine. He also wielded a specially designed rake to sweep the corn onto the rack as the mower moved forward, catching the cut corn before it could fall. The man's arms worked the rake in rhythm just like the sails of a binder or combine. Up, forward and back four times, then the fifth time he lifted his foot and dropped the rack and swept the corn onto the ground; this was enough for one sheaf. He then repeated this operation all day and every day until all the corn was cut. A second man would ride on the mower to drive the horses. The cut corn had to be tied into sheaves and thrown clear to make a path for the horses and mower to go round again. To do this, five men were needed. On a square field, each man cleared one side of the field, and when one reached the end of his side, the next man would be at the next corner, and so on. As there were five men for four sides, following each other round, it meant they all had a little rest in turn. The eighth man in the harvest field was my father, who sharpened the knives for the reaper and did all the odd jobs.

This was the method of cutting corn until I was ten years old, so I got used to the routine. We children were always with the men, thinking we were helping, when in fact we were really a hindrance.

I can still vividly picture those men tying the corn into sheaves. They would have their feet close to the corn that was to be tied up, reach over, pull it to their shins, whip out half a dozen straws and put them around the bundle. Then they would give them a twist, tuck in the ends and the sheaf was completed and thrown clear. I have seen them almost run to the next one. The faster they went, the longer they could rest. The reward, when completing the round of the field was to have a long draught of home-brewed beer from the gallon stone bottle that they took with them.

One of these men was extra conscientious. His home was three-quarters of a mile from the farm building and one of the fields was a mile beyond the buildings. He had no means of transport apart from walking and when working in this particular field, he would go home to dinner and return to the field within an hour. This meant walking (or running) three and a half miles and having a meal. I have heard my brothers speak of this many times, and to me it seems almost a physical impossibility. We always knew him as Nobbler Garrod.

When recalling such incidents, I have very mixed feelings about 'the good old days.' When remembering the past, we ought not to be a slave to our sentiments and admit that all ages have their advantages and disadvantages.

Often, in a stormy season, when the crops were layed, all the barley had to be mown by hand. If it was good going, a man could scythe an acre in a day.

'Scythers' by Daniel Wright

Carting the corn home to the stockyard was our joy as children; we loved riding in the waggons. I tremble when I think of the dangers we were in, climbing up the wheels to get into the waggons. Often the horses were young and would move off before we were ready, then we had to jump clear. Usually there would be a boy of about fourteen or fifteen in charge of the horses. Following the loads home, we used to walk under the back of the load and try to swing on the odd pieces of rope. I do not know how we escaped swinging into the wheels.

So, with four men in the fields loading the waggons and four men in the stockyard unloading, and a lad taking back the empty waggons and fetching home the loaded ones, harvest was gathered in.

Nearly everyone employed one or two boys who could earn roughly two shillings and sixpence a week. It was a great satisfaction to everyone to know that the harvest was completed and that the stacks were thatched. The stacks would be thrashed during the winter when convenient or necessary. Usually one or two wheat stacks were left until the following summer as the price was higher then. A stack containing ten acres of corn took one day to thrash. This involved about a dozen men.

On average it needed five men to farm one hundred acres. What a contrast now, in the 1960s, when it is not unusual for the largest farms to employ one man or less to a hundred acres.

On most Sundays, brother Lucky and his wife Lily would cycle over to join the family for dinner and tea. Their farm was running on the same principal as Oak Farm, which meant that there was much comparing of progress to discuss.

Chapter 9

Following the harvest, all the farmyard muck had to be carted on to the fields - about two hundred and fifty tumbril loads of it - and laid out in heaps eight yards apart; five or six heaps to the load. This amounted to about twelve to fourteen tons per acre.

During this operation, my brothers provided me with an empty sack. This they placed on top of the load of muck, then I was lifted up and placed on the sack. I had no objection to what I rode on so long as I had a ride. It was not too unpleasant, being mainly rotted straw. Then there was the ride back from the field in the empty tumbril. When this job was finished, two men spread the muck evenly over the land, and two horsemen followed with ploughs to turn it all in.

The horsemen and horses were in the fields at 7.00 a.m. and the men ate at eleven which, appropriately enough, was called elevenses. The horses were taken home at three, given their food, and the men had another meal called 'three o'clock dinner'. After the dinner, the horses were groomed, fed again, then turned into the yards with hay to eat, and straw to lay on until the following morning.

I had now reached the age of five and a half and was capable of taking my brother's elevenses to the fields. I loved doing this. Mother would put a packet of food in the basket for me, and an extra cup. The hot cocoa was put into a blue enamel cup with a deep lid which was used for drinking. Sam and Jack were ploughing Sheep's Close when I began taking them their food. I had to go through two meadows to get there. The gate between the two meadows hung high from the ground and was difficult to open. I used to place the can and basket near to the gate, climb over, pull them under the gate and proceed on my way. We would sit on the border of the field with our legs resting on the side of the ditch, the grub on our laps and a cup of cocoa beside us. We nearly always had to fish out a fly or spider before having a sip of drink, and sometimes the cup would tip over and spill the contents onto the ground as it was so uneven.

After the refreshments were finished, I used to feel amply rewarded for taking them to the field when Jack made me a cushion with his overcoat and let me ride on the plough up and down the field. A few years later he let me hold the plough handles and go on my own a little way. I was thrilled beyond description.

Alfred

On one occasion, Jim was working in a field further away. Katie, being older than I, had instructions to take a meal to him. She got her orders mixed up and went to the wrong field. She could see brother Jim in the distance and took a short cut crossing a ditch. She slipped to the bottom but managed to get out on the other side. Jim was working towards her from the far end of the field. Katie did not wait for him, but left his food and went home. Brother sat down and prepared for the meal. Mother had sent meat, vegetables and gravy in one dish and some custard in a basin. When Jim took them from the basket, he found the custard mixed in with the meat and vegetables. Some of the gravy was in the custard, and half the drink was missing. It had happened when my sister slipped in the ditch. Jim was angry with disappointment. He perhaps would have felt better if Katie had waited and explained, but she was very young.

When Mother had several things to do at the same time, she used to get fuddled. Once she sent a similar dish, and of course it had to be Jim again. This time she omitted to pack any knives, forks or spoons. I suppose what he could not handle, he drank.

The autumn passed quickly on and everyone was busy. It was hurry to get the ploughing done, hurry to get the wheat in before the weather got bad, then hurry to get the cattle beet off before they were frozen, and keep on hurrying to finish the ploughing for spring corn so the land would get some frost on it.

Christmas soon came and went. Spring and Summer brought no outstanding events beyond the usual routine, which to me was always exciting. Some evening educational classes were started in the village and all my older brothers and sisters attended them in the winter evenings. It was a help for them as they had all left school at the age of twelve. These classes used to finish the session with a concert. I remember two of the songs sung by brother Jack. One was 'Yip I addie I aye' and the other was 'What a mouth what a mouth, what a north and south.' Practically all the entertainment fifty years ago was produced by the family for the family who provided both artists and audience. It amounted to dressing up, acting the fool then laughing at your own capers. Two sisters played the piano and many happy hours were spent round the piano singing, not forgetting to clap after each item. I venture to suggest that had there been an outside audience there would not have been very much applause.

left to right: Katie, Fanny, Alice, Mary, Alfred

The family had a mania for collecting musical instruments. The piano was by Collard and Collard - the table type - it was not new when we bought it, so it could easily be over one hundred years old at the time of writing. A member of the family still possesses it. It had quite a sweet tone, but had to be treated gently. If the keys were banged, the hammers would fly off. We younger kids sometimes imagined we were concert pianists, and 'properly got going.' In would rush Mother or older sisters shouting, "You'll have the hammers off!"

Sister Mary was the family pianist at this particular time; she was also organist at the village Methodist Chapel. When she had a session on the piano, I never felt it was complete unless the 'Battle March' was included, and I always requested it. The 'Battle March" was by John Pridham and was composed for the piano to describe the triumphant entry into Delhi during the Indian Mutiny. I could picture it all; the bugles assembling the troops, the drums of war in the distance, then the charge by the cavalry and the soothing mournful music after the battle. It stirred within me a mysterious imagination as did the music in the days of silent films.

We had an American organ for hymn singing and several Jews harps. To try to produce a note from them set my lips and teeth on edge. There were two or three mouth-organs, and an instrument we called correctly or incorrectly a melodion. I must confess I do not know the difference between melodions, concertinas and accordians. There were two violins, a flute, and some sort of concoction we called the dulcimer. This instrument was a long box, wide at one end and narrow at the other. In it were suspended two tapes; on the tapes, lengths of glass were placed beginning at about nine inches in length, and gradually shortening to about two inches. The notes were produced by striking the glass strips with a small wooden hammer. The long strips were the low notes, and the short were the high notes. Uncle Tom made this 'musical box.'

The odd thing was that with this collection of a dozen or so musical instruments and a family of twelve, only three of us were what might be described as musicians. Mary and Alice played the piano and Jack the violin. When I was twelve, I had three years lessons with the violin, and according to my tuition book, progressed as far as the 'shake!' If I now attempted to play 'The Blue Bells of Scotland' after forty-five years, it is just possible that a keen ear might detect it. Perhaps it would be a good idea to have violin lessons at the age of seventy-five when the shake would come naturally. With all this home-made entertainment, the winter passed quickly and happily by.

I think William must have finished helping Lucky at Honey Pots Farm and returned to Oak Farm during 1910, as I can remember Jack, Sam, Will and Jim all being at home at the same time.

Will caused an upheaval at this time. He was shooting at sparrows with a number three shot-gun. The cardboard case that contained the shot to form the cartridge would be ejected when the shot was fired. The day was hot and he fired at a sparrow on the roof of the cowshed. This shed was thatched and was quickly on fire. It also joined a large thatched barn. The house, with the same type of roof was six yards away, and the cattle-yards were all littered with dry straw.

Will & Jack

Poor Will did not know what to do first, whether to get help or try to put the fire out, so he tried to do both at once. He rushed to the house, banged on the windows and startled the family inside by shouting 'Fire in the yard.' A ladder happened to be nearby and this he placed on the roof. After giving the alarm, he grabbed a pail, filled it with water, ran up the ladder and managed to put the blaze out. Although the day was hot, the thatch below the surface was moist and smouldering, but the rapid action of my brother saved the situation, before it became too serious. When he had shouted to the family through the window his words were so incoherent that they misunderstood him and thought he had said, "Lion in the yard." They arrived at the scene of disaster armed with cudgels, pitch-forks and a gun. Mother had the yard broom. Will was coming down the ladder panting from fright and exertion. An old sow passed by at this moment covered in tar. She had been rubbing round some buildings freshly done. Jack remarked, "If a spark had fallen on her she would have wot you call burnt." Everyone roared with laughter turning a would-be disaster into a comedy.

This reminds me of another unpleasant incident concerning Will, but I cannot remember if it was during harvest of the same year, or at some other time. When my brothers returned from a hot and hard day's work in the fields, they would come into the kitchen, throw their hats on the copper just inside the door, and dump their bottles that had contained drink in the same place with anything else that would be needed when they went out again. Will was the last one home and it was customary for the last one, if he had finished his own drink and was still thirsty, to empty the other bottles. Twilight was falling, and the light was dim in the kitchen. Will tried the bottles for weight. "Ah!" thought he, "this one has some drink left in it."

He pulled out the cork and tossed it down. But alas! It was engine oil. I remember being wakened by his retching; he sicked and sicked. A few years later he went to Canada, and being a bad sailor was terribly sea-sick, but it did not come up to the engine-oil vomiting, he reckoned.

We had a tree in the orchard that bore sweet eating apples and after midday dinner, the boys would gather these apples to take back with them to the fields. Unfortunately the tree was so high it was difficult to get the fruit, and the only method of getting the apples was by throwing cudgels and knocking them down. Sometimes they would lodge in the tree then drop down unexpectedly, so we had to watch out. Usually there were plenty of cudgels about and there was always a race to get there first. Jack arrived to pick up his weapon. Jim, just behind, stooped to pick his up just as Jack was taking a mighty swing with his cudgel to reach the top of the tree. Poor Jim was struck a terrific blow on the nose. He always had a bump on his nose after that, which he claimed was the result of this blow.

One of the summer evening pastimes of my brothers was to tear about on ramshackle bikes. Before Lucky left home he rode a penny-farthing. I cannot remember this, but Katie can and recalls Lucky riding down a hill from the farm gate, hitting a stone and pitching over the handlebars headfirst into a ditch. She can particularly remember seeing the impression of his head left in the mud.

My first introduction to bikes was the bone-shaker. This had solid tyres and no accessories whatsoever such as mudguards and lamps. In fact, I do not believe there was a lamp bracket. There was no bell, wide handlebars and no hand grips. The boys would ride this skeleton machine anywhere, through the shrubbery, round the farm-yard, up the rough cart tracks and into the horse-pond where the horses drank. There was no fear of punctures, and in spite of being left in the most odd places, it was mobile for years.

Apart from the bikes for rough riding, five brothers and two sisters each had their own cycles in the first decade of this century. The boys often cycled to Stowmarket on Saturday evenings. This was a town nine miles from Oak Farm. As everyone worked six days a week, all the country people and town dwellers did their shopping on Saturday evenings which meant that the shops remained open until nine or ten o'clock at night.

This troupe of cyclists used to visit fêtes, flower-shows, sports and chapel meetings, and services of song in all the villages within a radius of seven to eight miles. Oil lamps were the only means of lighting, and more often than not the lamp glasses were so smoked up hardly a glimmer could be seen. The roads were in bad repair and stones picked from the fields were used for mending. The illuminations were not bright enough to show up the stones, and the riders were upon them before they were aware. The sudden bumping would put out the light, which really did not matter as it was so dim.

It was not unusual for five or six of the family to travel in one batch, and they rode close together in order not to miss any of the conversations. In addition to loose stones, dried horse-droppings and clods from farm carts, it was a common occurrence for a rider to hit an obstacle, swerve, over-balance and fall onto the next cyclist. This started a chain reaction and finished in a multiple pile-up.

Among the family photographs is one of sister Fanny at the age of eighteen taken in 1905. She is standing beside her bicycle in a dress down to her ankles, leg-of-mutton sleeves, a waist of twenty-one inches I expect, collar boned up to her ears, and embroidery on her hemline, neckline and cuffs. She wore a fashionable hat of the day to complete the picture.

The high-handled bike enabled the rider to effect an upright position when riding, the chain was completely encased, dress guards covered the top half of the back wheel. Never did the owner of a Rolls Royce caress his possession with more loving pride than Fan did her bicycle.

Chapter Ten

Cousin Lucky the soldier had been home from India a few years. He was now married with a daughter, Eva, two years old, and a son, Hugh Lucky, born August 4th 1910. They lived in married quarters in Colchester Barracks. I can well remember going with Mother to see them. The baby Hugh was six weeks old and I was six and a half years. The infant was in his cot and while I inspected him: he was sick and that made me feel sick too. I soon forgot my discomfort when Cousin Lucky took me to see the Artillery horses in the stables. There seemed to be rows and rows of them and so much noise from their feet stamping on the brick or cobble-stone floors. The chains on their head-stalls were sliding up and down through the rings and echoing through the huge buildings.

A few weeks after this visit, my cousin was sent to South Africa again, taking his wife and two children with him.

Another winter passed, and the cold lengthening days of spring 1911 arrived. At breakfast, on a bleak March morning, one chair was unoccupied; Jack was missing. He had confided in two brothers asking them to promise to keep quiet until he was gone. He packed what he needed or possessed the day before. On the morning of departure he rose early, left home at six to walk two and a half miles across the fields by footpath to Finningham station, to start the long trek to Canada and a new life.

Finningham station 1913

The secrecy was to avoid the emotional good-byes and any attempts to make him change his mind. Mother was terribly upset to lose another of her chickens. I always think of her as a loving protective old hen who wanted her brood with her always. Lucky had left the family nest to start farming on his own, but he was safely placed on a branch of the family tree, and could be contacted at any time. To Mother, it appeared that Jack had fallen out of the nest to be a victim of human birds and beasts of prey. She was constantly thinking about him, and was a long time accepting the fact that he was twenty-two and would soon learn to scratch for himself.

Being a family so closely united, and living as a community complete in itself, we missed him very much for a long time. Two days

Jack

after he left, Mother received a letter stating that when the letter arrived he would be in Liverpool, so it would be no use trying to catch him. We learnt later, when he arrived in Canada, that all he had left was two shillings and sixpence. It was customary for a number of employers to meet the emigrants off the boats with a view to hiring them, and Jack was fixed up with a job and a meal to fortify himself in the meantime.

This was the start of a long, hard life for Jack. After a few years in Canada he tried farming on his own. He lost three harvests by hailstorms, and one very hard winter, twelve of his horses died.

He was dogged by misfortune so took various jobs, living with the families. Most of the time he was with sheep, and as shepherd he used dogs which he loved, and had a gift for handling.

The forty-three years our brother has spent in this wild young untamed country would provide ample material for a book in itself. During these years his different jobs have taken him right across Canada, spending some time in Saskatchewan, Calgary and Edmonton in Alberta, then within the shadows of the Rocky Mountains, beyond to British Columbia, finally to settle in Vancouver on the Pacific coast. There was an interval when he returned to England to farm for about twelve years, but fortune did not come his way. He went back to Canada in 1937. He was always a good correspondent and kept us well informed of his experiences.

With the exception of Jack's twelve years farming in England, when two sisters kept house for him, he never had a real home of his own, such as we know it, since he ran away from Oak Farm at the age of twenty-two.

When he left Oak Farm, he had a good home, excellent parents, a sweetheart, an interesting job with the horses, and many friends in the locality. But Jack was not one to live within the barriers of his job; his visions did not stop at the fence of the field in which he worked. He looked at the distant woods, and wondered what lay beyond. What is it like on the other side of the Atlantic Ocean he wondered? He was like a lone wolf urged on by the haunting wail of its mate. Instinctively he had to go and leave his hunting ground of peace and plenty, and follow the trail to a distant bleak and unknown land.

When Jack left for Canada he told us in later years that it made him terribly unhappy to leave everyone he knew, and all those he loved. He thought of the horses he would never feed, groom and work with again. But the call came to him as it did to his Father thirty-five years previously, and he had to leave all and go.

In a letter to his mother, my father wrote in the 1880s, "If you know of anyone planning to come to India, please try and make them change their minds. This is a hard and cruel country. There is no place like England." In the next century Jack often stated in his letters, "If you can get a living in England, keep there." Yet neither of them regretted trying other lands. Although neither of them found wealth in their travels, they and thousands who did the same sort of thing were the empire-builders, and each did their bit, however small, in helping to tame those wild and raw countries.

Chapter Eleven

What of me, young Alfie, now seven years old? My world hasn't even started to grow. It still lies within the boundaries of Oak Farm, Wickham Skeith, and is still governed by the family. Father is the Prime Minister, Mother - Minister of Health and Welfare, Lucky, farming at Honey Pots Farm is Foreign Secretary, Jack in Canada is some kind of ambassador, Fan is under-secretary to the Minister of Health, Sam and Will seem to be joint Ministers of Agriculture. Jim is definitely Home Secretary because when I threw a piece of turf over a hedge and hit Katie in the face, he knew justice must be done, and punishment carried out. He boxed my ears so hard I rolled into the ditch. I never again threw grass turfs over hedges.

Mary is the Archbishop of Canterbury. She does her best to make me a good Christian. Allie is Minister of Education. She does her share in teaching me to write my name and lays the foundations of arithmetic. She also makes me do five-finger exercises on the piano, and tries to tell me what octaves, flats, sharps, bars, crotchets and quavers are (We had the Sankey and Moody hymn book from which I could nearly play Jesus bids us shine' and 'Sun of my Soul'). As a recreation Katie and I quarrel with each other. I am seven and have not started going to school yet.

One may well ask why, at the age of seven, I was not forced by law or otherwise to attend school. Well, you see, I did not feel well. I was well enough to run around the farm all day and to help with the sheep and cattle, but the mention of school really made me feel ill and when I told Mother, she believed me. She would take me to see Dr. Duffton, and he was a very kind family doctor. Mother told him I was finicky over my food. He would say, "Let him run about the farm and get plenty of fresh air." This went on until I was seven. I did feel ill but it was psychological. I could not stand being in a confined space. Often when in Chapel with the family and everyone was quiet, and I knew I must keep still for an hour, I began to feel suffocated. I would tug at my collar and nudge my mother with my elbow. I used to say "Mother, I fare funny." She understood and would take me outside. Perhaps it would have been better for me if she had been firm and made me stick it out.

What I actually think I suffered from was an over-active inferiority complex, under-active self confidence, and a high state of sensitivity, resulting in a tender heart. I have suffered from these ailments all my life, but they have affected me differently in later years. When I was very young, a harsh word would bring tears to my eyes. I could not endure anyone who was rough or cruel. If I was told off it would break my heart, and during my first few years at school the boys called me duck-hearted. Any family argument or quarrel would send my world to pieces.

In later years I gradually grew to be on the defensive. Never did I have any desire to be aggressive, and it would give me no pleasure to be so. I always had a yearning to create or produce something, but never wished to become a great leader; neither did I want to be in a position to be seen, and have always been content to stay in the background. Yet to be deliberately slighted or ignored to make others feel superior would create in me a disgust for such a person so as to result in pity for them. Many an inscrutable person, such as a hot salesman, who hoped to take advantage of my indecisive manner would be rudely awakened by my sudden temper. Like those who are nervous, I was harmless until cornered and someone tried to take away my rightful bone. Just like a puppy, I had followed my parents and members of the family who made up the litter. I followed them inquisitively and for security; it was just instinct and I was happy. Now I was to be parted from the litter with whom I had spent all my life, and taken to school. I was to be put with strange pups in a training kennel under a trainer to teach me obedience, discipline and to be useful. I think this must be one of the greatest ordeals in a person's life; at least it was in my experience.

It seems unbelievable, but at the age of seven I knew no swear words. I had never heard one. I was looked upon as a very good and sweet little boy. Being a good boy through ignorance cannot surely be called virtuous. The spirit within me was no better than the street urchins who helped drovers with the cattle on the markets. It has been my observation that it would be difficult to find any group of men to swear more fluently than these drovers, and boys are quick to pick it up. The words I heard from my family in place of swear words were, brute, beggar, muck, duzzy fool, crikey and darn. I well remember when in a temper, I would ring the changes as with a peal of bells, such as "Brute, beggar, muck...Muck, brute, beggar..." and so on.

I never remember ever hearing my Father use a swear word, neither did I hear my eldest brother swear. The next brother swore a few times, the next a few more, the next rather more, and the next beat the last, and I followed on!

So I began my education at the expense of the state. From the start to the finish it was a jumbled up course of education, all of it at the village school of Wickham Skeith. The total number of pupils was about ninety and there were three teachers. Mrs. Last the head-mistress took the senior children and a second teacher had the next grade; these were taught in the 'big room,' and there were two classes of infants. In the 'big room' the grades went from Standard I to Standard VI. I, being seven, missed the first infants' class and even then I was with six year olds. After a time I was moved to the 'big room' and put in Standard II. By missing Standard I, I did not get the preparation for the second standard, but was with my own age group. I progressed with the other pupils to about Standard V, when I was twelve years old.

The First World War had been going on for eighteen months. Nearly all the young men were taken from the farms for the army. There were no 'reserved occupations' as in the Second World War. Two of my brothers had gone. There were not enough men left to run the farms. The educational authorities, on account of this, gave permission for boys of twelve years and over to spend the six summer months working on the farms. As I had reached that age, I was taken from school for six months. The same thing happened the following year when I was thirteen; and at fourteen I left altogether. This meant that all my schooling was done in six years.

Mother pleaded with Father to let me go to the Grammar School at Eye, a small town five miles away for two years, but he was adamant in his refusal. He argued that working on the farm was my education and was preparing me to be a farmer. He left school at nine and had done very well. Schooling only put ideas into young children's heads and made them want to live above their station, and he added (and I have often heard him make the statement), "the more you educate a man, the bigger fool he becomes." He meant that common sense is often smothered by too much learning. Or again, while a so-called intelligent person is working it out in theory, the ordinary man would have completed the job. This would particularly apply to farming, especially fifty years ago, but of course this would not always apply to every occupation or profession.

Mother did insist however, that I should learn to play the violin; she thought there should be something in life besides just normal work. I had lessons for three years beginning when I was twelve. For these lessons I had to cycle three miles to the next village. Mrs. Last would let me leave school half an hour early for this purpose, as it was part of my education. By doing this, I missed the poetry lesson. I couldn't have both and finished with neither.

My music teacher taught in Finningham School, and when going for my lessons I met the children coming from this school. They used to jeer at me as I was not one of them. The boys tried to or pretended to stop me and shouted, "Can you fight?"
When I had reached a safe distance away, I yelled, "Yes, if you can catch me!"

I sensed Father did not approve of this sissy fiddling, so I am afraid I did not put much heart into it. Periodically, Mother would say, "Just let yer father hear you play so he knows you are progressing."

With much persuasion, I falteringly played my latest pieces. After I had finished and feeling very red, I dared not look up at him and waited for a bit of encouragement. Following an uncomfortable pause he would usually say, "Cor, you should hear old Jack Tarrent play (I am not sure if this was the man's name). He could regular make his old fiddle speak." I used to feel like smashing the darned thing into a hundred pieces and chucking it onto the fire.

That just about sums up the pattern of my learning. During playtime, and after school we played marbles, ran around with hoops, and used catapults. The roads not being tarred, there were plenty of loose stones that could be used for ammunition. We had pop-guns in the autumn made from elder wood, and used acorns for bullets; then there would be a spell of bows and arrows.

THE GREEN, WICKHAM SKEITH. (*Cullum's Series.*) J-1162.

Going back to 1910, the year before I began school, King Edward VII died, returned to earth and finished another reign. To me at six years, it meant very little. I had my own little world. Kings could die everyday as far as I was concerned. They were in another sphere. A far greater tragedy had happened in the village.

In subdued voices my family was discussing the suicide of one of the residents. He had drowned himself in his soft water-butt. I wanted to know why, how and what he looked like. By me, the King went unmourned, yet one story connected with the passing of Edward VII, dwelt in my memory.

Brother Sam used to meet the village lads on the green to hear the latest news and discuss events. A late-comer arrived at the gathering with the lining of his cap torn and hanging around his neck. One of the wits greeted him with, "Wot yer mournin' for the King bor - yar got yar blinds down?"

I was more conscious of the Coronation of King George V in 1911 because it broke into my territory. Celebrations were held in a meadow on one of the farms. My brothers took part in the races and we had a free meal. I won first prize for a bunch of wild flowers and was given a mug with the picture of the new King on one side, and his Queen on the other. It was the greatest crowd I had seen in the village, and out of the population of four hundred, no doubt two or three hundred were there.

After all the excitement, we soon settled down to the usual routine. Fanny and Mary stayed with Aunt Jane in London. She was very kind to us and was always asking some of the family to visit her. We used to look forward to their return home to hear about the wonders of the great Metropolis. Yet it was not the wonders but the ridiculous that my mind retained.

Once Fanny related how she had stayed at home while Aunt Jane took Mary around the big shops. Fan read for a while and then, looking round the room it struck her how grubby and fusty it was. I don't really suppose it was, but compared with the large farmhouse rooms with sparse furniture, kitchen, passages and pantry all with scrubbed brick floors, it looked so. The parrot was still there with Jim the Irish terrier, and lots of rugs, mats, ornaments and chairs packed closely together.

The railway was at the bottom of the small garden and the whole place appeared to be very dingy to my sister. She suddenly decided to give the room a good turn out. It was wrong of her to do so, but it was just the sort of thing Fan would do. She took the chairs into the garden, whipped up the mats, took them out and shook them then hung them up to air. Next she swept the floor and had a good dust all round. Now, she thinks, 'I will put everything back in its place.'

Fanny had not reckoned on Jim the terrier! As soon as she began to fetch the mats, the dog flew at her and guarded the possessions until his mistress returned. Aunt Jane found her room upset and poor Fan feeling such a fool. My sister mumbled something about trying to help. Aunt Jane answered with silence.

Whatever happened in London, life carried on the same as usual at Oak Farm. The routine was always the same, and anything just a little bit different was quite an event in our lives. It was now late July 1911. There was no sound of cars or motorcycles to disrupt the peace. We rarely saw motor transport pass through Wickham Skeith before the First World War. If one passed the school play-ground we would all rush to the gate to catch a glimpse of it. On this particular evening, the only sounds were the sleepy twittering of the birds, the possible grunt of a pig in the sty, and the contented groan of a cow as she flopped down to chew her cud after filling one of her stomachs with grass. Parents and children were just unwinding after a busy day; dusk was falling fast and the sun had disappeared, leaving some light still hanging in the west.

Suddenly, one of my brothers saw a balloon silhouetted against this light and coming in our direction. We gathered outside the back door and watched its approach. It looked a huge thing with a tiny basket hanging below. It was about four hundred feet up. Mother came from the house with a lighted candle and the balloonists, seeing there was life below shouted, "Where are we?" The brothers bellowed back, "Wickham Skeith." Father added with a shout, "near Eye."

I do not know if the information was of any assistance. We heard no more about the balloon that passed in the night. It was the first I had ever seen there, and the last. They were used as crowd attractions at fêtes sometimes. Once, one of my brothers cycled miles to see a balloon go up. Either weather conditions were unfavourable, or the balance between the gas and sand was incorrect; it never left the ground.

Chapter Twelve

Seven of my brothers and sisters had now left school. Mrs. Last the school-mistress thought Alice should sit for a scholarship. Mother agreed, but Father could not see much point in it. However, Alice went in for it and passed and attended Stowmarket Secondary School. That left Katie and myself at the village school. As I had spent most of my life with Mother and my sisters, it was natural that I should try not to let Katie out of my sight. The infant classes used to finish half an hour earlier than the seniors, and this meant that I was stranded without a sister to see me home.

I was not against a compromise so I hung on to Daisy Turner. She was my age and lived in the house next to Oak Farm. As she seemed able to provide me with company for a greater distance than anyone else, she seemed a good choice and we used to go home hand in hand.

There was another young lady I used to see at Sunday school. My brothers knew I did not like her and they often teased me about her just to make me ratty. I did not dislike Sally Booth, but could not bear the way she dressed. I think she was still using the fashion of a previous era when little girls wore drawers longer than their dresses, and the drawers were emphasised by having wonderful embroidery on the bottoms.

When my brothers said, "Have you seen Sally today?" I defended my honour by hotly replying, "I don't want her, she shows her britches!" Sally and I were Methodists; Daisy was Church of England. That was no disadvantage to my mind. We went to day school more times than to Sunday School, so she answered my purpose very well. Although I did not see Daisy on Sundays, I did enjoy the Sunday School and never felt that I was made to go. My sisters used to say, "Come on Alfie, it's time for Sunday School." There are times when a command is necessary, but a duty carried out by invitation gives more joy and satisfaction.

From childhood, I was brought up to accept that there was a God, a God you could believe in. I was taught to pray and live by faith. These things were never forced upon me. If they were, I might have doubted their existence. I accepted the glory of God as a spiritual food, just as a plant accepts the glory of the sunshine to live and grow; one cannot actually see the rays from the sun any more than one can see the power of the spirit of God. Yet we see the results of both around us, and feel the power within us.

The circumstances in which I was brought up make it so easy for me to believe in spiritual things. Had I been reared in the slums of London, or had wealthy worldly parents, or even lived next door to a village pub, my outlook could easily have been different.

The Sunday School Superintendant, my teacher, was actually like Christ, and Christ-like. His name was Walter Bean. In appearance his resemblance was very much like a picture of Jesus we had pasted on a cupboard door in one of the bedrooms. His beard was the same, and he had that same calm, passive expression. His occupation was woodwork, being a wheelwright and undertaker. Mr. Bean was a zealous follower of his Master. He lived about four miles from Chapel, but walking footpaths through the fields the distance was just over two miles. He did this journey twice every Sunday to talk to a handful of children, and we read passages from the Bible and sang hymns together. Yet his loyalty, devotion and example made a far deeper impression than would eloquent words from a less sincere person.

It is strange how we form mental pictures of life and eternity, and they could be nothing like the actual thing. The geographical outlay of Wickham Skeith left me in no doubt whatsoever of being on the right road for heaven.

In addition to Sunday School, I used to attend two services with my family. The services were generally conducted by laymen. I did not look upon them as humans with human weaknesses like everyone else. Whatever they said from the pulpit, I believed and accepted literally.

To reach our Chapel, the last hundred yards or so was a straight, narrow path about five feet wide. When the preachers spoke of keeping on the straight and narrow path that leads to heaven, I honestly felt that my destination was assured.

Then again, another speaker would tell us that the way is winding and difficult, with obstructions that must be encountered before reaching Paradise. My mind would instantly follow the route to the village church, a twisting uphill lane just wide enough for a hearse or wedding cabs, by brushing past the boughs. At the end of the lane, a gate had to be opened and closed, as a meadow had to be passed through where a pony and donkey often grazed. Then a second gate was opened before reaching the churchyard, which made me think that no doubt church people also went to heaven.

In my early years I could not quite fathom things out. I looked upon members of the Church of England as wealthy people, including the farmers who kept maids, the shopkeeper, girls who had left the village a few years and risen to be cooks, housekeepers and even the gardener at the Hall. I thought of them as rich as they all went to church and had a certain bearing. They walked with confidence. The chapel people seemed to think they must act with humility and appeared as if they were constantly apologising for being born.

Our preachers would read from the Bible about it being easier for a camel to go through the eye of a needle than a rich man to enter heaven. Some enlarged upon it. My mind was confused with the idea that rich people went to church, but could not go to heaven. What a pity adults do not realise more the tumult of a child's mind and explain things more clearly. I am still not sure if some of us ever get these things in their proper perspective at any age.

Having got it rooted firmly in my mind that as my father took me to chapel by the straight and narrow path, it must be the best way to get to heaven. As second best, we could get there through the church if we were not rich. These problems being solved to my satisfaction, the material part of life had to be faced. This was well cared for in our village, as just beyond the chapel was the village green. Here stood the day school and the general stores. Around the green there were three farms, two pork-butchers, the windmill and several cottages, so this part of the village supplied the needs of the body.

Beyond the green, the road continued, being the widest piece of roadway we had: it went downhill and we called it the 'Broadway.' My mind accepted that the way of the righteous is hard, and as explained previously, evidence supported it. I felt it was right, healthy and necessary to go to the green to have our wants supplied.

But our preachers told us not to go the way of the un-Godly. It was easy, they said, to yield to temptation, and they warned us most emphatically not to take the broad way that led to destruction. At the age of seven or eight, I thought they meant our road 'The Broadway,' which by a strange coincidence led to 'The Swan.' This was the village pub which I thought was an evil place and had to be avoided. To my tender mind, the layout of the village plainly illustrated, 'the way of the sinners,' 'the way of life,' and finally, 'the way of the saints.'

The former Swan Public House

Although I lost two years of schooling, perhaps by going around with my Father, hearing him converse with different people on various subjects, I learnt a little. As he was my Father, his views I believed were always right, but I also listened to the other person's point of view. These talks were pigeon-holed in my memory to be drawn out later to fit into some sort of jigsaw of life. Many of his statements are as fresh in my mind as the day they were spoken fifty years ago. In spite of the fact that he left school at the age of nine, he was a philosopher in his way. What he knew, he had learnt the hard way, and by observing other people he was always ready to improve himself. One of his many sayings was 'Correct yourself by other people's mistakes,' and another, 'Don't stop after a sprat if you can get a mackerel, but if there is no mackerel don't despise a sprat.'

It never bored me to go with my Father on his business trips, or visiting adult friends and relations. It never occurred to me to interrupt; I was content to listen. When any of these people addressed me directly, I became self-conscious at once and could never find words to answer. Even after half a century, I am still the same in a small gathering of people.

March 1912 came and Will decided to emigrate and join Jack in Canada. I can remember seeing him go off with Father in the horse and cart to the railway station. Oak Farm was a doleful place that morning; it meant that three of the six boys had left home. We heard, in due course that Will, being a bad sailor, did not enjoy the voyage. He had Jack's address, which I think was in Manitoba. Will arrived at his destination on a Sunday and not knowing where to contact his brother, noticed a service going on at a place of worship. He thought he would go in, and stepped inside and took a seat. He casually surveyed the man sitting beside him. It was brother Jack: the two had met 3,000 miles from home, in a place where their mutual interests led them. I bet their minds were not on the gospel at this particular meeting.

Sam also left the family home at about this time. By nature, he was a dealer. When at school he would have dealings with the other boys, and as he grew up he would buy and bring home unusual things, which annoyed Father. On one occasion he bought a donkey which was not very practical. I remember one very wet, miserable morning we had just finished breakfast. Sam was there and Father came into the room leading a long lurcher-cross greyhound-type of dog by a piece of rope. He had found it tied up at the back of the cart-shed. It was Sam's. Father was furious and a terrible row ensued. Other arguments followed other such dealings until Sam left home and went to live with a farmer with whom he was friendly.

This farmer let him have the use of a meadow on which Sam could put his unusual purchases. He also had a gift for carpentry and used to make poultry houses to sell. I believe Sam would come home to help on the farm during the busy spells. Once, either the farmer or another acquaintance bought a horse in London and asked Sam if he would go to London and ride it back for him. My brother loved doing anything unusual and readily agreed. He rode this horse bare-back from London to Suffolk, a distance of eighty miles. He said at the end of the journey that he was so stiff and sore, he could neither walk nor sit.

Sam was by no means a black sheep, but his nature would not allow him to plod on day after day in a monotonous routine. When he started a job, he would do the work of two men. He liked to get it finished and start on something else. Actually, he almost had the strength of two men. He was the strong man of the family. I have often seen him pick up a four-stone weight in each hand and slowly raise them full length above his head. Then he would gently lower them.

When I was nineteen, I thought I would try my strength. I was alone in the barn, and after a tremendous struggle I managed to get a four-stone weight above my head. Just at that moment I heard Father's footsteps approaching. I dared not lower the weight quickly for fear of dropping it on my head, but tried to resume an elegant posture as soon as possible. Instead, I came down with my burden and finished on the floor at a peculiar angle, just as Father entered the barn. If he had jeered me, mobbed me or warned me I might strain myself, it would not have seemed so bad, but he just ignored the whole affair as if it was the most usual thing to find me laying on the barn floor gripping a four-stone weight.

Leaving my weakness and returning to Sam's strength, he could lift a sack of barley weighing two hundredweight off the ground and put it in a cart three feet high. A sack full of grain is just about as awkward a thing to lift as you will find, as there seems nowhere to get a firm grip.

I had it related to me that one day three men were trying to lift a fair-sized tree out of a ditch with little success. Sam came along. "Get out of my way," he said. He got hold of the tree and stood it vertically, pushed it to the side of the ditch, and then lifting the other end of it, rolled it on to level ground.

So we pass along to another harvest. I pause a moment because it has just floated through my memory that it was this year, 1912 that the 'Titanic' was lost with about twelve hundred lives. The only thing that connected our family with this tragedy was, I remember hearing it said, "What a blessing Will did not book his passage on this ship."

However, in spite of national disasters, world wars, and earthquakes, seed-time and harvest, winter and summer never failed to return. After the Great Flood, when Noah and his family were spared, the Creator set His bow in the sky and promised never to flood the earth again, and it has been so ever since. But there are still floods locally and some prove very disastrous. In 1912 we had our flood. Towards the end of harvest it rained and rained heavily for two days. The ditches filled, the streams overflowed, the river rose. The sheaves on the lower lands were swept away, and chickens and their huts floated down the river. Wickham Skeith street where stood the 'Swan' was under water. The houses of Messrs. Hoyland, Gowland, Lambert, Mayes, Hayward and others were flooded. Instead of liquid being delivered to the 'Swan' in barrels, it was freely flowing in one door and out of the other.

The road from the 'Swan' to 'The Horseshoes' in the next village of Thornham, ran along by the river and was under several feet of water. For a wager, Putch Cattermole swam from one pub to the other, a distance of over a mile. From this it was alleged he caught a cold and died of pneumonia.

I well remember Sam driving us younger ones in the horse and cart to see the waters after they had subsided quite a bit. They still came over the wheel hubs.

Our flood drained itself away and we needed no dove with an olive branch to inform us. Time, as with all material things, soon obliterated even the scars left by the water, and the memory of it soon faded too.

The autumn followed, fresh and yet the same as those gone before. All writers of country life describe the smell of burning rubbish, the horsemen with their outfits for cultivation, the changing colours of the leaves, blackberries, wild hazelnuts, conkers, fallen leaves, flocks of birds passing overhead, the call of a cock pheasant, the notes of the partridge before they settle for the night and in those days there seemed to be a covey in every field.

I am not merely writing about these things. I was a part of them, as a partridge is a member of a covey. I was a member of a country family. It was my territory, my life, and I knew nothing else. I did not look upon this sort of life, I looked out from it.

With my pop-gun in my pocket I sauntered home from school, dragging my feet through the fallen oak leaves, picking up the acorns to shoot through the gun. They could produce quite a loud report, and if the target was someone's face, it could create a nasty sting.

I could hear the sound of a threshing tackle working at old Button Barker's farm, the almost mystic hum of the drum, (whence its name I would imagine) as the sheaves of corn passed through. The sound was rather mournful but was harmonised by the bright click of the elevator taking away the straw. It sounded like a beat in a musical group; but the most exciting sound was the powerful bark of the steam-engine with its loud chuff, chuff, chuff when the drums were working at full capacity, and dying away when the man feeding the machine was sorting out another sheaf. The steam-engine was not only the leader of the band but the driving force of the whole outfit. Governed by its governers it produced the power when needed, and kept the tackle and the team of about a dozen men working at a regular pace.

We all knew each other in the village and all that was going on. I knew the threshing machine would next call at Ernie Hammond's then Sandy Elsden's, Will Martin's and Stanley Cutting's before coming to Oak Farm. Katie and I used to be so excited when we saw it coming up our lane, and we would have to wait about another ten days for it.

I used to think the best time for threshing was February. The rats and mice had had time to breed and the stacks were full of them. We had the time of our lives killing them; it sounds sordid, but it's true. Some of the village boys followed the engine from farm to farm for this purpose. The old cats got wise to it and joined in, and the fox-terrier Tiny was doing her bit. It was quite usual for the mice to run up inside the men's trouser legs, so as a precaution they would tie string round the bottoms. As darkness fell, the old barn owls could be seen silently flying around for their pickings.

For this dusty work, it was a recognised thing for the farmers to supply ample home-brewed beer. For this, all operations came to a halt at mid-morning and again mid-afternoon. Sometimes, home-baked shortcakes were added.

The tackle's next call would be Carlos Mutimer's. Then Oak Farm would be silent again. A few mice would have taken refuge under odd heaps of straw, but to kill them was not the same; the excitement had gone. They are vermin and should be destroyed but I never got much satisfaction in taking life just for the sake of killing.

It was the custom at this period for most farmers to stack about ten acres of beans in the barn to be threshed with flails. The object of this was to provide work for the men during very bad weather. Katie and I used to sit and watch the men put a layer of unthreshed beans on the barn floor. Two or three men would thrash all over it with flails until all the corn was out. The straw was then taken away and the beans swept into a heap to be put into a dressing machine later to blow the short pieces of straw away.

The cost of these flails would be just a few pence. They were often made from young saplings grown on the farms, I do not suppose the three men would thrash more than a few hundredweight in a day. Little did I think that in my lifetime I would see one man manipulate a huge machine costing three thousand pounds which would harvest and thrash up to fifty tons of grain in one day.

Another job that was done when it was wet was sweeping chimneys. I have never heard of or seen anyone use such peculiar methods as my family did. They used a holly-bush which was like a small Christmas tree, and attached to it a long line. A man then took the other end of the line, which was weighted with a piece of iron, up the roof to the chimney stack. Using a long pole, he dropped the weight into the pot then down into the fireplace, where a second man gently pulled the line until holly bush and soot came tumbling down. For the copper flues they had a very unique idea that nearly ended in disaster for Jim. This was done with gunpowder. A measured amount was wrapped in several layers of paper which was lighted and thrown into the copper hole (as we called it). Before the flame reached the powder, the copper door was shut and firmly held with a broom against the shoulder, which could be a very anxious moment. After the explosion, the soot was removed from around the copper.

The unfortunate occasion happened when Jim did not wrap the gun powder securely. As he threw it into the copper hole, the paper loosened and before he could shut the door the explosion occurred. It singed his hair, removed his eyebrows and took the hair off the back of his hands.

Jim

Wickham Skeith is one of those villages that does not lie on a route connecting two towns. A few people from adjoining villages pass through the street, which is not the main part of the village, to get on to the main Ipswich-Norwich road. Therefore, apart from the residents, we only saw people who came to the village for business such as Mr Jolly. He was the carrier who brought supplies from Ipswich to the shop. Then there was the oil tanker drawn by two heavy horses with their nose bags swinging under the vehicle. This used to deliver paraffin oil in bulk.

During the spring, two or three stallions would call at their respective farms for breeding purposes. Usually their grooms rode in a cart drawn by a small pony. The stallion walked behind with his huge arched neck, and braided mane and tail all adorned with ribbons. They made a beautiful picture and we used to call them 'Show Horses.'

Our parish, with its population of four hundred was a community within itself and every movement was an event, even the weekly delivery of grocery. Mr. David Cullum kept the general stores and did his own deliveries while his wife served. He finished nearly all his sentences with, "Did you see?" but abbreviated, such as, "I'm late this morning, dee see." It seemed as if he was finishing all his statements with his own initials, D.C.

Sometimes we had tragedies that stunned us for days, like the one concerning a man who ran a business employing four others. We looked upon him as a figure of prosperity. One of the men arrived one morning to begin work. He unlocked the door, entered the building to find his boss with a rope round his neck and hanging from a beam. I remember that my Father was one of the jury at the inquest, but do not recollect the verdict.

At the age of nine this tragedy was pushed from my mind by the fact that it was now my turn to accompany Mother to London to visit Aunt Jane again. She met us at Liverpool Street station and we went through the usual routine. I was reacquainted with the parrot and Jim the terrier. He was getting old and peevish and had to be treated with respect. Mother and Aunt Jane extended my education by taking me to the places where children are usually taken, such as St Paul's Cathedral, the Zoo, Westminster Abbey and The Tower of London.

I appreciate London and all it represents and still gaze at the great buildings and their fine architecture with awe. Its huge population contains brains, brawn, ignorance, cleanliness, filth, wealth, poverty, crime, virtue and anything one could think of. It has been the hub of the empire and is still the hub of the world in some things, yet it would not make me feel important or superior if it happened to be my home. I should feel that I was one insignificant individual helping to make up the masses of humans, equal perhaps to one brick in the Houses of Parliament, or in fact about one ten-millionth part of London.

I am far more content to be one four-hundredth part of Wickham Skeith. We can claim just as high a percentage per hundred persons of crime, tragedy, divorces, virtue, immorality, wealth and poverty. In the country fifty years ago, we did not have to join the rat race to exist. We just simply existed and finished equal to the people in big towns minus the mad race. In the same era, most of the Londoners in the lower income class used to say that they could not live in the country as there is 'nothing to do.' They still did not do anything until their country visitors arrived. Then they would all go to a show or something, and we were equal again.

Could we reflect for a moment; the last sentences have suggested to me the striking similarity of extremes. Country folk are considered slow-moving, slow-witted and therefore ignorant. The bright boy makes money, accumulates a fortune with his head office in London. What is the next thing he does? - Buys a house in the country with some land, takes up shooting, horse-riding, and pretends he is a farmer. He imitates the countryman and tries to get back where he started.

Then there are the types of extremely wealthy people. Perhaps riches have come to them suddenly; they indulge to the full with food, drink, all-night parties and everything else that is done by the gay set. Their stomachs are ruined, resulting in a strict diet. They are so wealthy that they can get away with wearing any old clothes, and often die young.

The poor man is enjoying good, wholesome food; his clothes are serviceable, he can expect to live longer, and if he has a contented mind he is better off.

Please forgive me for that diversion. I am afraid I have strayed from the family, so will quickly return to Oak Farm. It was about ten o'clock on a December evening in 1913. Father and Jim had gone to bed. They were tired after working with the threshing tackle all day. Everyone else had gone upstairs except Fan and another sister who

were having a quiet read before retiring. Fan thought she heard rain beating on the window. She looked up and saw a light outside.
"My goodness," she gasped, "The stackyard is on fire!" She shouted upstairs, "Fire in the stackyard!"

Everyone came tumbling down and by the time Father and Jim got outside, sightseers and helpers were arriving. Someone was sent on a bicycle to Mendlesham, two miles away, for the fire engine. There was no telephone or motor transport and the bike was the quickest way to take a message.

Two horses were used for drawing the fire engine and the man who contracted to supply them had to be contacted. The men who pumped the engine had to be gathered together as it was a manual contraption. In the meantime, the fire was raging and the wind was blowing it towards the house. A gang of men fetched ladders and organised themselves in passing buckets of water and damping the roof of the thatched house. Burning straw was floating towards the house but was caught in a row of horse-chestnut trees growing nearby, which saved our homestead.

Father was getting panicky as the fire engine had not arrived. He told Jim to take the two fastest horses and go to meet them, but by the time he reached the road, the engine arrived. The firemen layed the hose from the horse-pond to the blaze while six men pumped for all they were worth and produced something a little bigger than a dribble. One good old beer drinker, Jum Stringer, who left the pub to attend the fire said he could have done better than the fire engine by himself.

Six-man horse-drawn fire pump circa 1913

Judging by the cans of home-brewed beer my family were taking to the firemen, I now think it was unnecessary to bring the fire engine. One straw stack that had been erected the same day and laid lightly, burned with such fury that the flames were seen by people from Ipswich eighteen miles away. Someone drove the traction engine to a safe distance, but the rest of the tackle and one or two corn-stacks were destroyed. The fire was caused by simmering cinders igniting some straw.

During all this commotion, Mother thought Katie and I would be better out of the way, so she sent us to Mrs Davey's in the village. I well remember grabbing my wooden money box containing about thirty shillings, and taking it with me. The money box itself was a present from brother Sam. He had written on the bottom, 'Started Alfred Burrows three years of age and hope he will get it full to buy a farm.' I have used this same money box daily for sixty years, and as I write I can see it standing on my desk.

We will pass along to spring 1914, as nothing of importance happened following the fire: that is apart from the tragedy of Fred Martin's horse. Fred did a bit of dealing, buying a few ducks and chickens. He used to drive his horse fast, then pull it up suddenly. One day, he swung into our yard, stopped abruptly and down went the horse. Fred leapt from the cart and sat on the horse's head. This was the usual thing to do to prevent the nag from injuring its head by struggling to get up. He sat there some time. There was no movement and he looked at the horse's eyes. It was dead; stone dead. "Huh," said Fred, "He's never done that before."

That same spring, Will returned from Canada. He had been there nearly two years. Father said that it had made a man of him, and the experience he had gained was worth more than a thousand pounds to him. This was a high figure in those days and I think father proved to be right.

We watched Will unpack his personal belongings and exhibit his treasures. There was only one trophy that dwelt in my memory. It was the head of a full grown bison, in skeleton form of course. My brother had found it on the prairie. It was such a cumbersome thing to bring home and it was complete with horns.

Chapter 13

It is now 1914, and twenty six years since Father took his wife and two children from his native village of Cretingham to begin farming on his own. From the time he left, until he was prevented by old age, which was a period of nearly fifty years, my Father loyally and sentimentally revisited once or twice a year the village of Cretingham where he was born. There were no relations on his side living there, but several of Mother's relatives were living there and in the adjoining villages. Some were farming on their own, and some working for other farmers.

Father had prospered and continued to do so, but he never forsook the people he knew as a boy, or relations, however humble. He never forgot that he was one of them, and he would not let us forget it either. In memory I look upon him with admiration for his humility, and appreciate it in others wherever it can be found.

In spring and autumn, a Saturday was given up to cleaning the harness, polishing the brasses, and washing the pony trap ready for those regular visits to Cretingham. Being the baby of the family, it was my lot to be chosen to accompany my parents on these journeys. The distance was fourteen miles and the travelling time about two hours as Father never hurried his horse. In consideration for the nag she was allowed to walk up and down the hills. He always quoted, "A righteous man regardeth his beast."

I used to feel very cosy and safe sitting between Father and Mother, with the cart rug over our laps. Father always seemed relaxed on these travels and would talk to Mother more freely. He would entertain me by pointing out everything of interest, such as a branch railway we passed that was started and never finished as the cost was incorrectly estimated and therefore funds ran out. There were the ruins of a church or castle standing near to a farmhouse. Passing a farm gate on one of these trips, Father unexpectedly stopped his horse. He had noticed a tiny chicken, about a week old, caught up in some wire netting.

"Alfred," he said, "Get out and release that poor little thing." This I did and climbed back into the trap. "There," he said, "If that chicken could speak, he would thank you for the kindness."

As we approached the respective birth places of my parents, there were the usual reminiscences. I really loved to hear these conversations although I could not always understand the trend. There were snatches of past events that remained a mystery to me for years. They often referred to the year of the murder, which seemed to be a kind of landmark of time with the locals. "Yes," Father would say, "It must be twenty six years since we moved from here to Stowupland, because it was the year following the murder." Details of gruesome happenings were strictly kept from the ears of us children. So this tragedy, veiled in mystery, faded away as a sort of village fable, and with the current events of passing years, the memory of it was lost in time.

But, in the year 1967, on a quiet September Sunday evening, I had a great urge to re-visit Cretingham, and to see the cottage in which my Father was born one hundred and nine years previously. With my wife, I called on the granddaughter of my Mother's sister whom I had not seen for over forty years. She, like myself, had passed the three-score year mark. After making ourselves known, I remarked

The former 'Bell'
Cretingham

how I was hoping to make a few notes on my Father's early life in the village. Quickly she said, "Don't forget the murder." I actually had forgotten hearing about it.

Two, and in some cases, three generations have passed away since the day Father was born, but the village has hardly changed. The same farmhouses and cottages still stand and are occupied. Most of the roads are the same width as when used by only horse transport. The only additions, according to my observations, are tarmac on the roads, electricity, telephone, television, and a few new bungalows. The Bell Inn where, according to Father's estimations, Grandfather spent too much time and money, is now a private house. Four very old cottages belonging to my half-cousin Charlie Mays, (and brother to the lady whose acquaintance I have now renewed), have been sold to an enterprising man, who has made them into a modern 'olde worlde' free house and called it "The New Bell."

The New Bell Public House, Cretingham

The week in which I was making this visit, the tiny school in which my Father received his scrap of education, was sold for conversion to a bungalow. Elsie, my new found half-cousin, has been a widow for over thirty years. She lost her husband when he slipped off a stack on to a sharp piece of hedgewood resulting in septicaemia. She was left with two small children.

We were escorted to Kittles Corner and with nostalgia on his behalf, I gazed at the cottage in which my Father was born; then on to

Friday Street in the next village of Brandeston where Mother was born. I could not look upon the house of her birth because it had been reduced to ashes by fire long since, and on that spot a new bungalow had been erected. I saw the school where Mother sat ninety-five years ago, and where she had designed a sampler which my sisters still possess. She left at the age of eleven. The school is now a private bungalow.

Then it was back to Cretingham to view 'Pot Ash,' the cottage where my parents had begun their married life and where their first two children were born. I truly felt I was treading where they had trod, and was literally following in their footsteps.

We returned with Elsie to her home.

"What about the murder?" I ventured.

"I don't know the details," she said, "but I'm sure a relation of mine still has the newspapers with the full account of it." How I longed to see those papers, but dared not ask, so went home unsatisfied. Elsie said that they were so fragile with age and could scarcely be handled. I did so want to know about the murder. After a few weeks, I wrote to Elsie, saying that we would like to visit Cretingham again to see her, and get further acquainted with the past, and would it also be possible to have a peep at the old newspapers?

"I shall be pleased to see you," she replied. When we arrived she said, "I've got the papers and you can borrow them and take them home with you."

There were three editions, 'Police News, Law Courts and Weekly Record', 'East Anglian Daily Times' and 'Suffolk Times and Mercury.' These papers were respectively dated October 15th 1887, October 3rd 1887, and October 7th 1887. Each paper gave a full account of the tragedy with details of the inquest and names of all the jury. It was a tragedy practically unequalled in the annals of crime and was described as 'a horrible tragedy,' and 'an appalling tragedy,' but I did not notice any of the papers referring to it as a crime. Whether we call it a tragedy or a crime, it is nevertheless a fact that the vicar of Cretingham was murdered by his own curate.

The vicarage where this awful deed was done stands less than one hundred yards from the cottage in which my Father was born.

At this particular time my parents were living in the same village and within half a mile of this startling event. As I write these notes, it misses three days of being eighty years since this terrible happening. People still living in the village, so I'm told, had parents who were closely connected with the vicar through the church. With such an outstanding tragedy in a small village of about three hundred inhabitants, it is not surprising that stories handed down, got slightly distorted through the years and were verging on the supernatural. But the facts were recorded in these newspapers, which are for the time being in my possession, as follows.

The vicar, whose health was not too good, engaged a curate to assist with his duties and the curate lived in the vicarage as one of the family. At first the two men had differences of opinions, but became more friendly as time wore on. After about a year the curate became unwell and went away for three weeks for a change. On his return the vicar, through ill health,

The extract to the left is taken from the Framlingham Weekly News for October 8th 1887. For the story in more detail, read Sheila Hardy's book, 'The Cretingham Murder', published 1998 was confined to bed. He was an old man of seventy-three with a very thick, bushy beard. The curate was thirty-three years old. In one newspaper he is photographed with a moustache, and in another he is clean-shaven, no doubt taken from an earlier photograph. He was a bachelor. The vicar's wife was much younger than her husband; she was in her prime and was his third wife. The first wife had died before the vicar acquired this living, and the second who died at Cretingham is buried there.

THE VICARAGE CRETINGHAM SUFFOLK

On Saturday evening, October 1st 1887, Mrs 'Vicar' had been reading to her husband. She came downstairs at about 9.30 p.m. to join the curate, the groom and the maid-servant in prayers. After prayers the young clergyman said to his hostess, "I could hear you reading to your husband and it irritated me." He was still feeling ill, in fact not well enough to take the church services the following day. The vicar's wife said, "I will go back and read to my husband until he falls asleep. Then I'll read to you"

She returned to the old man's bedroom where she had what is described as a crib at the bottom of his bed, on which she could rest when not attending to her husband. Having had two nights of broken rest, the vicar's wife apparently fell into a deep sleep and did not fulfil her promise to read to the young man.

Just after midnight this woman was awakened by a lot of rattling outside the bedroom door. She opened it expecting to see the maid; instead it was the curate. He said, "I want to speak to the vicar. Can I come in?" She was wearing just her nightdress, so she pushed him out and locked the door. After a short time this disturbed man returned, and again knocked loudly saying, "I must speak to the vicar." He seemed very persistent so the old vicar said, "Let the poor fellow in and see what he wants." This time the lady put on her dressing-gown before unlocking the door.

The curate entered the room carrying a candle in his right hand. He passed the wife and went to the bedside of the husband. The wife heard her husband say to the curate, "Now don't be foolish," and chuckled as if it were some sort of joke. The younger man left and went to his own bedroom which adjoined. Awaking from a deep sleep, the woman could not seem to follow the curate's movements in detail, but could remember hearing her husband say, "He's cut my throat." She went into the curate's room. "What have you got in your hand?" she demanded. "Nothing," he replied.

Returning, she found her husband on the floor with blood gushing from a wound. She called to the young man, "You had better come and see what you have done." She tried to stem the flow. The groom was sent on horseback to Framlingham four miles away, to fetch the doctor. Two hours elapsed before the doctor arrived but in the meantime the vicar had died. His throat had been cut practically from ear to ear, and a bloodstained razor was found under the looking glass in the curate's room.

While this treachery was going in, the murderer was wearing his dressing gown. After the deed, he dressed in his clerical garb and left the house. Evidently he wandered about for several hours, and was seen approaching the vicarage from the direction of Ipswich at 5.00 a.m. He returned to the vicarage, entered the hall to find a policeman standing there. The curate spoke to him saying, "Can I go up to my room?" "But I must accompany you," replied the constable.

He took him in custody and had him removed to Framlingham where he was placed in an ordinary cell. He was tired, sullen and very quiet.

The vicar's body was taken to the Bell Inn where grandfather used to sup his beer. The inquest was held there and the body and wound inspected by the jury. I imagine there must have been a trial; if so, it was in later editions of the newspapers. It was reported in the account I read, that at the inquest the deceased's wife was stringently questioned about her relationship with the condemned man. One juryman in particular would not let it rest. His questions came thick and fast as one would expect from a barrister. But the victim's widow answered openly and promptly and without embarrassment, every time. If I could judge by the detailed account of the whole affair, I would say she had been innocent of anything immoral.

The curate was eventually found guilty but insane. His past history revealed that he had been mentally affected, and ten years previously had had treatment in a mental institution.

One correspondent, reporting on the tragedy apparently felt that it needed a bit more drama as dessert. Evidently he searched through the history of Cretingham church and found: I quote his words as follows: 'In "White's Directory for Suffolk" it was narrated that in a vault in the chancel in 1826, the skull of Lady Cornwallis who was buried in 1603, was found perfect with long plaited hair.'

When I began this chapter I was jogging along with my parents in a horse and trap and nearing the village of Cretingham and then somehow drifted back to 1887.

We will come forward again to 1914; the visit to the relatives was over once more and we were on our way home. Kitty mare never needed any urging when homeward bound. She knew the way and needed no guidance with the reins. The wheels rattled over the loose stones where the roads had been recently patched up. Usually, we would be about halfway home at lighting-up time. Getting the cart lamps lighted was quite an operation, especially if it was windy. Mother held the reins while Father performed it. Father always took spare candles with him to replace the burnt-out ones.

Nearing home we left the narrow lanes and came on to the turnpike, the Ipswich-Norwich main road, originally made by the Romans. This was well maintained and easier travelling for the horse. But only half a mile brought us to Thwaite 'Buck's Head,' one of the stopping places for the stage coaches where they changed to a fresh team of horses not so many years before. We took a turn to the left here, leaving one mile to go to Oak Farm and home.

Chapter 14

Seven years had passed since Father started Lucky in farming. He was well established and was getting along comfortably. The one time farm-worker, maltster, fisherman and soldier now considered that he was able to launch another son into business. During the summer he looked around for another farm to hire. At the same time, the Kaiser was looking around for some countries to conquer. By harvest time, Father had selected a farm, but had not begun operating on it as the recognised date to start a fresh farm was October 11th. Kaiser Bill had selected a country and could not wait until October 11th, and he started his war operations on August 4th 1914.

I was ten and can vividly remember this date. Father had bought two new self-binders, one for Lucky and one for himself. These 'up to date' machines reduced the labour force by three men to the one hundred acres, by doing away with the job of running behind the reapers tying every sheaf by hand.

On this particular 4th August, the new machine, drawn by two horses, was cutting wheat in Sheeps Close near to our main breeding place for wild rabbits. As the field was being finished, this meant the sport of the harvest of rabbit-catching. They usually took thirty or forty, which was plenty for everyone to take home to make rabbit pies with pork added.

Will had his twelve bore gun, (I'm sure it was Will; the same brother who nearly set fire to house and buildings when shooting sparrows). He discharged both barrels directly behind the horses which startled them out of control. They went full gallop to the end of the field and were stopped by another brother. Only a small part of the binder was broken, but it spoiled the day. The horses were taken off the machine, and while covering it up, a very dark thunder cloud came up from the Abbey Farm direction. I clearly recollect one brother saying, "There's a black cloud hanging over England," to which another brother mournfully replied, "Yes, and there'll be a darker one yet." To me this seemed the end of the world. I could not decide which was the bigger catastrophe, the broken binder, or the war that was starting that same day.

However, war or no war, harvest must be completed and preparations made for the next one. Plans had to be made; extra livestock and implements bought to equip the new farm. Father could not choose the son next in line according to age to manage the new project, as this should have been Jack, who was still in Canada. So the lot fell to Will, the fourth son.

At the age of twenty-four, brother Will took charge of Harts Hall Farm, Walsham-le-Willows, twelve miles from Bury St. Edmunds.

At the age of fifty-five, Kaiser Bill had overrun Belgium and was trying to take charge of France. But I must leave the war and its history in better hands than mine and just concentrate on my family.

The same procedure that was taken when Lucky went to Honey Pots Farm, Worlingworth, was repeated in similar pattern by Will going to Harts Hall, even to taking sister Fanny as his house-keeper.

Father's beginnings in a smallholding of twenty-six acres had now grown to four hundred acres. In doing this he seemed to have a unique method of his own design. At least, I have never heard of such a method being adopted. But then, I would not know, perhaps that was how it was done up to the beginning of this century. In the first place, Father never told us what he had in his mind. We had no idea for what object we were working, apart from just working for our clothes and food. We did not dream that he would be able to afford to start us all off in farming. Of course, after the first two or three boys had become established in farming, we in turn expected the pattern to be repeated; in fact it nearly got to the point of our demanding it. Even allowing for the time Jack and Will were in Canada and Sam was away from home, from the time we left school until we began farming on our own, we six sons worked for Father for an average of eleven years each. During these eleven years we never received a penny in the way of wages, allowances or pocket money, but if we were willing to build our own pig sty or chicken house in the orchard or corner of a meadow, and make a few pounds for ourselves we were allowed to do so. By using this method I am absolutely convinced that it was not done for the purpose of employing cheap labour. It may have been to make us value money. Father did not want us to take the attitude of 'Let us eat, drink and be merry for tomorrow we get another wage packet.'

The affluent way of life was not even heard of in this age, unless it was by the very few of whom the many would never come in contact. We had to be trained to go without things in the present so that we could enjoy comforts in the future. One could always hear people saying, "I like to put a bit away for a rainy day" or "You never know what you might want." It was on this doctrine that Father had to form his plan, which I feel was to keep everything within the family for the family, and not just for himself. If only he had told us this plan, I am sure we would have worked with more vigour and co-operation.

We were provided with food and clothes, and these were bought with money Mother made from the produce of about three or four cows, and the eggs from about two hundred hens. For extras such as carpets and furniture replacements, a batch of turkeys were reared for Christmas trade. I think most farmer's wives provided for the housekeeping in this way at that period. The farmer of course provided the food for the cows and poultry.

Now when Father decided to start a son in farming, he did it in his way. His aim, by the way, was to get each of his sons into a four horse farm - that is a holding of about one hundred and thirty acres. In practically every case he could provide the horses by breeding his own working horses. The value of the four horses was written on a piece of paper, and added to this list was the price of seed corn in going valuation, machinery, cattle mangers, breeding sows and anything else that was needed. Then a sufficient sum of money was placed in a current account in the bank in the name of the particular son who was taking the farm. This money was for labour, first half-year's rent and running costs. The total of these items in those days was about twelve to fifteen hundred pounds, equal in purchasing power to fifteen thousand pounds at today's price. The hiring of the farm was done legally through a solicitor and valuer.

The rest of the transactions between Father and son were done by deed of faith and trust, with no witnessed documents to prove anything. Sometimes Father did not even have a copy of the capital involved. He would casually say, "You can use this money for as long as you like, free of interest, and pay me back when you can." So according to the state of farming prosperity, good fortune, and the ability of the borrower, each one repaid the money when, or if they could. I heard it suggested as the money was paid back, Father had not actually helped his sons.

But looking at the facts, had he paid us the wages in force at that time and we paid for our board and clothes, by skimping and scraping it might have been possible to have saved around sixty pounds in about twenty years. The prospects of starting a farm on this would have been very bleak.

Letting us have this money free of interest, Father was losing for himself about five hundred pounds on each son. For a man in my Father's position, and for that period, this was a very large sum, and there were six sons. I do not think we appreciated to the full all that he did for us, or thanked him as we ought. Even with the help we had, not one of us accomplished anything comparable to his achievements.

* * * * * * * * * *

Although Father had served seven years in the army and was very patriotic, surprisingly he would say to his sons who were eligible for the army, "Now don't volunteer to fight in this war, but when your country sends for you, go. If you offer your services, and feel you are not being useful you will think 'what a fool I was to volunteer.' If you wait for conscription, you can say, when my country needed me, I went."

The war, and farm work went on. 1915 came, and my sister Mary, who was now twenty, worked on the farm milking the cows, feeding the other stock and working in the fields. She loved the outdoor life. During harvest, she was suddenly taken very ill with violent pains. The doctor was sent for and he ordered her to hospital immediately; it was appendicitis. Either through the delay in getting her there, or the lack of advanced operating, sad to say she died.

Mary with her class at Wickham Skeith school

This was my first experience of bereavement within the family. Mother was heart-broken, and the whole household was cast into sudden mourning. It was the worst happening of my life, at the age of eleven. The smell of varnish and wood of the coffin standing in the parlour, mingled with the scent of flowers was a combination I shall never forget. Even today, similar smells always take my mind back to this very sad occasion.

The conflict, to be known as World War 1, was growing more serious, and my brothers were expecting to be conscripted at any time. But the war department remembered that they had our cousin Lucky in South Africa; they sent for him and his field artillery early in the year. His family was brought to England and Corporal Lucky Lockwood was sent to France just in time to win the Mons Medal. With such a man holding the fort, Sam and Jim had not yet been sent for.

Actually, I wanted them to go. Not because I wanted to get rid of them, neither did I hope they would fight. I just longed to see them in uniform. A lot of the village lads kept coming home on leave in uniform, and I was sure my brothers would look better than they did. Everything they did I thought was wonderful, and I was sure they would make marvellous soldiers.

Sam did not like to volunteer against Father's advice, but he had an urge to see some action, so decided on a middle course and joined a Remount Depot in Ilford, Essex. I shall have to make a guess at the nature of this Depot. It was either a kind of horse hospital, or convalescent home for getting horses fit again for war, or a gathering place for civilian horses before being sent to various horse regiments, or both. In any case there were some pretty unmanageable animals to deal with, which Sam enjoyed.

My world was still Wickham Skeith and all my interests in the war were either through my family or our village, such as comments like , "George Davey is on leave. He's a Sergeant now." Then we heard that Jack Martin had been killed. Through these sorts of things I learnt about war. Meanwhile, we each carried on with our daily tasks and individual duties. I was keeping rabbits, which was a paying proposition, and also had a fresh girlfriend. No! I don't mean I was keeping a 'fresh' girlfriend. Daisy Turner and I had somehow drifted apart, perhaps into different classes at school. Then she was not so necessary to me as I was now brave enough to go home from school alone: besides, I had a bicycle.

Ruby Day was the girl who sat in front of me at school. When the lesson did not hold my interest, my attention was drawn to her hair hanging over my ink-well. When one sees something hanging, who can resist pulling it? It may not have met with her approval, but certainly gave me satisfaction and proved that the instinct of the Ancient Briton was not yet extinct. If she did not approve of my approach, it had the desired effect of making her conscious of my presence. I had not diamonds to give to Ruby, which would be too much like giving coals to Newcastle, so I gave her my attention, which was cheaper. We became friendly; I always felt safe when I was with a girlfriend, deriving I think, from the fact of being protected by so many sisters. It was a haven, away from the aggressive, harsh and unsentimental boys.

Some of the children said we were sweethearts. I didn't know; the relationship was pleasant, and that was the main thing. I think it is right to take happiness as it comes so long as it is not at someone else's expense.

At about this time, tragedy struck our small community again. As I have never kept a diary, I have no idea of the exact date, and will not try to find out. The span of time that I would remember these sort of things could not have been more than seven years, and this was the third suicide in this small village. It is a mystery why people should take their own lives, and what happens to their minds. This man had a thriving little business, then suddenly we learn that he had shot himself. It was reported that there was quite a large sum of money in cash about the house.

Sam & Jim in uniform

Having been sent to the next village of Finningham on an errand, I got caught up in the full glamour of war. Approaching was the sound of hundreds of horses and as they came nearer, I could hear the jingle of the horses' bits. They were rounding the White Horse corner. Six hundred mounted men (so I was later told), were moving to another camp in Norfolk. The women were bringing out aprons full of apples and throwing them to the men as they passed. The children by their sides were waving enthusiastically. I took in every detail at the time - the harness, the spurs and the men's overcoats rolled and strapped on the saddles.

Had I been old enough, I am sure I would have enlisted right away, and more than likely found myself peeling potatoes in the cookhouse. I wished my brothers were among them to share the glory.

It was not long before my wishes were granted. Sam had given his name in for service when needed, and was soon called up. He joined the 17th. Lancers: their motto is 'Death or Glory.' It was a peace-time crack regiment, but with the short war training no regiment could claim to be superior to another. I remember when Sam came home on leave how he demonstrated the charge with the Lancers using bags of straw for the enemy. They rode at full gallop, thrusting the lance through the 'body' and then letting it drop off behind them ready for the next one.

However, to my knowledge the cavalry were never used in World War 1, so Sam was transferred to a machine-gun regiment. After a very short time, Jim was called up. He chose the Royal Field Artillery and was accepted as a gunner, but later he became a signalman.

We at home did not feel the effects of war very much. There were food shortages which we did not notice, living on a farm. The zeppelins sometimes came within hearing distance and I saw the outline of one on a clear night looking like a huge cigar. One was brought down not so far away, and people in the village could see it burning in the sky before it eventually came down. It happened on a Saturday evening. A young man who worked for Father came in on Sunday morning to feed the stock and said to me, "Shall we go on our bikes and see the wreckage?" I readily agreed. We had no idea where it had fallen. As we pedalled along, people kept telling us which direction to go. On and on we went and knew we had covered over twenty miles. We then met some fellows on bikes.

"Where's the zeppelin?" we asked.

"At Theberton," they said, "We've just been."

"How far is that?" my pal enquired.

"You've got over ten miles to do as yet," they beamed.

Walter turned to me: "Can you stick it, shall we go on?"

"Yes," I said, "I'm alright."

THE STRAFED ZEP.

DISMANTLING THE WRECK

TWO SURVIVORS.

In East Anglia where the 'strafed' Zep. fell on June 17, tho' the excitement has died down considerably, a lively recollection of the events of Sunday week still exists and thousands of pilgrims have visited the spot.' On Sunday last the crowds all day were enormous and the Police, who were there in force had all their work cut out to regulate the relic searchers. These very thoughtlessly invaded the neighbouring lands and trampled down the corn in places before they were discovered, thus adding to the damage already sustained by the farmer occupier.

The work of dismantling the derelict has proceeded ever since its fall—and continues. To facilitate the work a well-known firm of tractor manufacturers were asked to send one of their engines, as it was desired to recover two or three more bodies which could not be readily got at owing to the superimposed weight of metal. But the engine was found to be too strong for the purpose and would have torn the Zep. framework to pieces. So this brilliant idea had to be abandoned and the naval contingent went on with their more leisurely method. The meaning of the old saying, 'Slow and sure' was thus once more exemplified.

We finished the journey and saw the heap of twisted metal. We brought home a piece as a souvenir. Checking the distance we gathered we had completed over sixty miles. I was twelve years old, saddle-sore but not too tired. Just as we arrived home, Father and Mother were leaving for chapel three miles away. They were in the cart ready to go, so I left my bike and went with them. Walter went home for tea, then returned to feed the pigs and cattle.

The newspaper extract to the left appeared in the Leiston, Aldeburgh & Saxmundham Observer on Saturday June 30th 1917. The picture above is from one of a number of postcards produced and shows the team of men sent to dismantle the wreck. Indeed there were only 2 survivors from a crew of 23.

With Sam and Jim in the army, Oak Farm was short of labour with only two men and Father. Walter Barker, nicknamed Kee Kor was the horseman, and Walter Wade, nicknamed Coddy was stockman and labourer. They were both young men in their twenties, married with children. Father had to attend a tribunal from time to time, to keep them exempt from army service. Someone had to remain on the farms to produce food for the army to march on. To keep the farm going, Father had to be his own second horseman. Kee Kor used the first pair of horses, and in that capacity was senior to his boss. Father would start at seven in the morning just like a farm-worker and do a full day's work in the fields with the horses. In addition to that he shepherded his flock of one hundred sheep in the early morning and evenings.

To reinforce the labour problems at the age of twelve, and with the permission of the educational authorities, I was kept from school for the six summer months to help on our farm. It is surprising what a boy of twelve can do. In connection with the sheep, they were folded on sanfoin. Father would make a fresh fold in the evening, and I would let them in the next morning. In the hot, dry weather, I would let them run on the meadows so that they could drink at the ponds. After harvest, the sheep would have the run of the stubble and I had to keep them from straying off the farm.

The pigs and young cattle were practically in my charge under Father's supervision. During the early summer there was the horse to lead on the hoes, with a man at the back to guide the hoes. This job lasted several weeks.

At harvest time I would take the empty waggons to the fields and bring the loaded ones home. Father would not allow me to lead the horses for this job as he believed it was too dangerous. The horses might tread on my feet or I could be kicked when they were worried by flies. In either case it was more than possible that I would fall in front of the waggon wheels. This meant that I had to ride every time using three waggons and three different horses. Every horse had a character of its own. Gypsy was a stubby built mare, always in a hurry and taking the shorter cut everywhere. If you wanted to pull her to the right or left, she went all in one piece, like a wooden horse.

Then there was old Depper; she was more flexible, moving her head from side to side and inclined to follow her head and roam about. She had to be constantly kept on a straight course. Depper had a kindly eye, and you could even imagine a kindly smile. She used to turn her head right round to watch me climb on the shaft, then on to her back. If she had spoken, I don't believe I would have been surprised, I almost expected her to say, "You're a funny little ol' thing. You don't know much." When I clambered down from her back, she would smile again as much as to say, "Here you are again. I should get on just as well without you."

For the third waggon, the horseman would change the horses around. If we were carting from a difficult field with bad gateways and undulating land, it would be Smiler. He was a fine upstanding, intelligent gelding, and very reliable although he was only six years old.

When it was level ground and straight gateways, I was trusted with a four year old named Tinker. At that age, he had not formed a definite character, and his movements were unpredictable. His four years and my twelve years only totalled sixteen, so did not represent much wisdom, and certainly no experience. No wonder Depper smiled.

Being in charge of such a young horse was a man's job, and I was very conscious of it. After a long day, I looked back on it with self-satisfied importance and went to bed with a very big head and a very sore bottom!

The War Office thought that as Jim had not completed his training for active service, the British Expeditionary Force in France could manage a few weeks without him. They decided to send him home to help Father get the harvest in. It was an exceptionally wet harvest, and at the end of Jim's twenty eight days the corn was cut but not carted, and it was sprouting badly in the stooks or shocks as we called them. On behalf of our King and Country, and through many channels, someone in authority said in effect, "You can keep Jim another fourteen days, and get that harvest gathered in." With the benefit of this extension and the help of an old navy pensioner, the harvest of 1916 was completed.

This was Will's second harvest in his new farm at Walsham-le-Willows. He also was short of men and was allowed to have two soldiers to help him. They were Welshmen: they lived in the house, and Fan cooked for them. Having completed their job, they returned to their unit, leaving my brother and sister on their own again. Both were very nice fellows.

Hart's Hall Farm house was very isolated, standing nearly a mile from the public road. The road itself was a very minor one and little used. The long drive was no more than a rough cart track. Where it was not patched up with stones, water stood in the tracks, three or four inches deep. Close behind the house, a green lane ran that once connected two roads, but was now grown over with only enough room left to walk along. Down this lane poachers often prowled who were not against picking up a few fowls from lonely farms.

It was here that Fan frequently spent the evenings alone, as Will had begun courting. No television, telephone or wireless in those days; no traffic within hearing distance, just quietness. A large English sheep-dog with a bob-tail roamed around to guard the place supported by a terrier. When they broke the stillness with their combined barking, it could be even more nerve-wracking than the quietness itself.

The name of the large dog was Bob as would be expected, and the small one was called Brownie because of her colour: not very imaginative names, but suitable nevertheless. Wherever Bob went, Brownie followed on three legs; one of her feet was cut off by a grass-cutting machine. It had healed and a pad formed which was nearly as tough as the toes she had lost. The stump used to come to ground occasionally when taking a sharp bend on that side to support the body weight. Bob and Brownie sometimes became bored guarding the farm against poachers, so for a change, they went poaching themselves. Brownie did the ditches while Bob stayed on top, hoping to catch whatever came out.

It must have been while they were on one of these jaunts in the late evening that a mysterious sound approached the house. Fanny was alone and could hear it coming; the clinking of a chain being dragged slowly over the stoned yard. No other sound, no footsteps to be heard. The dogs were not there to frighten it away, or to cover up the weird noise with their barking. Nearer it came, right to the front window, paused, and then went round the house to the back door. Here the rattling chain stopped.

Fan was terrified. She dared not go out and investigate. Figuratively she froze in her chair, but thawed out when Will arrived home. He went out again to find that one of the cats was caught in an iron rabbit trap that was used in those days. The chain was used to fix the trap to the ground. The cat had been caught by the foot. She had managed to pull the trap clear and dragged it home to the back door knowing she would get human aid for her release.

My sister had several scares whilst at Harts Hall. One was in the middle of the night when she heard banging coming from a room downstairs. She went to Will's room and awakened him. They went downstairs together expecting to see the unexpected, and couldn't even see that for some time; then they saw it sitting on the curtain-rail regarding them with thoughtful eyes. An owl - it had entered the chimney and had apparently fluttered all the way down bringing the soot with it.

On another occasion Will was called to sit on a jury in Ipswich, and was unable to return home that night. It had to happen when my sister was alone, that in the early hours of the morning she was awakened by a man shouting and banging on the front door. She plucked up courage to ask what he wanted.

He answered, "Is your brother there?" She dare not say that he wasn't, so replied, "Who is it?" The man shouted back, "My name is Fountain. I am a neighbour and I have a cow calving and cannot manage alone." Fan explained the situation. I am sure Mr. Fountain was more distressed about giving my sister such a shock than he was over the condition of his cow.

I used to spend many weekends and parts of school holidays with my brother and sister, when they related everything that had happened at Harts Hall.

By early 1917, Sam, Jim and Cousin Lucky were all fighting in the front line in various parts of France. I cannot resist including our cousin as he always seemed to be one of the family. His wife, Mabel, and their children spent the full length of every school holiday with us. I hero-worshipped him. He was a born soldier, trained and experienced, with Indian and South African service behind him and the ordeal of the Boer War. He was fearless, reckless and a bit of a blunderbuss.

He seemed to be promoted to a higher rank every few weeks. In fact, he rose from Corporal to Captain in five months, which was or is a record in the artillery to reach the rank of a Captain in such a short time. He was mentioned in dispatches four times and awarded the military cross.

We watched for the post daily to learn if our brothers were safe and well, often with dread in case they were not. Jim was caught in a gas attack, which affected his eyes. He recovered after a short time, but the effects from it still troubled him from time to time.

On another occasion, he was thrown from an army waggon injuring his head on the hard road. He was sent home to England for treatment. Sam received one slight wound, otherwise they both remained in active service to the end of the war.

Father, Lucky and Will were trying to produce all they could from their farms. Food was scarce and precious so they helped with the war effort and benefited themselves as the prices were high. Even my rabbit project was flourishing with the prices at about ten shillings a rabbit, and rising to one pound. Father gave me a pitman pig, (that is the diddy one of the litter) as a reward for my first harvest. I brought another from him to keep it company. They proved to be very profitable. The money I gained was invested in the school war-savings effort as fifteen-shilling certificates. My teacher, Mrs Last, complained because I did not take in a regular weekly sum. I had to explain to her that I had no money until I sold my pigs or rabbits.

Another sideline I had would bring me in vast amounts of money: these were rats' tails at twopence each, hen-sparrow-heads at one penny, and cock sparrows at about a farthing each. This was paid by the local council, and a person in the village was authorised to pay out the money. The object of this scheme was to destroy vermin and save valuable grain.

Often I would build up my supply for a week or two before presenting them for payment. By this time, the smell was so unbearable that the treasurer took my word for the quantity rather than count them. I also caught moles and sold them for ninepence each. These were then skinned and sold at one and threepence a skin. So, at the age of thirteen, I was quite a tycoon.

During the same year, Will and his girl decided to marry. Owing to the war, it was a quiet affair, but it answered the same purpose. It released Fan, so she packed her belongings and returned home again. The war was making itself felt and was very real to us. In spite of the hardships and sorrows, it did not make us less shocked to learn that another villager had taken his own life. This was the fourth tragedy of this nature to happen within my short memory. In

Will & Doreen with daughter Dorothy

sympathy and consideration for the families of the victims of these acts, I make no effort to find out details or exact dates.

While my brothers were in the army, and after the farm men had finished work and gone home, I was Father's right hand man, there being no one else around until the men returned to work the next day. When a job cropped up that needed two pairs of hands, I felt very important to be called upon to assist. While I was still only twelve, Father said, "One of the heifers is just about ready to calve. I shall want you to come and hold the lantern."

Mother was disgusted. "You're never taking that boy out there are you?" she said. Father continued lighting the lantern, and not looking up he replied, "Why not, he's got to learn some time."

I did not want to hurt Mother but was afraid to disobey Father, so I followed Father to receive first hand knowledge of the birth of a new life.

It was rather difficult to deliver the calf, as the heifer was small and the calf more than average in size. When the mother had recovered her strength she got up to inspect her off-spring. She began to lick it, but when the calf shook its head the young cow went mad. With her mouth open, and frothing, she began to bellow like a mad bull. One moment she was stamping on her newly born calf, and the next moment she was butting it about the shed with her short horns. I was most prompt in finding the nearest way to the door. Father was shouting, "Show a light." So I exposed the least possible part of my body to the dangers of the moment by holding the lantern in one small hand on the dangerous side of the door. The rest of my body I kept on the safe side.

When I recovered my composure enough to peer through the crevice made by my wrist which was joined to the hand holding the lantern, I could see Father battering the beast about the head with a wooden stake five feet long and two inches in diameter. Where Father had found this weapon I had no knowledge. Perhaps he had it ready for such an emergency. He tried for some time to get the animal to own its young without success. Her brain seemed temporarily upset by the ordeal of the confinement, so Father put the calf in a separate shed, hoping the heifer would settle down before morning.

In the morning, with the help of the men, a halter was put on this awkward mother and she was tied to a post. The calf was brought out and held against its mother until it began sucking at the teat. This gave comfort to the cow which instinctively turned her hatred into mother-love and brought happiness to both, and to me - my first lesson in midwifery.

Naturally I expected this to be the routine every time, but usually the calves arrived easily and were accepted happily by their mothers. The following spring, two mares were due to foal and again I was present to help and gain experience. I was thirteen years old and accepted these things as just another job in a day's work. It never occurred to me to tell my school pals what I did. Actually about all I did in these maternity cases was to hold the lantern. We could not expect these expectant mothers to be in the best place in the labour ward for light and convenience, so we had to take the light and manipulate it wherever the animal decided to have her offspring, which sometimes was in the most awkward part of the buildings. Father's instructions for the positioning of the light was rarely much more than , "Higher, lower, right or left." He used to say, "That's right Alfred, show the light. If you can see, I can see."

When everything was over, and mother and baby were doing well, I honestly felt that **we** had done a good job.

Father never tried to minimise my importance over this. He knew that anyone could have done my job, yet he could not have managed without an assistant. I was equal to a boy pumping the bellows for a piped organ; necessary, but not very skilful.

When I returned to school in the autumn, after my summer away helping on the farm, I discovered that I had lost Ruby. Harry Potter had won her love, and it must have been very sincere as they eventually married.

To heal my wounds I tried to charm another young lady by giving her sweets and showing her my watch. I always carried a watch. Teacher used to ask me the time when the school clock stopped. The boys did their best to get me to tell her the wrong time so that we could come out of school earlier. But I could not forfeit her trust: besides, it might have jeopardised my chances with Iva Hammond.

Iva's father was a wealthy farmer and lived in the third best house in the village, according to my opinion. I thought the Hall and the Vicarage might place it in the third position. It was in one of Mr. Hammond's bullock-yards a few years back, that an employee of his hung himself. My friendship with Iva developed very much to my satisfaction. We passed letters to each other under the school desks and even got as far as sending one or two through the post. Iva Kate had a very attractive hoarse voice, and a crackling laugh. According to my memory, her hair was a light gold in colour and hung round her head in ringlets. On Tuesday afternoons I went to Finningham for violin lessons and she agreed to meet me outside her house on my way home in the twilight of the winter afternoons. If I kept Iva out beyond her usual tea-time she did not have to give an account of where she had been, as her parents did not arrive home from Ipswich Market until early evening. As for explaining to my own people of the delay on my part, I could always say that there was a head wind, even if it was behind me.

Iva was two years my junior, which made her eleven years old, so I was superior in age if nothing else. Another thing I noticed about my little friend was that her hands were always cold. According to the adage, cold hands denote a warm heart. As I did not discover the temperature of her heart, I could not vouch for the truth of the saying. It was not long before Iva's parents moved her from Wickham Skeith school to the grammar school at Eye, so our paths divided for all time.

Six summer months working on the farm brought me to the autumn of 1917. Six winter months at school brought me to the spring of 1918 when, at the age of fourteen, I had finished with school completely. With my broken spells of schooling amounting in all to six years behind me, I began farm-work in earnest.

Time marched on and the war began to wear off. About October 1918, Sam was allowed home on leave. He had been in France for over two years. We were very glad to see him, and he of course was delighted to be at home again. The flu epidemic was raging at this time and our entire family with the exception of Father, went down with it. Fan managed to crawl around to look after us: five of us were in bed with high temperatures. Sam suffered the most, as he had pneumonia which affected both lungs. Although I did not realise it, the family thought he would die. A pal of his from the next village, who came home with him, caught the same complaint and did die. The story went round the village that 'poor old Sam had come home to die.' However, he recovered, and while he was convalescing the war ended, so Sam never had to return to France.

What a wonderful feeling when a war ends! You can look forward and plan although it needs a great deal of readjustment. The dark cloud that had hung over England when war was declared, and became darker as one of my brothers foretold, was now showing a silver lining. In fact, one could see the sunshine of hope behind it.

Oak Farm, Wickham Skeith in 2011

Honey Pots Farm, Worlingworth, where Lucky Jnr. farmed. The house was built in 1908 by Hugh Lockwood, cousin Lucky's father.

Harts Hall Farm, Walsham-le Willows, where Will began farming. He later bought this farm, and sold it to buy Wattisfield Hall, pictured below.

The Burrows Family Farms

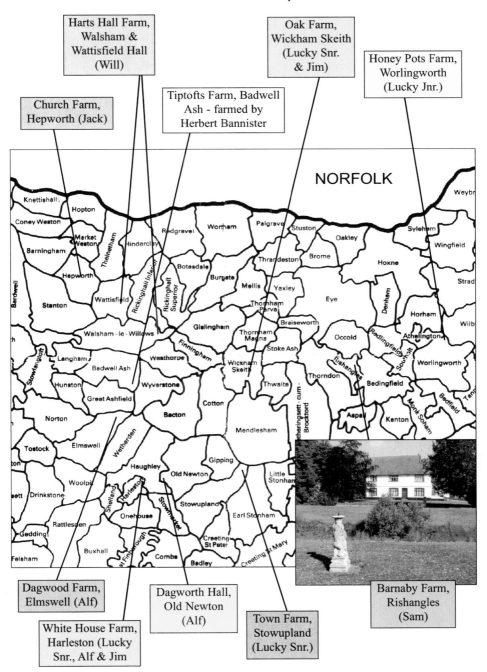

Harts Hall Farm, Walsham & Wattisfield Hall (Will)

Oak Farm, Wickham Skeith (Lucky Snr. & Jim)

Honey Pots Farm, Worlingworth (Lucky Jnr.)

Church Farm, Hepworth (Jack)

Tiptofts Farm, Badwell Ash - farmed by Herbert Bannister

NORFOLK

Dagwood Farm, Elmswell (Alf)

Dagworth Hall, Old Newton (Alf)

Town Farm, Stowupland (Lucky Snr.)

Barnaby Farm, Rishangles (Sam)

White House Farm, Harleston (Lucky Snr., Alf & Jim)

White House Farm - an early colour photograph. Below, the house in 2011.

Chapter 15

Sam and Jim are now fully demobbed. The war is finished and pigeon-holed to join history, but it is still fresh in the minds of my brothers. They relate their experiences and I listen eagerly, and take in every detail so much, so that after nearly fifty years I can still remember Jim's army number: 148032.

The past was soon smothered by the duties of the present. Jim again took his place at Oak Farm, and Sam went to live with Will at Harts Hall, working there where he was needed. During the war, Father had been able to accumulate more money with the high prices of farm products. In 1919 he hired another farm for Sam. This was Barnaby Farm at Rishangles, consisting of 120 acres.

Sam & his wife Lily

The same procedure was adopted as with Lucky and Will. There was one difference in this case however. Sister Fanny did not go as house-keeper as Sam married a few weeks after taking possession of the farm.

There seemed to be happenings in the village from time to time to remind us that there was a world outside the family. One of these diversions occurred at about this time. The widow of a doctor living in Wickham Skeith advertised her house for sale. It was oak-beamed, plastered and thatched; a picturesque 'olde worlde' dwelling. Amongst the prospective buyers to view the property was a man very interesting to converse with. The conversation drifted away from the property for sale to the Lady's private possessions.

She picked up a revolver to show him. It was alleged that she slept with it under her pillow. She handed it to the man to examine. It was loaded. In passing it to the expectant house buyer, the fire-arm went off, and the bullet entered the woman's body resulting in her death. The whole affair was purely accidental.

SERIOUS ACCIDENT AT WICKHAM SKEITH.

A distressing accident occurred at Wickham Skeith on Monday afternoon, Mrs. Gowland, of Summerseat, widow of the late Dr. Gowland, being accidentally shot. It appears that Mrs. Gowland has recently disposed of her residence, and was handing a revolver over to the purchaser when the weapon went off, Mrs. Gowland being seriously wounded in the body. Medical assistance was sent for, and Messrs. Spencer, C. F. Wright, H. V. Mitchell, and H. E. Burns, M.D., were quickly in attendance and ordered the patient's removal to the East Suffolk and Ipswich Hospital.

from Suffolk Chronicle: November 1919

These tragedies do not stop life carrying on, and the villagers, including the Burrows, went about their daily duties.

Father said, "Alfred, I want you to take some seed corn to Harts Hall in the tumbril. Kee Kor will tell you which horse to take."
"Oh, can I have Matchett?" I pleaded.
"I don't think you ought to take her. She's only three years old and hasn't been in the shafts many times. It's seven miles to Walsham-le-Willows, and you are only fifteen," he answered. "Anyway, I will ask the horseman."

The reason I wanted Matchett was that she was the first chestnut horse we'd had. The other horses were all black. Besides Father's four blacks, Lucky, Will and Sam had all started farming with four black horses. Then Father began using a Suffolk stallion and Matchett was the result. She was a showy little mare with arched neck and full of life, picking up her feet and taking three steps where two would have done. She was sweet tempered and harmless. When asked, Walter Barker alias Kee Kor, the horseman, said, "The boy Alf will manage her alright. They'll be alright."

Was I proud to drive that outfit through the village! No one noticed me. This did rob me of a little of my importance. I just felt as if the eyes of the world were upon me. Matchett and I got on very well, and became great friends. We worked together for the next ten years.

At this present time, I was learning to use those cameras I had been given, and to try and develop and print the plates. This is the equipment that Aunt Jane gave me that had once belonged to her son Percy. A photographer friend of mine gave me some instructions on the matter.

I did not indulge much in social life, having no wages. My evenings were occupied in attending to my rabbits, pigs and chickens in order to make a little money; by the time I had made a few shillings, there was no time to spend it. Even if I had some leisure time, I felt it was wrong to let my hard-earned money go easily. I would have liked to join in more sport, but always felt that Father thought it was a waste of time.

Alfred

For a while, I belonged to the Scout Movement and learnt to tie a few knots behind my back. This particular scout troop was run by a Church of England rector from an adjoining village. This Rev. Bennett, who to me seemed an elderly gentleman, invariably wore shorts on any occasion and wherever he went. This looked rather odd, especially walking in Ipswich on a cold day, and he drew many enquiring glances. It was difficult to decide whether he had just dropped in from the tropics or was a lost highland piper. One look at his clerical collar belied both these suppositions.

A non-conformist church began a Boys Brigade company nearby, and I decided to transfer to that company as most of my pals were members. The only thing I can remember learning from this organisation was that I was a bigger fool than I thought I was. On a very special occasion, all the surrounding villages joined the Stowmarket Company on the Recreation Ground for an inspection by some Army General. There must have been nearly two hundred of us lined up and nearly falling over backwards in smartness. We had to jump to attention at the appropriate command while the General took the salute. When the command rang out, "The General's Salute," I took it to be 'the general salute.' Consequently I stood in the front row of the ranks doing a lonely salute, while the rest of the company stood to attention. I felt like a worm on a pin, and prayed that the General did not think I considered myself his equal.

I had my special friends, the ones I could speak to on an equal footing about rabbits, pigs and chickens, and we would sometimes compare our opinions and admirations of farmers' daughters. It sometimes leaked out where our affections lay.

One of these special pals and myself were discussing our possessions one evening and we tried to find out which of us was the wealthiest. We began confiding in each other, and it transpired that he was worth one hundred pounds and was fourteen years old. Then we began to make a valuation of my assets. I had some investments in War Savings Certificates; there might have been a dribble in the Post Office Savings Bank. There were the rabbits and their hutches, thirty laying hens and a few cockerels shacking on the stubbles. My total did not quite reach one hundred pounds, so we valued my bike and that just brought my wealth equal to my pal's. My friend was proved the better man because I was one year his senior. Considering the purchasing power, what we had then was equal to about eight hundred pounds at today's prices. Of course we had the war to help us reach this target.

Most of the men had returned from the forces and had settled into various jobs. The life of the village had taken on its normal pattern and Oak Farm had the regular gang of men again. Mother was still cooking and feeding the family; she was the mainspring of the works. Father may have controlled the outfit, but Mother's absence would be felt sooner than his.

All men should remember, 'The hand that rocks the cradle rules the world,' and never forget the years when we were entirely dependent on our mothers. My father was a good-living man, typically Victorian, a person we, his children, greatly admired, but we found it very difficult to demonstrate our love for him. He seemed to be completely unapproachable. It may have been necessary because of his large family, and he was absolutely just and never physically cruel. It would have been lovely if he had been able to show more tenderness towards Mother. She would have responded so readily and truly deserved it. He did not show his appreciations for her qualities as a good wife and a real mother, but was not slow in revealing his irritation when she could not match him in the business outlook.

Father was steward at the little chapel in Wickham Skeith, and mainly as there was no one else to do it, he took on the job as secretary and treasurer. Having left school at the age of nine, he was not equipped for these offices, so Mother became the secretary's secretary, and sister Allie the treasurer's treasurer.

The old chapel at Wickham Skeith pictured in 2008

Allie succeeded Mary as organist. Taking the twenty-one years my family lived at Wickham Skeith, I do not believe it would be an exaggeration to say that we accounted for one quarter of the congregation. Mother sometimes became mixed up with her secretaryship and farm correspondence. She would write several letters, and later address the envelopes, and it was not unusual for her to put the letters in the wrong envelopes. One letter was to a lay preacher, asking if he would be able to conduct the service at the chapel on the following Sunday. If he was able, she would be pleased to entertain him for tea. Another letter to Messrs. Quinton and Son Ltd, corn-merchants and suppliers of animal food at Needham Market was sent asking them if they would kindly deliver, as soon as possible, pig food, calf meal and cooked maize in quantities as stated. The preacher received the order for feeding stuff and Messrs. Quinton and Son were asked to preach and be entertained to tea.

Sunday school picnic at Oak Farm

Oak Farm was approached by a lane from the east, and would be considered, even by a countryman, as rather a lonely spot. It was roughly quarter of a mile from the little-used road that connected the two villages. Situated north-west of Oak Farm was a second farm, and not many could have been more isolated. It was completely surrounded by neighbouring farms, so that none of the land joined a public road. Not even a footpath crossed the farms, and when the occupiers entered their land from a narrow lane and closed the gate, any unauthorised person passing this spot would be trespassing. To reach the farmhouse from there would be to follow the farm drive or track through the meadows and between the fields for about one mile. It was in this house that a family of five spent a night of terror, with not a hope of human help. The nearest occupied dwelling was a farm cottage standing three quarters of a mile across fields to the west. At about the same distance was Oak Farm from a north-easterly direction. Neither my family, nor the cottage people heard their cries for help, and there was no chance of anyone else hearing them either.

From six o'clock one evening until past seven the following morning, this family locked themselves in a bedroom while an armed, would-be murderer, prowled inside and outside the house with a gun. It was autumn, at six o'clock in the evening, and the light was fading. The family were sitting round the table having tea. The room was lighted by an oil-lamp standing in the centre of the tea table and the curtains were not drawn.

For obvious reasons I will give the family the fictitious name of Wood, and the man who kept these people imprisoned in a bedroom all night I will call Oldman. As Mr. and Mrs. Wood, their two sons and one daughter sat having their meal, two or three shots were fired at them through the window. The mother and daughter were wounded. The entire family rushed to the door, across the hall, up the stairs, and into a bedroom, locking themselves in. I do not know if they remained in darkness the whole time, but I imagine they would be afraid to show a light, and may not have had any means of doing so.

In terror they could hear Oldman's footsteps outside and if possible, they felt worse when the sound of the footsteps entered the house and wandered from room to room. They thought he might shoot at the lamp standing on the tea table, and so set fire to the house and perhaps shoot them down like rats if they tried to escape. Their lips were parched with fear and their throats dry, but they had no liquid to ease the discomfort and no food to aid their feelings of faintness. Although they were all one family, it must have been embarrassing to spend thirteen hours in one room with no preparation for such an ordeal. At intervals during the evening and into the night, Mr. Wood opened the window and yelled at the top of his voice, "Help, help, murder!" But his voice just faded in the breeze before reaching human ears.

With the dread of what the next moments might bring, the time must have seemed to stop. At the same time, we 'Burrows' were carrying on in our usual way oblivious of the plight of our neighbours. We had been thrashing corn all day, and in the evening a special meeting was being held in the chapel. Either through duty, desire or inspiration, we all trooped off to these affairs in one body. After washing the traction engine's smoke and corn-dust from ourselves, we had our tea and then set off at about six o'clock for this Methodist gathering. Jim did not join us; he had a cold and was full of dust and phlegm, so he would stay at home and hope to keep well enough to help with the threshing next day.

The rest of us returned from the meeting full of the details of our evening out. Brother Jim seemed thoughtful. "I can't make out what has been going on outside there," he said. "Just after you left, I heard a gunshot. I didn't bother to go outside not feeling very well, so I settled down to read. After a time the old turkey cock began calling out."

Cock turkeys, cock pheasants, guinea fowls, and ganders are all very good at giving the alarm when something unusual is happening. Jim, being a countryman, knew this old gobbler sensed that something was wrong. "I put my hat and overcoat and went out. Two more shots rang out," he continued. "They appeared to come from the direction of Wood's farm. No one could see to shoot rabbits. Anyway, I decided the shooting was not on this farm and so I came in again."

Jim settled down once more. The house was quiet. Only those who have spent some time in a lonely farmhouse know the silence I mean. There were no neighbours, road-traffic or trains within hearing distance; no television, radio or the expected ring of the telephone. Jim would possibly hear a mouse nibbling behind the skirting board, or the first drops of rain splashing on the window pane. My brother would be able to identify all the farmyard noises and he told us that he had heard the old gobbler give his cry of alarm two or three times during the evening. I imagine that the birds have very keen hearing and that after we knew the facts of the tragedy, we came to the conclusion that every time the besieged family cried out for help, our old turkey cock heard them and gobbled.

We all went to bed. Next morning we were ready for threshing again, with the exception of Jim whose cold was worse. He was not up to remind us of the previous evening's gun shots and turkey warnings, so we all forgot about the happenings. At breakfast Father said, "I shall not have enough sacks to put the corn in, so Alfred would you go to Mr Wood's and ask him if he would lend me a few. If he can, I will fetch them later."
This was 6.45 in the morning.

Ignorant of what was happening to the Wood family, Father was sending me right to the scene of the terror. I was about fourteen years old. I took the short cut across two meadows and down beside two fields to reach this farm. It was a frosty morning and the meadows were really white with it, and who, young or old, can help getting a thrill to be the first at making a footprint in the great expanse of pure white. This might strike you as a desecration of something pure.

I remember this particular morning as clearly as if it were fifty days ago instead of nearly fifty years. Crossing the middle of the second meadow, I felt like an explorer walking where no other human had trod. I was within forty or fifty yards of the gateway leading to the first field when my dream was shattered. Someone had been there before me. Coming towards me were other footprints. I have always been interested in footprints; human, birds or animals. These were made by a man. If my errand was urgent, I forgot about it. I turned around and tried to walk in them. I could not. They were too far apart. I tried looping into a run, and by doing this I could step into them. So the man who made them was running. Boy scout teaching came out. They branched off from the way I had come and headed towards the gate of another field in the direction of the village. In my mind I had formed a clear picture of someone running away from the farm to which I was going, with the object of reaching the village as soon as possible. I left my detective work and continued my journey to execute my Father's orders.

I reached the further end of the first field which left me about a hundred yards to the farm of Mr Wood. A gun went off. "Huh!" I thought. "Someone is shooting in the farmyard." My brothers were always shooting at rabbits and pigeons - all farm people did the same, and it meant no more to me than stepping on a dry stick.

At last I arrived at the back door of the house where the family were still locked in the bedroom, and where they had spent thirteen hours of fearful agony. They still did not know in which part of the house Oldman was, but they knew that the shot I had heard had been fired somewhere in the house. Less than five minutes after this shot, I was knocking at the door. I received no reply, so I hammered away again. The besieged family would not have been surprised if the gunman had come round the house and blown my brains out.

After knocking at the door for the second time I stepped back to ascertain if the family were up. I was seen from the window behind which they were trapped. Mr. Wood opened the window gently and gesticulated frantically for me to keep quiet. He whispered down to me, "Go home as quick as you can and tell your brother to come at once." I came away through the hedge and over a railway sleeper used as a bridge into the field and started for home. Then I remembered that Jim was ill. I returned to the farm, knocked at the door, stepped back and looked up at the window again. Mr. Wood opened the window and I started to talk to him. He looked scared and again motioned me not to make any noise, so I breathed up to him, "My brother is ill; who shall I send?" In a panic he replied, "Anybody, anybody, send somebody." Off I went in full ignorance of the tragic urgency of the case, imagining that someone had broken a leg accidentally which would need urgent attention.

The threshing team was one short as Jim was ill and I cannot remember who went to answer the call. In the days that followed, my family including myself received full and first-hand particulars of the whole affair, not because we happened to be the nearest neighbours, but mainly because Mother was so kind-hearted. Mrs. Wood and her daughter were taken away for treatment, which left the husband, a grown-up son and a younger son not yet twelve to fend for themselves in an atmosphere of morbid memories.

In her generosity, Mother told these three that they were welcome to come and live with us, which increased the family to ten and after a while threw the household out of balance. Then the older son and his father were asked if they could find other accommodation and that the younger boy could stay until his Mother returned home. This was accepted. While staying with us, their experiences were related in detail.

According to my memory, the facts were as follows...
Oldman was married and was not a native of the village, but was working in Wickham Skeith and living in a caravan until his job was completed. He became acquainted with Miss Wood and it developed into a friendship which reached a point where she realised that there would be no future for her. What was in that man's mind on that fateful night no one will ever know. He may have thought that if he could not have her, neither would anyone else. By taking a gun and firing it through a window proved that he meant to take drastic actions to satisfy himself.

The misery he brought to this family has been described and can be better imagined. No hope of rescue came to these people all through that night. At seven o'clock in the morning, the farm men appeared for work and one of them went to the door for the day's orders. Mr. Wood spoke to him from the bedroom window as he had done to me. This man was sent to fetch police, doctor and help.

It was this man's footprints I had seen passing over our meadow. I imagine Oldman saw these men appearing for work, and may have gathered that one of them was dispatched for aid. He realised the game was up. Evidently he turned it over in his mind for ten minutes or so, and then turned the gun on himself. This was the shot I heard a few minutes before I hammered on the door. Little did I know that a man lay dead behind that door, warm and perhaps still twitching.

The mother and daughter recovered from their wounds. The lonely farmhouse story appealed to newspaper reporters, and locally it was a sensation. It made good reading for Londoners as a lone farm all-night siege story. Several reporters called at our farm hoping to pick up crumbs of news. As I only missed being in at the kill by only a few minutes, I could picture myself as headline news in all the papers. I searched through all the London papers and the only reference I could find was, 'A boy from the village on business bent, heard the last shot.'

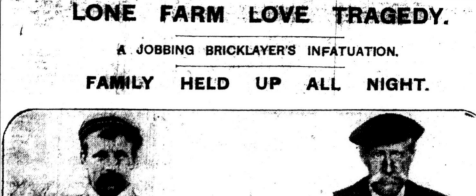

LONE FARM LOVE TRAGEDY.

A JOBBING BRICKLAYER'S INFATUATION.

FAMILY HELD UP ALL NIGHT.

In the above photograph is seen the farmhouse which was the scene of this tragedy. Through the lower window on the left Youngman first fired and failed, and it was in the lower room on the right that he fired when Mrs. Reeve received her arm injury. The kitchen through which the assailant attacked, when he went to the rear of the premises, and injured mother and daughter, is immediately behind the front door. Inset on left is the dead man, Alfred John Youngman, and inset on the right the farm bailiff, Mr. Reeve.

from the Suffolk Chronicle & Mercury: March 5th 1920

Lucky & Alice Snr.

We are now passing through the year 1920. Father decides to take life easier as he is now sixty two. He does not want to retire completely: for him to live in a town house would be like trying to keep a cuckoo in a canary's cage. He looks around for a small farm of about seventy acres which could be worked by himself, one employee and myself.

In the 'Farms for Sale' column appeared what looked like the ideal place. Father viewed the land and buildings, Mother viewed the house and gardens, my sisters viewed the distance to the nearest chapel and shop, and I viewed the distance to the nearest town.

What Father saw was exactly what he wanted; good land, excellent buildings, just the right situation up a narrow quiet lane, and only three other houses within a mile. What Mother saw was a typical farmhouse with a pump over the sink. It was as it had been for three hundred years, very picturesque with a beautiful pond in front. She, at the time, was hoping for something a little more convenient. What my sisters saw was a mile and a quarter to the nearest letter box, bakehouse, groceries and chapel. What I saw was the possibility of getting my hand in at shooting. There were some good prospects of game about as it joined a sporting estate. It would be a nice little bike ride into Stowmarket - only three and a half miles. Just right for Saturday evenings. I could take my choice of shops to buy long pants, long-sleeved vests, sock suspenders, braces, nice baggy flannel trousers, wide-brimmed trilbys, caps with huge peaks and double-breasted suits. I should be able to finish the evening at the cinema, gaze at the silent film, listen to the accompanying piano, and imagine I was a cowboy, cunning crook or handsome lover.

I did not tell Father I could see life opening up for me. He decided that the farm was what we all wanted and bought it.

Chapter 16

Lucky Burrows, senior, became the owner of White House Farm, Harleston, Stowmarket, Suffolk: it was just under seventy acres. This was the first time he had become a land-owner as all the other farms had been hired. It was bought at the rate of about thirty-six pounds per acre. All the land, an excellent range of farm buildings, a good, substantial farmhouse and two cottages were included, and purchased for one thousand pounds less than it would now cost to build a very small bungalow.

Farmer friends remarked that Father would live to regret paying all that money for a farm. He never regretted buying it, although he lived to see the value drop. He never lived to see prices rise to such an extent as to make his farm worth about ten times more than he gave for it.

He arranged for Jim to take over Oak Farm, Wickham Skeith, on the same principle as his other three sons did with their farms. Even sister Fanny went again as housekeeper to a brother.

from left to right: Jim, Alice (jnr.), Katie, Fanny

When Father left his native village of Cretingham to start farming on his own, I have every reason to believe he did not possess one hundred pounds. By his effort and initiative, and his particular method, he and his sons were, by 1920, farming nearly six hundred acres.

Michaelmas Day, October 11th was the day for moving into White House Farm. To many of us the horse was the only means of road transport still, and the power for farming was the horse. Very few changes had taken place in the way of farming. The distance we had to move was nine miles, but the turkeys and sows were not driven on the road this time. All the household effects and farm equipment were moved by horse-power. Jim and the horseman took several loads and I made several journeys to and fro.

One of the most uncomfortable trips was when I moved eight iron hurdles. Iron hurdles could be described as gates on wheels, and they were supported by their four wheels. They could be dragged around to make sheep folds in a very few minutes and some of these hurdles were between twelve and fifteen feet in length. To move the hurdles to Harleston from Wickham Skeith I had a horse and tumbril. Attached to the rear of the tumbril on the left hand side, was a train of four hurdles, and on the right were the other four making two trains side by side.

I was a worried sixteen year old in charge of a mobile contraption of about seventy five feet in length and running on thirty four wheels. These wheels had not tasted a drop of lubricant since they were made, and for the first half mile they were running on rust and fairly quiet. By turning at the rate of about two thousand times to the mile, the axles dried and brightened, and began squeaking louder and louder until they sounded like a litter of fifty hungry pigs fighting for one teat. No two squeaks were on the same note. Nearly all the wheels were at an angle of forty-five degrees from upright on their worn axles. The loose chains on the hurdles were jingling and rattling like forty little devils.

The wheels were held onto the axles by a nail in a slot, and as the nails wore through, so the wheels dropped off. I had to continually watch out for fallen wheels and put them back on again. When they were completely lost, the front of the hurdle had to be chained high on to the one in front so it just ran on its back wheels. Negotiating corners successfully needed great skill, aided by an equal amount of luck. To take a left hand corner, I had to drive all my tackle over to the right and stay close to that side, and when the horse and tumbril were well round the bend the last hurdles were rounding the left hand verge so I needed all the road for quite a long distance. The possibility of meeting a motor vehicle was very remote, and other road users had ample warning of the approach of something unusual. Another load made me very concerned; this was a fowl house loaded on a waggon. It was roughly fifteen feet from the ground. With this load, I had to pass under an iron railway arch, and the headroom specified seemed to be lower than my load. I could picture everything becoming stuck underneath. However, I took a chance and kept the waggon wheels in the lowest part. There was less than half-an-inch to spare.

There was one more trip that gave me no pleasure. On this occasion I had a tumbril piled high with a mixture of pigs' troughs, cattle mangers and other odd stuff, with my bicycle tied on the top. I had a different horse and was not familiar with her as she came from one of my brother's farms. Her name was Doughty. This brother said, "Apart from one thing, she's as quiet as a lamb. She is terrified of a donkey, but you're not likely to see a donkey, so there's nothing to worry about." This was one of the last loads. I had done the journey many times and had never seen a donkey so there was no portending worry.

About two miles along the road, what did I see coming towards me? You've guessed - a donkey! I had no idea what would happen; Doughty might bolt, rear or back my load in the ditch. The little animal came jogging along pulling a tiny cart in which was seated a large man, looking bigger than the donkey and cart put together.

The distance between us became shorter and I kept talking to my steed to assure her that there was nothing to fear. We were now thirty yards apart - Doughty's ears were moving in all directions. We were nearly level, when Doughty stopped. She was trembling with fear and dared not move backwards or forwards. Her four feet were stamping to form a square and her rump was sinking to the level of the shafts. The donkey was passing, and to get away from the danger, my horse gave a sudden plunge. This upset the tipping apparatus of the tumbril and my entire load shot onto the ground. A good Samaritan passing by helped me to reload and I continued my journey.

Approaching some crossroads a few miles further on, I saw coming from the opposite direction - yes - another donkey! Stopping my horse, I waited until the man in charge was close enough to hear, then I bellowed out, "Which way are you going?"

I daresay he thought I was making too much noise to be inquisitive; more likely thought I was balmy. Anyhow, he turned down a by-road and left the way clear for Doughty.

As soon as we began moving out from Oak Farm, Tiny the fox-terrier became restless. After a few loads had gone she knew evacuation was in progress. She had no intention of being left behind so while the waggons were being loaded, she would go down to where the roads forked, and wait. Whoever came along first would pick her up.

We eventually finished moving and got house and farm settled. It very quickly became home for us, and I had no regrets about leaving Wickham Skeith. The five suicides, the revolver death and the near murders were left behind.

White House Farm stood on very high ground, and the air was so fresh and clean. It was just like starting school after the holidays, with new boots and Sunday suit taken in for everyday wear. You wondered how long it would be before your copy book would become blotted.

Mother wanted a few alterations done in the house as is usual when one moves. Father engaged Jim Meakings to do the work. He married Mary Scarlett, a dear friend of the family, and as a friend he had his meals with us, and would proudly tell us of his experiences while doing his prison sentence. He was a conscientious objector during the First World War and was locked up for refusing to fight.

The previous owner of White House Farm was a keen, ambitious man. He was a widower. After leaving the civil service, he became landlord of a public house, then he bought this farm. With five years of high prices he prospered to the extent of then taking a farm of about three-hundred acres.

One Saturday morning, after we had been at the farm about six weeks, our predecessor married his second wife. Jim Meakings brought us the news when he came to work the following Monday. Just one week later Mr. Meakings brought us some more news.

"What do you think had happened now?" he said. "The man who sold you this farm shot himself last Saturday. Just fancy that. Married one Saturday and dead the next." I thought we had left all the tragedies behind. Surely they were not still going to follow us around.

This little village of Harleston in Suffolk, not to be confused with the town of Harleston in Norfolk, is one of the smallest villages I know. It covers an area of six hundred and twelve acres, and at the 1921 census, its population was fifty people living in four farm houses and seven cottages. There is a sweet little thatched church, and we would often hear its one bell tinkling away. I wonder if it is still rung? Father, Mother and sister

Fan are now resting in the churchyard amongst the fields and meadows of Harleston Hall.

Looking again at Harleston, even now it could hardly be called a village with its eleven houses dotted over the six-hundred and twelve acres. There was not even a letter box. To have our bodily needs supplied, we had to travel over one mile to the next village of Haughley with not a house between. On the way to Haughley we had to pass over Rush Green which was roughly two acres of coarse grass with a few hawthorn bushes scattered about and surrounded by high hedges. Here gypsies loved to camp. There seemed to be a fresh company of them every other week in various stages of wealth. The poorest would be an elderly husband and wife with just a covered waggon and an old horse. Others had better caravans and good horses. Most of them used to search the hedges for suitable wood and sit around a camp fire making the wood into linen pegs.

Rush Green where the lane to White House Farm leaves the Haughley Road

One rather large company visited this site annually. They were wealthy, with four or five magnificent caravans painted in bright colours with lots of brass fittings. They had fifteen horses of various ages: some were foals that had been born beside the road where they would stop on their travels. There were horses of all colours, but the majority were piebalds. These gypsies were undoubtedly horse-dealers.

Some of these roving people stayed on the spot for several days, others stayed several weeks and had lines of washing out to dry. Most of them were very clean people. They lived their lives in the way they liked and some had dogs that looked capable of overtaking a hare in a few hundred yards. An occasional family took their hens with them that ran about freely. Like their owners they looked upon the caravan as their home and did not roam far from it.

We never tried to move them on or interfere with their way of life, and they never molested us, or to my knowledge, stole anything apart from one old boy who helped himself to some hay for his horse on a cold day when the ground was covered in snow. Father was annoyed because the gypsy did not ask first. Often Father had long conversations with them. If anyone showed friendliness towards him, he would return it, be the person gentry or gypsy, duke or dustman.

Although Lucky Burrows prospered, he never changed towards people in any walk of life. The established farmers who could boast of coming from two or three generations of farming the same land were looked upon as of some importance and fifty years ago some of them took the same view of themselves. As is natural, they would gather in a group at whatever function they happened to be, this being understandable as they shared the same interests.

But to use their position as a social status symbol was rather ridiculous as the position was not so wonderful after all. My Father's mind was far too big to indulge in this petty competition however necessary it appeared to be. He would never attempt to creep into certain company with the subtle hope that their glamour would reflect on to him and his subordinates to give himself false glory. He was always himself, and to be one's real self is not an achievement, but a natural gift.

* * * * * * * * * *

Father and Mother are now settling in at White House Farm, and with them just two children, Alice and myself. They, as far as their family is concerned, are back to where they were when they left Cretingham. The eternal cycle again - with four boys in farms, Fanny with Jim, Jack still in Canada and Katie a children's nurse.

Each member of our family will to the end of their days look back on Oak Farm, Wickham Skeith as the real home because it was there that the family was complete with Father, Mother and ten children. We momentarily live in a ridiculous nostalgic dream, and looking back, wish that time could stop at that moment. We suddenly awake, realise where we are and sensibly look forward. There would be no present without the past, and no future without the present.

Young Alf

Alice Jnr.

This land that Father now owns, once belonged to Harold. You remember; he was the man who was shot through the eye with an arrow at the Battle of Hastings in 1066, and his armies defeated by William the Conqueror. Yes, King Harold II, who was king for so short a time, once had large possessions in this area owning a great part of Haughley and possibly all Harleston, hence its name, deriving from Harold's Town.

Leading from Rush Green where the gypsies camp, is a lane. In winter it is a slushy track and in summer a grassy drift. This lane leads to an old barn known as 'Gally Barn.' Hearsay has it that this is the spot where people were put to death on the gallows. I have not found the proof of this.

Again, many people have told us that Martyrs were burnt on Rush Green and when we were new at Harleston we were informed that if we looked under a certain clump where blackberries grew, we would see a large stone to denote the spot. We looked. Sure enough, a stone lay there half buried. It was oval and about two and a half feet in diameter and I imagine it weighed around three hundredweight. I believe you will find it still there.

Editor's note: There are several historical items in this book that may not be entirely true. Regarding the burning of martyrs at Rush Green, this is unlikely. Nearby, there appears to have been a place where, once, hanged men's bodies were gibbeted - hence references to a gallows. Martyrs from this part of Suffolk were burned in the reign of Mary I, but most were burned at Bury or Ipswich. None from Harleston or Haughley are listed. However one of the Mendlesham martyrs was named Simon Harleston, which may be where the confusion originates. We did try to find the stone, but much of the area is covered in brambles and it was impossible.

So, in an atmosphere of burnt saints and hanged criminals with gypsies camping near to the martyrs stone as neighbours, Father and I worked together for the next nine years, on the land which nine hundred years previously had been the hunting ground of Edward the Confessor's brother-in-law before he became King Harold II.

Farming was still carried on in practically the same method as had been used for over one hundred years. I can think of only three ways of improvement we were now using in the 1920s.

We were cutting the corn with a self-binder which tied the sheaves as they were cut. The corn and seed drill did away with dibbling in seed or broadcasting it. Both these machines were drawn by horses, and threshing with a flail had gone forever.

Although I do not really feel old in 1967, I can clearly remember these jobs being carried out in the old way.

Now I was sixteen, working on the farm and doing the same amount of work and hours as the farm workers. Under Father's system, I, like my brothers, received no wages or pocket money. Any money I needed would have to be made in my own time so I had one hundred laying hens and a few pigs. Mother kept her fowls in the stackyard and near the farm buildings. I kept my poultry in the meadows as far from the buildings as possible so that our respective flocks could not become mixed. They were all free-range.

When Mother, or my sister fed the hens they called them in the usual way, in a kind of soprano voice at about middle C range, "Coop, coop, coooopeee!"

I trained mine to come when I whistled, otherwise when Allie "Coopeeed," my hens would all run home. One disadvantage I had by having my fowls so far from the house was the temptation to poultry thieves. I lost several this way. They always disappeared in fives and always on a Sunday night. Someone must have known we usually went to chapel on Sunday evenings and this somebody must have walked or cycled, and five was all he could manage at one time. We never found out who stole them, but the thieving stopped after I had strong locks and bolts fitted on the doors.

One autumn, Mother had fifty of the best rhode-island red pullets I had ever seen and these were kept away from her other fowls. She fussed over them and their feathers shone with a rich golden hue. Their combs were as red as poppies and they had just started to lay. She opened the door to let them out one morning and stood back to avoid the rush as they always come out like children leaving school. She waited several seconds - just one came out. Mother looked in the hut - the other forty nine lay dead.

Father sent for the policeman who knew no more than we did. "Had we enemies?" he asked. "Who would do it for spite?" No, as far as we knew, we had not acted towards anyone in such a way as to demand such drastic retaliation. A poultry advising expert was sent for. "What do you feed them on?" he enquired.

"They have nothing but the best," Mother said.

"What do you call the best?" he asked.

"They had a special treat yesterday," the expert was told. "After making the butter and salting it, we wash it in running water. The first water that comes off is like milk and the hens love it. We call it buttermilk. I mixed their food with it and the remainder was put in the trough. They gobbled up the food and drank all the liquid, and thoroughly enjoyed it."

"Ah," said the advisor, "you have killed them with kindness. It was the excessive salt they had consumed that caused the trouble."

The verdict was accepted in good faith. If he was wrong, it would not have brought the pullets back to life. The life of the single survivor was spared because she never stopped to feed with this batch, but always spent the day with the old hens, so no doubt the man was right.

These little tragedies seemed great to us and it was difficult to get back to the routine of work after they were over. We felt better when we began our respective jobs. As there was a man to do the horse work, I would go hedge-cutting, mangold-pulling and muck-spreading.

When I look back, I marvel how we used to get around in the clothes we wore, let alone work in them. At a certain time during the autumn, Mother would say, "You must start your winter clothes. I've got them all ready." She always went by the date and not the temperature. I was warned that I would 'get my death of cold' if I didn't dress suitably. Actually, I was rarely free from colds for long in the winter. I wonder what would have happened if I had not put on long-sleeved thick vests, long-tailed flannel shirts and long woollen pants ankle-length? Then I would begin the next layer... A pair of cavalry-twill riding breeches with buckskin strappings reaching to within six inches of my ankles, thick, heavy land boots: then as all land workers were wearing some relic of the past war, I finished protecting my legs with a pair of khaki puttees. At least I could boast of a marvellous pair of calves when fully adorned. For my top half, apart from braces, I had a thick, leather belt, a cloth waistcoat, a leather waistcoat and then a jacket made from some heavy material. We then had the audacity to say we were hardy, did not feel the cold much, and rarely wore an overcoat. Not being content with such a simple statement, we added in all seriousness we thought we ate more because we always seemed to put on weight to the extent of about one and a half stones in the winter.

When we weighed ourselves on the barn scales in our winter attire, we got as near to our actual weight as the chap who could not find all the weights, and when asked how heavy he was, he replied, "The last time I got on the scales I weighed eleven and a half stones, two bricks and a stable lantern."

It was very unusual for Father to have a cold, for the simple reason that he never changed into winter clothes. The fact was, he never got out of them. He wore long-sleeved vest and long pants all the year round, and very thick stockings. These were kept up above the calves with a piece of horse ribbon and the tops turned down like cycling stockings. Actually, on hot summer days he looked cooler than the boys of today with bare torsos. He used to say, "What keeps the cold out keeps the heat out."

Thus we carried on through the seasons until I approached the age of eighteen. I do not know how I managed these last four years without the protection of girlfriends. I suppose the period between school sweethearts and more serious girlfriends is rather awkward as you are neither one thing nor the other. The time was almost filled with my farm life and I had become friendly with a farmer's son called Gerald. We went around together attending and visiting anything in which we were interested. On our Sunday evening walks we encountered a couple of girls. As we passed them we coughed and they giggled. We went a certain distance then turned back. They went a certain distance in the opposite direction and turned back and we passed again. They tittered and we grinned. We went home well satisfied with our mutual advances. A few days later, Gerald and I were walking in the meadows of White House Farm when we saw Belle and Nancy coming up the lane. Gerald said, "Whatever shall we say to them?" He was younger than I.

"I know," said I, "I'll show them this leveret we've caught. It's in my pocket. That will give us a start." So we got a start and all walked together. As we parted, another meeting was arranged. In the meantime, I bought some sweets thinking I must offer the young ladies something.

When we met, Belle was offered a sweet. "No thanks," she said, so I tried Nancy. "No thanks."
"Don't you girls like sweets?" I asked.
"Very much," they replied, "but we don't like sweets that have been carried around in the same pocket as young hares."
I was nonplussed. We had a lot to learn.

Our acquaintances did not blossom much, so Gerald and I reverted to the 'looking around' stage. I decided the best thing I could do would be to buy a motor cycle. I was crazy about motorbikes and the one I bought cost eighteen pounds. It looked as if it was in the process of growing into a motorbike, and had stopped half way - something like a tadpole when it is nearly a frog. The thing had pedals in case it broke down. I don't mean the tadpole, I mean the bike. It had long, narrow handlebars and carried a squeaky hooter that must have come from a penny bazaar. The petrol tank was about three inches square and held about four pints. On the tank was printed the word DREADNOUGHT. I believe it was the make of the bike, but have wondered since if the previous owner put it there in commemoration of the day he met such a fool as myself to buy it, thinking that he would never dread anything again.

As for me, sometimes 'the thing' would go, and sometimes I had to pedal it home. I took it out one Sunday evening after I had tuned it up and it was in a fit state to be put through its paces. I dressed for the part. There were not many motorbikes about in 1922 and I had seen their riders wearing goggles and so on. I put on my trench-coat and goggles, and wore my cap back to front and felt equal to any test pilot that ever was or will be.

I took the first few miles at half throttle. Not many of the secondary and byroads were tarred at this time. Turning my head sideways I noticed with great satisfaction that I was raising a small cloud of dust. There were not many cycles speedy enough to do this. Coming to a straight mile (I was now three and a half miles from home), I thought, this is the time to see what she will do. I went into full throttle and kept it there: I could do no more. No one had heard of supersonic speeds, but I do not suppose I was far away from the centre of my own sound waves. Had there been a slight back breeze no doubt I would have been outpaced by my own dust trail. The bike had no speedometer so I could not record my feat for posterity to appreciate.

But I was enjoying it. I felt like the God of Speed until I saw a shadow behind me. It was overtaking me! I couldn't catch it, and it looked familiar in shape. Then I recognised the figure of George Lee, a chap about my own age. He waved and passed on. He was on a push bike, the racing type, and he was doing nearly thirty miles an hour.

I felt humiliated, ashamed and overdressed. The name on the petrol tank rose before me - DREADNOUGHT. I thought, 'I shall dread everything for evermore. The Thing must be got rid of.' So I saw a motor cycle agent. "What will you allow me for this motor-bike if I buy another?" I asked. "That isn't a motorbike," he said. "It's an auto-cycle." I knew I 'ought to cycle' and apparently it would be faster,

142

but I was determined to have a real motorcycle and agreed to buy a 250 cc two stroke Connaught for fifty pounds.

My savings were greatly depleted by the purchase. I had it for several years: it would travel at fifty miles an hour and I was content. Some means of paying for the running costs had to be found. This was met by selling game - I was getting a little handier with a gun now. Father warned me that on no account must I shoot over the hedge onto other people's property, and if I kept strictly within the law no-one would have any reason to complain. So in fear of the law and Father, I went straight.

Although my conscience was clear, it did not stop the game-keeper on the adjoining estate from watching all my movements. As I walked around with my dog and gun, my eyes used to sweep over the estate often, and I could discern half his figure. The other half was concealed behind a tree. Sometimes it was a misty shape behind a hedge, and I could picture his eyes as expressionless as an owl's, tirelessly waiting for his prey, even if it took years.

I can honestly say that I never broke any of the game laws, but this keeper was so bitter about me lawfully shooting on my father's land that he would neither look nor speak to me if we met on the road. This began when I was only sixteen and continued for years. He was convinced that it was only a matter of time before he would catch me out.

One day he pounced, but when he looked in his claws, he found no prey. This embittered him more than ever. It happened when I was sauntering round the boundary fence. Seeing a rabbit sitting on the bank, I shot at it. Bess went to retrieve it, but actually I had missed. The dog jumped the ditch and searched for it on the 'holy land.' The vigilant keeper appeared from nowhere. "You have shot over my land." At last he had spoken to me. I could not convince him that I had shot at a rabbit on our bank, and would not accept my invitation to come over and see the shot marks in the hedge. He said, "Never will I set foot on your land."

After this, I had a feeling of being watched all the time. This was his idea of course. I could feel his eyes on me even if he was a mile away drinking beer in 'The White Horse.' Strangely enough it was from behind the White Horse window that he struck the next time. From this vantage point he could see me pass, with my game hanging on my bicycle handlebars. I was taking them to a poultry dealer for dispatch to London. On two consecutive days I passed this pub with four brace of partridges. This was too much for the man who watched. "I believe I've got him," he thought. "This young fool is disposing of his birds illegally."

I had a visit from the police while I was feeding my hens. The constable and I knew each other very well. He said, "Your hens look well." I had no reason to wonder why he was there and almost innocently accepted the fact that he had actually cycled over a mile with his notebook to tell me my hens looked well.

Casually he said, "You do a bit of game-shooting?"   "Yes."
"Hum. You have a licence to kill?"   "Oh yes."
"Ah. What do you do with the birds you kill?"
"Oh, I take them to Mr. Diaper the poultry dealer."
The policeman had a statement already made out. He said, "Read this, and if you agree with it, sign it." It tallied with what I had just said so I signed it.

I gathered later, he had then proceeded to Mr. Diaper's and had said in effect, "I know you are taking game from young Burrows and that you have no game-dealer's licence." Jimmy Diaper told the 'law' he did not need a licence. He had packed game for his customers ever since he had been in business. He did not buy them. He just arranged the transport and gave his customers whatever money they fetched. The game-keeper gave up the chase as it always led to a dead end.

The owner of the estate had for years hired the shooting rights on our little farm, and when he did not have it, he seemed more concerned with what he hadn't got than about all the farms and woods he owned. When I look back on this keeper, I have no bitter feeling whatsoever towards him. Although he acted in a stupid manner, he was only trying to do the job for which he was paid in the way he thought best. Had he been friendly and found out the facts, he would have had no cause to worry.

My average yearly bag for the nine years was about twelve brace of pheasant and fifteen brace of partridge. This was not nearly the number that hatched and grew up on our land. I had no time to try and hold them on the land by feeding them.

Should these lines get into the hands of any shooting men, I should like to record the following for their interest. The year in which I was watched from the White Horse window was in the middle 1920's and in that particular season I shot over forty brace of partridge on our under seventy acres. Now, over forty years later there are many estates of over one or two thousand acres, where one would not even see that number of partridges.

With the help of my gun I managed to keep my bike going. I hate to look upon the lives of the birds in such a commercial manner. It was not a case of necessity being the mother of invention but more a case of my needs being the father of my actions. All my life I have loved wildlife, loved the woods, the trees themselves and the lives they shelter. To be alone, surrounded by the dictates of nature opens your mind and fills your heart and soul with the majesty of our Maker. The detailed planning of survival of plant, bird and animal life without the help of puny humans is beyond our conception. Had there been no prospect of becoming a farmer, I would certainly have trained to be a game-keeper, and been an individual in a world of my own.

I know exactly how the estate owner felt about our little piece of land and remember him with sympathy. I would have been just the same if our circumstances had been reversed. Among the strange people around, I think shooters and anglers are the most weird. An angler will sit all night in a biting, freezing wind without catching a thing, and then spend the following evening in the pub, telling everyone about what he did not catch.

Whether we have fifty or five thousand acres on which to shoot is all the same. We all envy that little bit beyond the boundary. When our neighbours have their shoot, we place ourselves in a position to see if anyone will put a foot on our land. We suspect everyone and follow our best friend like a sleuth. That is the attitude of most game preservers, and I have been just the same in spirit if not in possession. We know the origin of every gun report within hearing distance. We know who it is and whether they are after rabbits, pigeons or the odd pheasant. No stone is left unturned to find out all details of any mystery shot. We lie awake at night wondering if anyone is after our birds. Many patrol their lands in search of poachers in the early hours of the morning.

I guarantee that people indulging in this sport spend more anxious hours over their game birds than they do about their herds of cattle, or flocks of sheep. No doubt they feel that the farm animals are more controllable. But should these animals stray on to their neighbour's land and cause great damage, are the owners of them watched and followed about? Oh no; he is shaken by the hand and told not to worry and not to think of paying any compensation, the situation might be reversed someday.

For the lovers of this kind of life, shooting days are the times when all men are equal. Everyone is happy and there is no thought of a status symbol, rat race, or 'keeping up with the Jones.' One minute you are walking with a grave digger and you certainly do not look upon him as a symbol of death. Your next companion might be a doctor. As he makes a clean kill, it never enters your head that he should preserve life. So wealth and poverty, learning and illiteracy, age and youth, move in equality until the end of the day when they return home and prepare to take up their respective duties again.

Chapter 17

I have often complained about the lack of freedom during my day, compared with the present time. In my saner moments, I realise that it was the best way. We were kept from dangers and evils by strict control, but our lives were dull according to present day standards. We really were not unhappy. If there was no chance of getting what was wanted, we valued more what we had. Easily come-by wealth is never appreciated until there is a fear of losing it.

What am I doing at the age of eighteen and a half? Nothing very exciting; walking through the corn crops with Father and his one man, hoeing up the big weeds and clean-hoeing the root crops, otherwise the weeds will smother the beet and swedes.

Most evenings are spent attending to my pigs and poultry. Then there is the motor-bike to clean. I expect more time is spent cleaning it than riding it. Two or three times a week I see my friend Gerald. Thursday is market day at Stowmarket. Father likes me to spend an hour or two there to keep my mind and interests in the right directions for farming.

The auctioneers have portable pens for fowls and these are dragged into the street on market days. The vendor's poultry is placed in these pens from which the auctioneers sells them. The buyers take up all the pavement space and half the roadway. Chicken crates are standing in the gutters and feathers fly all over the place.

After the sales, large herds of pigs are driven through the town to be loaded up at the railway station. There are always plenty of back-street urchins in rags helping the drovers and hoping to make a few coppers. They have shoes and socks now; ten years previously, half of them were bare-footed.

Practically all the traffic is still horse-drawn. The pigs are going between the legs of the horses and under the carts and waggons. Some of the horses are snorting and rearing; the waggoners are trying to quieten them. The boys are shouting, the pigs shrieking and the

drovers swearing. It is sheer pandemonium.

The streets have barely time to quieten down before a herd of cattle appears, bound for the same destination. These are preceeded by drover boys flashing past to take up their positions for guiding the bullocks along the desired route. The cattle on these occasions never seem to be driven. They are so relieved to get away from the market cattle pens that they usually travel at full trot, and the drovers have difficulty in keeping up with them. With their smocks flowing out behind them, you realise with relief they have no wind left for swearing.

Now another herd is following on. And people tell us that traffic jams were unheard of until cars appeared. I suppose modern jams are more organised with their every-conceivable road sign. I am afraid one-way streets, white lines, zebra-crossings, traffic lights and no-parking signs would have been utterly ignored by the road-hogs that were causing the trouble in Stowmarket on market days in the 1920s.

As for 'Keeping Britain Tidy,' there was nothing to be done about it apart from clearing up all the horse-droppings and pig and cattle manure. The town did have a good farmyard smell about it.

Not quite the environment one would choose or expect a romance to bud, but I saw her coming up the street with golden hair hanging in ringlets and touching her shoulders. Genuine curls. She was walking with a girl-friend, laughing and talking, pink and white complexion with deep dimples in her cheeks. Not much more than a school girl; seventeen perhaps. I looked - you do, don't you, whether you are eighteen or eighty? I had looked at several, but I would not forget this one.

There was not much I could do about it. I had no idea who she was. A few weeks later, I saw the same girl driving towards Stowmarket. She was with a bearded man who was obviously her father. When I saw an acquaintance who lived in the direction from which the object of my interest had come I asked in a disinterested manner, "What is the name of that man who lives somewhere out your way? He has a beard and drives a chestnut hackney with three white socks. He has a light-brown varnished rubber-tyred trap to match."

"Oh," he said, "That's Herbert Bannister. He farms Tiptofts Farm, Badwell Ash." "Is it?" I said. "I'll tell you one thing; he's got the prettiest high-stepping hackney I have ever seen."

"Yes, he always drives a good horse," he agreed.

I did not tell the fellow it was not the horse I was interested in. If it had been a donkey, I would not have objected. Still, even a flower looks better in good surroundings.

Discreet enquiries revealed that they were chapel people. This was very fortunate because my family were also chapel people and liked their children to mix with other chapel people.

I felt encouraged. There was nothing to stop me leaving the Methodists and attending a Baptist Church. The denomination did not bother me or my conscience. My motive was obvious and I have never felt any shame over my actions. Better men than I have forgotten their soul when seeking their heart's desire, and I would rather be honestly weak than deceitfully righteous.

Herbert Bannister

So, I wended my way to a particular Baptist Chapel and directed my steps to a seat behind a pew containing the family from Tiptofts Farm. By now I had learnt that the name of the girl with the golden hair was Eva. She was the youngest of the family, having two sisters and one brother James, whom I shall hereafter refer to as Jimmy in order to distinguish him from my brother James.

One of the sisters was the organist. A few meetings later, Eva was at the organ as deputy-organist to her sister. "Oh," I thought, "besides driving a high stepping, high spirited hackney through the busy streets of Stowmarket in a very commercial atmosphere, she can also play the organ in the worshipful quietness of a country chapel."

Wetherden Baptist Chapel in 2011

I appreciated her adaptability, but secretly hoped she would not be capable of doing too much, feeling it might minimise my chances. As yet, I had made no contact; just living in a world of hopeful dreams. Even thinking in this way is the beginning of the breakaway from your own family and I imagined I was exploring an unknown world.

I did not realise that my father knew Herbert Bannister well; even though he knew nothing of the family. They were both self-made men and had much in common. While I was still dallying, Father came home from Stowmarket one Thursday in February with a marble-white look on his face as he did when he was upset. After putting his horse in the stable, he came in and said, "I've just heard that Herbert Bannister is dead. I was told it was a heart-attack after a short bout of flu. He was only fifty-four."

"This must be my end too," I thought. "The family will no doubt sell out and I cannot now even attempt to make contact for a long time."

Mr. Bannister was buried in the cemetery at Badwell Ash and a memorial service was held at Wetherden Chapel where the family attended. I decided that I should go to the service. To my knowledge I had never spoken to the family, so I had no reason to go. I went.

The lectern was draped in black, as were the family in their pews. The absent one was very conspicuous and in everyone's thoughts. Eva seemed more attractive than ever, dressed in black. Of course, even at eighteen I was grieved for the sorrowing family. Perhaps it might be more truthful to say that I was sympathetic. To analyse my feelings in perfect truth, I have to admit I was really sorry for myself. I was mourning for my lost hopes.

The farm work continued half heartedly and my evenings were spent making hen coops for bringing up broods of chickens. I made sixteen from wooden packing cases obtained from the grocers. The finished articles cost about half-a-crown complete, and they would all together enable me to rear one hundred and fifty chickens. The pullets from these replenished my laying flock and with two breeding sows to keep up a steady outflow of pigs, I was getting my foot on the first rung of the farming ladder. Full occupation, if not a complete cure, is a great solace to a dejected mind.

The bursting forth of spring and early summer lifts the heart and it is not easily kept down by gloomy thoughts. The scent of the bean blossoms make hoeing a joy and stirs the instincts of youth.

I was a regular attender for morning service at the Baptist Chapel, feeling that if there was any truth in the saying, 'out of sight, out of mind,' it would be better to place myself in sight. Eva was beginning to smile again and walk with a friend after service. It took weeks for me to get into conversation as I did not want to spoil my chances by being too bold. I almost erred on the side of caution.

If it was merely a girl I was seeking, I would have been satisfied with the first that came along, or the next best thing. But by that time, it was one or none, so I moved carefully. I 'got my foot in' so to speak by way of the brother. We had many mutual interests including motor-bikes, and I became a regular visitor without making my intentions too obvious.

Tiptofts Farm - then and now

It soon became clear that this brother Jim had several friends with exactly the same interests as myself in every way. There were at least three farmers' sons, an insurance trainee fast becoming a preacher and a blacksmith. Casual and business visitors were anxious to get further acquainted. There were so many keen to get their knees under the Tiptofts' table that I would be lucky to keep my foot in the door. My position was very precarious.

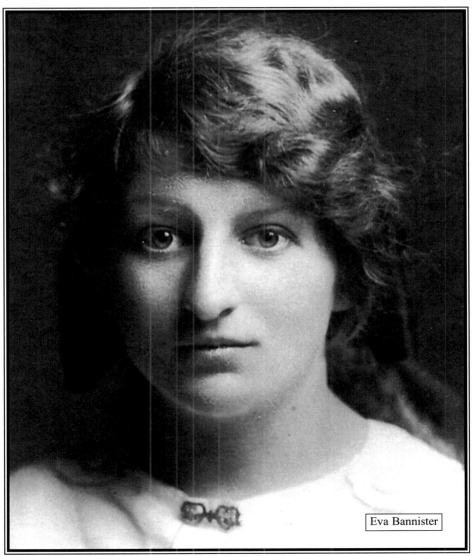

Eva Bannister

There was no talk of the Bannisters getting out of farming. One sister was married and the other was just about to do the same. This would then leave Mrs. Bannister, Jimmy and Eva with shares in farming the two hundred and eighteen acres.

By management, mutual interests or coincidence, the Bannister and Burrows families began visiting each other. This was gratifying as it kept the acquaintance alive, although it did not bring certainty to my aims. So the friendship continued in this way.

As I neared the age of nineteen, it became apparent there would be no change in the occupiers of Tiptofts Farm and about this time they bought a new car. This, I felt sure, would weaken the threads of our friendship, especially as within a few weeks, Eva was driving it, she being keen on all outdoor activities.

Cars were so rare, with perhaps an average of two to a village that they were looked upon as a luxury and sheer extravagance. In the countryside, each car was known over a wide area and many people had never seen a lady driver. When a golden-haired girl of eighteen was seen driving around in an open car in 1923, it drew a great deal of attention. Added interest was attracted by the fact she had benefited financially by her father's death - not a large sum by today's standard of purchasing power - but enough in those days to rent, equip and run a hundred acre farm.

These circumstances interested another set of ambitious lads. The first list I mentioned were genuine schoolday pals. How grateful was I that my attention was made manifest before the death of her father. I doggedly pursued, not knowing whether I would ultimately be dismissed or chucked out.

* * * * * * * * * *

We left my four brothers getting on with their respective farms about three years hence. They each continued to visit the parents regularly It was not unusual to see the four sons talking to Father outside the Corn Hall at Stowmarket on market days, and myself trying to push in to listen. By this time, Lucky had hired more land and was farming over two hundred acres.

Will had bought Harts Hall, the farm where he started, and after a few years sold it to buy another farm in the next village called Wattisfield Hall. This brought with it about three hundred acres. These two boys had the World War I prices to help them. Sam and Jim meanwhile were comparative beginners and were discovering that good prospects in farming were gradually declining. Sam would often combine his market business with a visit home. I would meet him at Haughley Railway Station with the horse and trap. After lunch, he would ride to Stowmarket with Father.

I remember meeting him on one of these visits: waiting at the level crossing, I had a good view of the platform. This was the time when the railways were used and railway shares were sought after. Haughley, being a junction for London, Norwich and Cambridge and a terminus for a light railway, was a busy station and it was not unusual to see forty or fifty people on the platform. Through this crowd came Sam, as unconcerned as if he was hunting the hedgerows on this farm. The eyes of everyone, porters and passengers alike, were upon him.

He was carrying his twelve-bore shotgun in the crook of his left arm and a seemingly heavy burden over his right shoulder. It was an otter which he was grabbing by the tail, slung over his shoulder

with its nose reaching to the back of his knees.

Neither gun nor otter had any covering and, to complete the picture, my brother's dog was following at his heels.

Sam was taking it to a taxidermist in Stowmarket to get it preserved. This otter had found its way to my brother's pond. There was no river within two miles and it was evidently hungry. There were no fish in the pond and it was killing the young ducks. Sam had no choice but to shoot it. Oh, the reason for the gun and the dog was that we often went over our little farm together on his visits.

Jack returned from Canada that year after roughing it for twelve years. More than half this time, he had lived in log cabins doing all his own cooking and washing. He was still a bachelor. Most of the time he was working on ranches, mainly with sheep. He tried farming on his own, but was beaten by the climatic conditions. He was not one of the few who came home with a large fortune. After getting through the family welcomes and renewing old acquaintances, he made his abode with Sam and helped on the farm.

At White House Farm, our horseman had to give up work owing to ill health, which gave me the opportunity of using the horses, the job I'd been hankering after for a long time. There is something wonderful about working with horses. Like dogs, they do not just recognise your voice, but actually know what you say. By talking to them they will turn right or left, move forwards, walk backwards, stop and go. A horseman I had in later years could work with horses all day without using reins.

Dogs and horses love your company and after a real understanding has been acquired, it is much more than cupboard-love. I was with Matchett all the time then. She is the chestnut mare I was allowed to take on the road when I was fifteen and she was three. Moggy, her mother, made up the pair. Some of the horse-brasses I carefully shined and adorned them with are still in my possession.

For many weeks and months of every year for five years, my only companions were the horses until we returned to the stables from the fields in the late afternoon, and never for one moment was I lonely. I was so happy and whistled and sang at the top of my voice. I would sing hymns from Sankey & Moody's 'Ancient and Modern;' also songs ancient and modern all mixed up together. I quite probably began early in the morning with a rendering of 'Now the day is over.' Words lost all meaning in the jubilation of my spirits.

Old Moggy and Matchett thought I had a most beautiful voice. They were unhappy when I was quiet. Of course there were miserable days when singing would be out of keeping with the conditions.

Ploughing with a pair of horses at four acres a week is slow progress and you have to keep going in practically all weathers to get the land up in time for the frosts. There were days of cold, thin driving rain where it was not heavy enough to make you pack up. I always took some empty sacks to keep out the wet and the cold. One sack was used as an apron to keep my knees dry and another as a cape to protect my shoulders. The dent in the trilby was turned inside out to shoot the water. With enough changes of sacks, I was proof against the elements.

All field work done by horses necessitated walking between eight and ten miles a day. In my case, this was in addition to feeding my pigs and poultry, milking two cows and grooming and feeding the horses, morning and night. The good days far outweighed the bad when I could dream of my love life and make elaborate plans for the future. Farming, of course, would be my career, and my ambition was to farm one thousand acres... not own it - that would be out of the question - but to hire the land and farm it. I was sure it could be done. Lots of men have done it. To spare the reader disappointment later on, I must confess that my goal was not attained.

To farm a four-figure acreage would have brought me more worry than gratification, but the planning and dreaming gave me great pleasure. It was not an idle dream. In a practical way, I worked out the possibility of the achievement and actually nearly touched the halfway mark. I could have moved higher but was reminded by events that riches are not found in acres of land.

The only real wealth worth having is found in a contented mind, grateful heart and harmony with your partner. Had I stubbornly followed my star, the result would definitely have been excess worry, irritability, no time to build up a peaceful home atmosphere, and a frayed relationship with my partner. "Better a dry morsel and quietness therewith than a house full of sacrifices with strife."

There is no place in my experience where you can think better than behind a pair of horses working in the fields with no humans in sight. It is different from walking in the woods alone. There you have to walk round the trees and dodge the boughs; your concentration is broken.

Now, with a pair of horses, especially ploughing, there is nothing to divert your attention. They need no guidance as they follow the furrow; they are company for each other and are happy, so you do not think about their feelings. You hold the plough mechanically by the feel of it and you have no fear of being watched as you know you are doing your duty and earning your keep. So your mind drifts away in most unusual channels. No wonder some plough-boys become poets.

The horses drew up to the hedge, snapping a few twigs off as they turned. I set the plough and the horses moved forward a few yards. The plough was held in an upright position. Moggy and Matchett took a step back to slacken their traces and rest for a few minutes. It was a repetitious act and they knew the routine.

I sagged back on the plough handles and took in the extent of the view available. Five churches could be seen. Without leaving the farm, two more were visible. The houses in view did not outnumber the churches by very much either.

Concerning the five churches, I knew beneath the steeples of Wetherden and Haughley lay a cluster of houses. These steeples looked relaxed like a hen pheasant who had raised her brood to the point of independence. The spires of Stowmarket and Great

Finborough stood up alert and anxious-looking, like the heads of pheasants above the grass, watching for enemies that might harm their young. Harleston church stood quietly alone in the meadows. She had no spire, no steeple; just a little shelter above her one bell. There were no dwellings within protective distance of her thatched roof. She was like a tiring, thin pheasant who had been robbed of her eggs just before they were due to hatch. There she waited, disappointed and resigned, hoping to pick up a lost soul that had wandered from another brood.

"Come on Moggy. Get up there Matchett. We must do a few more rounds before bait." The traces tightened, the seals creaked as they pulled into the collars, the stones squeaked when the metal mould-board pushed past them and we moved off. I wanted this day to finish. Christmas was drawing near and the animals must be fed and littered down for the night. There was excitement in the air because our young half-cousin Hugh was coming for the holidays as he always did. Although he was seven years younger than I, he was nearer my age and shared my interests more than my brothers and besides, I never lived with my brothers for very long.

Hugh was the son of cousin Lucky Lockwood the warrior, who had been retired from the army for four years. Lucky Lockwood was so proud of his Christian name that he chose Hugh Lucky for his elder son. The younger son, born in 1920, he named Alfred Lucky which made five Luckys in the family.

My foot was still in the door at Tiptofts Farm and I even had an invitation for tea on Christmas Day. Feeling very nervous and honoured, I went. Two of the before-mentioned farmers' sons were amongst the party; also the young blacksmith. I did not feel confident of much success once the party was over. Considering these three young men were about twenty-one and I was a boy of nineteen, looking seventeen and feeling fifteen, there was at least the consolation of knowing I was still running level.

Although Eva had her mother's car to ride about in, because of her exceptional love of animals, Polly the chestnut Hackney with the three white socks was in no way neglected. Eva used to drive out with her mother in the trap. One day, Polly shied and tipped them both out of the cart. It did not stop them continuing with their journey. This young lady used the mare for riding and had even travelled on horseback to the Baptist chapel which was six miles away, leaving Polly in the young blacksmith's shed during the service.

Jimmy, being more mechanically minded, bought himself a big Ariel motor-cycle and side-car. He probably had the idea of being independent and free to offer a lift to someone else's sister while his own sister was travelling pillion on my rather insignificant two-stroke Connaught. I was now accepted by the family as a weekly visitor.

And so life and the family carried on in this same pattern for the next two years.

My twenty-first birthday came and, as I was the youngest, Mother and my sisters arranged a party for me. All my five brothers, three sisters and four sisters-in-law came and wished me well.

Mrs. Elizabeth Bannister

Not long after my boyhood (that is, in years) was left behind, Father began looking for a farm for Jack. Together they inspected several; then one farm that was begging for a tenant particularly took Jack's eye. It was a one hundred and eighty acre farm in the village of Hepworth. Farming at this time was getting worse and this farm had lain one or two years with little attention. This really appealed to my brother, he having been in Canada so long and used to breaking up the Prairie. He would rather have this, he said, than a neat well organised holding, but Father was not so keen about it. Eventually he decided to take the place and so his fifth son was set up in farming.

This brought the little empire of Lucky Burrows and his sons to exactly one thousand acres; three hundred and sixty of which he owned. Should these scribblings by any chance be read by someone who thinks I am boasting, I would not be in the least bit worried. My brothers and myself have achieved nothing outstanding on our own, any more than the average working farmer, and we have worked hard like millions of other people. Had Father not put his first two sons into farms before the First World war, they would definitely have been called up for active service. If our father had remained a farmworker, there would have been very little hope of his sons getting into farms, as farmworkers' weekly wages were as follows...

Before 1914: thirteen shillings
1915: fifteen shillings
1918: twenty-five shillings
1924: twenty-five shillings
...and not reaching two pounds until World War II

How close to failure comes success. They hang equally balanced for a time, then some little circumstance, decision or will-power tips the scales in favour of success. On the other side of the scales are those for whom the balance of success is against them, but one cannot call them failures. They may indeed be good men with characters better than the prosperous. Their minds may be wider and their characters strengthened by adversity. It is truly remarkable that two persons travelling side by side could be divided by a tiny act of fate to be destined to finish poles apart.

My paternal grandfather finished his working career in the bar of Cretingham Bell. His domestic independence was in the cottage at Kittles Corner where, no doubt, he began his life. His possessions were never more than a few sticks of furniture, and for the comfort of his remaining years he had to rely on the kindness of his son and daughter-in-law, my mother and father.

Kittles Corner, Cretingham in 2008

Father began his life in the same house and finished patriarch of a family with over one thousand acres. Taking this case as an example, what was the deciding factor? I would say the deciding factor that created the great divide in the destinies of these two men was a few pints of beer. While grandfather spent his shilling to sit and sup his beer, Father saved his shilling, investing it in livestock. So, he worked and earned while grandfather sat and spent. That was the beginning of the great divide.

Placing Jack in the new project took on much the same pattern as was adopted for the four other boys, namely Lucky, Will, Sam and Jim. Again, Fanny went as housekeeper. This time, Katie went also for company. They of course helped with the fowls and Jack built up a flock of about two thousand. Fanny and Katie invested jointly in a flock of sheep to eat the rough grass. The profit from these they accepted as remuneration for housekeeping.

The three toiled away and the farm gradually improved. The prices of farm products were falling and what little profit was made had to be ploughed back into the land. Farmers who had only known the good times were slow in adjusting to the bad and were going bankrupt.

Industry was suffering too and consequently low wages followed, which brought about the General Strike in 1926.

As I was working in one of the fields adjoining the Harleston - Haughley road, our local police constable pulled up on his bike and dismounted. Leaning his machine against the hedge and adopting the proper stance, he rose on his toes, descended on his heels, bent his knees and returned to the position from which he had just started. "Can I put your name down to be sworn in as a Special Constable?" he said. Apparently the government wanted to get as many as possible on their side in case the strike became really serious. I told him I wouldn't make a very good policeman. He said, "You'll mix in with the rest. Bill Scarfe from Green Farm and several others are joining." So, we all went to Stowmarket police station to be sworn in. In due course, we were all equipped with a warrant-card, badge, arm-band and truncheon. The situation quietened down without our assistance.

Everything jogged along at Whitehouse Farm in the normal way. I was working in a cart-shed facing the horse-pond when I saw the lady from the cottages running towards the farm. "Have you seen my little boy?" she called out. "No," I answered, and I went out on to the road to help her look for him. He was only a little toddler about two and a half years old. We looked around. Then I saw him at the edge of the pond. He was lying face-downwards and I rushed to lift him out of the water. A neighbour then arrived and applied artificial respiration for a long time. But Willie was dead. The poor little fellow had just wandered up the road and had been attracted by the water. It was very shallow, but he had fallen forwards and could not get up.

It was awful to see the mother in distress. She had other children and more came to fill Willie's place and to take away the grief.

Spring of 1927 opened out before us. It was then I discovered a new motor-bike was needed. This was a big decision to make as most definitely, Father would be against it. Therefore it was pointless to seek his advice. In determination, I settled on a 498 cc A.J.S. with overhead valves, twist-grip control, electric lights, pillion-seat and foot-rests with leg-shields for the winter. The price of this complete outfit was seventy-six pounds. At that time, this money would have bought ten young bullocks, two working horses or four fat bullocks.

Of course Father thought, 'Whatever are things coming to? Young people are getting out of hand.' I always worried about what he thought. In this respect I knew he was much older than I before he had even owned a penny-farthing bike. It does hurt some of us to go against our parents' wishes, but you also have that feeling of being held back when you are champing at the bit to get forward. You just have to take the bit between your teeth and bolt, otherwise there would be no progress. It matters not if mistakes are made: the man who never made a mistake never made anything.

Father gave me no lecture on my purchase. He had no grounds to do so as I had bought the bike with my own hard-earned money, but I must confess it made a large hole in my savings.

Chapter 18

It was about five years since I had first taken an interest in Eva Bannister, and by now I should have felt I was her accepted partner. We met regularly and went around together, but I did not feel sure of our relationship. She was purely an individual and would be the chattel of no-one. On one occasion I well remember she and her brother Jimmy had been having an argument. As I approached the house, I met Jimmy coming away and as we passed one another he said, "She's a rummun'. You'll never twist her round your finger." The warning had no meaning for me. I was looking for a partner, not a slave.

I have never had any interest in a woman who was willing to be kept down and definitely had no desire to keep a woman down. Where such tactics have to be applied clearly denotes a lack of intelligence, understanding or self-control on the part of one partner, or both.

Eva would never be taken for granted; she had the spirit of a suffragette. She stood out from her family, her religious group and most of her sex as having a will of her own. She had no fear of parent, priest or partner. There was no need of fear because for these people she had great respect and treated them accordingly.

I emphasise that this was 1927, forty years before the writing of this book and she was already half a century ahead of her time, living the life of freedom and equality of the sexes as it should be. But she never violated her rights or advantages by indulging in petty or peevish demands.

Baptist ministers were often entertained by the Bannister family, being invited for meals and, the more distant ones, to stay for the weekend. These men were accepted by Eva with respect for their knowledge and experience, but as equals, worshipping the same God. Should they appear to put a barrier around themselves or give the impression they expected a pedestal to be provided to keep them aloof, she would quite likely meet them gaily in the morning by pulling their thin grey locks and saying, "Hello darling, did you sleep well?" You could see the robes of self-righteousness fall away and reveal the heart of a child and the weakness of a human male. So why try to camouflage themselves anyway?

Anyone of the Victorian order, believing that women should not do men's work, should not whistle like errand-boys and think it is 'not nice' to see a woman using two horses, one in the shafts and the other as trace horse to cart muck to the fields; think it wrong for ladies to smoke, ride astride fat hackneys, sing the latest songs or travel on the back of motor bikes, and so on... Well, if people with such restricted outlooks had visited Tiptofts Farm in the 1920s, they could have seen a very pretty girl doing any or all of these things. An elderly frown would then have been greeted with a hearty young laugh and a puff of cigarette smoke.

Eva loved her life on the farm surrounded by animals. Their welfare came before people; people could speak for themselves. It took a long time to realise that under her gay and light-hearted exterior, she had a serious and practical mind.

Well, I was still a regular at Tiptofts and chief escort to that fair maiden. The early hopefuls were fading away and later hopefuls exhibited their manliness without much success. After five years of constancy and no definite dismissal, I ought to have felt like a conquering hero, full of self-confidence. But I was still uncertain.

How I wished I was tall, dark and handsome with a smooth flow of speech. Had I been the possessor of these four merits, they would surely have been my downfall. Happily, my uncertainty was my redeeming feature. A few years later, Eva told me she did not like handsome men and as for the self-important smooth talkers - she had no time for them. I had the pleasure of witnessing in later years the truth of her words. Anyone trying a haughty, superior, downward slanting glance on her slunk away with their eyes to the ground and their tail between their legs.

I was now a good halfway to becoming one of the family and the deep thud from the exhaust of the AJS was becoming known for its regularity en route. There were three routes I could take to Tiptofts if I wished to make my visits appear less frequent. Turning an ordinary thing into a mystery makes one feel important. I used to go and see my girlfriend in the spirit of a Knight Errant, if not in appearance, and wanted everyone to see me and know where I went.

As I thought I was not attracting enough attention, I took the fishtail off the end of the exhaust pipe to get as much from it as possible. This did not altogether satisfy me. I wanted to justify my existence to the ears of more people so, when approaching a built-up area, I would accelerate to full throttle, shut off suddenly and produce a report to echo between the houses like a shot from a twelve-bore gun.

This used to happen when going on my visits, but returning home was different. It was done quietly and that was when I changed my route home. You see, as I went to Tiptofts, I felt like that brave knight previously mentioned going to protect a damsel from undesirable suitors, but I left with the attitude of leaving treasure, and did not want to draw attention to the time it was left unguarded.

These tactics did not quite work according to plan to cover up my retreat, as it gradually extended to well past midnight. One evening, my expectant mother-in-law quietly said to me, "I would like a word with you." She was very tiny, quietly spoken and ladylike.

"Yes," I said, my five feet, eight and a third inches towering above her four feet seven. In fact I seemed to be sinking into the ground up to my neck and was inclined to hope I could go under and come up somewhere else. Mrs. Bannister in the meantime was growing to such proportions that her voice and figure filled the universe. Whilst the world and all creation stood still, she spoke... "Would you mind leaving a little earlier in the evenings? It is often rather late when you go home you know." I sent up my reply from ground level in many, measured, casual tones, but by the time my words had risen to ear-level, they sounded hoarse, faltering and guilty.

"What would you consider a reasonable time to leave?"

"When my husband was alive, he insisted his daughters must be in by nine-thirty, but I will extend it to ten o'clock." I thanked her and said I would try and comply with her request. When the clocks advanced for summer, this meant leaving before sunset. It wasn't natural.

Ten minutes past midnight at Tiptofts Farm, Badwell Ash in the 1920s was altogether different from other country folks' midnight. Tiptofts farmhouse stood about one hundred and fifty yards back from the road. It nestled amongst the shrubberies with its ornamental pond and surrounded by meadows. The midnight picture would be the dark outline of a large house, the eerie movement of the trees and the feeling that all activity became bed-ridden when the workmen went home at five-thirty and died when the occupants went to bed at nine-thirty. You would imagine the entire place laying dormant, awaiting the resurrection of morning, with a feeble pulse of life in the form of the squeaks of bats and a mournful wail from an owl. One's sympathy would be with the mother of a pretty and attractive young woman, and would agree it was right to keep her daughter away from an ardent lover in an atmosphere where the past was dead and the future held no dread, and the present lay cushioned in the dark velvet of the night.

Jimmy, Eva's brother, had a system of living that was original and entirely his own. Some time in his early life, he lost four hours. It might have been a delay in his birth. His life was so full, he just could not recover those lost four hours. Consequently, he began his days late and finished late. He did his routine like other people, only it was about four hours later. When I arrived at seven o'clock in the evening, Jimmy was more or less halfway through his day's work. It was like arriving in America. If I had put my watch back four or five hours, we would have been on the same wavelength.

He could be found most evenings with his sheep, grinding corn into meal for the animals or gardening. Then of course he had the cows to milk, several calves to rear with which Eva helped, and she could not feed the cats and dogs until the milk was ready. Then the dairy utensils had to be washed up. It is no exaggeration to say that it was often eleven at night before the chores were completed. And I was expected to leave for home at ten o'clock... if you see my point.

I made some kind of effort to leave at ten. On a typical night, Eva used to walk to the orchard gate with me where I had left my bike. The cats and dogs had not been fed, so they followed too. As we leaned against the gate, the pets sat about in a semi-circle with their eyes on their mistress, thinking about supper.

They got tired of waiting: there were about six cats so some of them washed their faces, some rolled in the grass; the older ones sat patiently with their tails wrapped round their front feet and purred. Old Pip, the spaniel, sat and solemnly gazed.

I was just about to tell my girlfriend how pretty she was, but she got the first word in. "Look at those darlings - aren't they sweet?" I love cats but at that moment I could not raise much enthusiasm. I gazed to where the sun had just set. It looked distant and quiet until one of the calves began to bleat. Half a dozen more joined in, most unhappy and rasping. Talk about being chaperoned!

There was no alternative but to go. I shifted uneasily; the cats got up and stretched. 'Now for supper,' they thought. I started to kiss my sweetheart goodnight and at the same time, the pussies began to snug round our legs purring - and when cats are really happy, their tails shoot up straight. So, to the strains of hungry calves and cats' tails going up my trouser-leg, we parted for the night.

And as I fumbled for the motor-bike controls and tickled the carburettor, the last thing I would hear was, "Come along my little putsy-wootsies; poor old Pippy-wippy. I know you all want your suppy-wuppy."

I am sure if I had produced a petition for an hour's extension, every lover in the land would have signed it.

All evenings were very much the same at Tiptofts. Indoors and outdoors were not distinct from one another. The window curtains were rarely drawn, so inside was carried outside with the lights. The milking, calf-rearing, sow farrowing, corn sack mending and various other jobs went on during the winter evenings. If no-one was outside using the hurricane lantern, it stood on the copper alight and ready to be taken out.

The family consisted of Mrs. Bannister, Jimmy and Eva. Darkness meant nothing to any of them as they went in and out during the evenings. None of the house doors was ever locked, night or day; not even when all the family were away from home. Perhaps the windows would be closed to keep the cats out.

Everything was so free and open; no subtle suspicions. No-one moved about at any time during the night with a furtive feeling. It was in this wonderful atmosphere that I was doing my courting. Can you wonder I lost acount of the time.

After light refreshments and coffee, we would be accompanied to my machine by the lingering and vibrating notes of a harp. Yes, a harp, a real harp. One of those instruments that stands about five and a half feet high with two pedals to produce the sharps and flats. This particular harp took me away from the material to the sublime - away from the milking and calf-rearing, rattling pails and hobnailed boots stumping up concrete paths - night after night, those discordant noises were replaced by liquid notes which carried on until midnight.

But who was the angel behind these chords? (I always think of angels as females.) This heavenly body was certainly no female, even if he was an angel; it was Jimmy.

He had bought a harp and was learning to play it. It was a long time before it sounded like a stream rippling over pebbles. At first, you were reminded of a tap just turned off. The water drops were well spaced out and just when you decided it had finished, another plopped into the hand-basin.

Hugging this instrument sat Jimmy in his shirt-sleeves and waistcoat. His trousers were caked with calf saliva, dried milk and meal and he was still wearing his hob-nailed boots.

I began to get carried away with this time that seemed to belong to Tiptofts alone. Midnight was respectable: even to break into the next day did not seem out of the way, until I realised Mrs. Bannister had been in bed for over three hours. My noisy bike had to be started. I was alarmed. I did not want another warning. The best thing to do was to push it half a mile down the road away from the house and cottages before kicking off.

I stuck my toes in and shoved it to a spot called Cutting Hole Arch. Here a stream went under the road and through an arch. This was as far as I could get from habitation. It was supposed to be haunted, but the story did not bear much weight with me. Besides, I would rather get wrong with a ghost than a future mother-in-law.

After taking the precaution of pushing the motor-bike so far in order to make a quiet getaway, the first kick or two usually had no result. Then more often than not, the next attempt brought forth an explosion that echoed throughout the countryside just as a new day was being born. What one might call the crack of dawn.

During our courting career, one event in particular springs to my mind which could have resulted in being one of the most embarassing times of my life.

One very cold windy evening had been spent indoors. Jimmy was visiting his girlfriend and had not returned home. It was time for me to go and I had my hot drink. Even after putting on my motor-cycling outfit, it was not very inviting to go out. We leaned on the copper for a spell. "Come on," Eva said, "You must go. I'll come out with you. I shall have to put the dog to bed." The dog always slept in the meal shed. We went out. The wind was funnelled between the buildings where we went. Eva opened the meal-house door and the dog shot in. Eva popped in to make him more comfortable and I dived in to get under the wind.

The yard gate clicked. Jim was home and his footsteps were coming towards our door. "Keep quiet," I whispered. "Let him go

171

past." There was no reason at all why I said that. It was quite legitimate for us to put the dog to bed, but I was overcome by a sense of guilt being in a dark shed alone with a girl. I knew I was not guilty of anything, but Jimmy would think I was.

As he walked smartly past the door, he turned the key and locked us in; one of the few occasions when a door was ever locked at Tiptofts Farm. Eva panicked and was about to call out.
"Don't make a noise," I said, "We'll get out somehow."
She said in despair, "There's no way out."

By this time, Jimmy was safely in the house and with the wind blowing, there was not much hope of making him hear. I never knew why he locked the door because he left the key in the lock. Eva was getting in a right old state; her mind was going round.
"Whatever will the men say when Sid the pigman tells them he found us here when he came to work?"

There were eight men working on the farm. It looked like being a good tale for the pubs.
"Well," Eva said, "how are you going to get us out?"
"I can take some tiles off and drop down on the garden at the back."
"You can't get to the roof - there's a granary above us."
"There must be some stairs to the granary," I said.
"Yes, but you can't drop from the granary roof onto the ground."
"Is there no other outlet from the next floor?"
"There is a door but that opens onto nothing as that is where the waggons are unloaded. The sacks of meal are pulled up on to the granary floor. It must be ten feet from the ground."

I could see this was our only means of escape. "Let's go up into the granary," I said. We had a dim torch. We opened the door onto nothing and looked down. "Lovely," I muttered. I dragged three bags of bran to the opening and pushed them out; then I jumped down on to them and unlocked the door. This was when I found Jim had conveniently left us the key. Out walked the other prisoner to freedom. We then dragged the three sacks of bran through the door we had first entered.

Sid must have been mystified why these three bags of bran laid there, covered in mud.

We became engaged in 1928. Jimmy was moving towards marriage also, so the Bannister family were talking about selling up. I could not see where my future lay, or what to aim at. At this time, I was brought to see the bigness of my father's mind, or perhaps it would be more correct to say, his hopes of a completion of his plan.

By this time, it was obvious beyond doubt that it was his dream to see all his sons in farms. It must have been to this end he planned when buying White House Farm. I was only sixteen at the time and it was some time after he had bought it that he revealed the fact he had bought it in my name and confirmed the gift of it to me.

He must have calculated that by the time I was ready to farm, he would be over seventy, and would have the satisfaction of knowing his last son was provided for. He did not want the satisfaction of seeing his name on the deeds. I think he looked beyond the immediate future to the time when people would say, "There goes the man who started with nothing and finished up by seeing all his sons with a farm each."

Whilst on the subject of the Deeds of Conveyance of White House Farm, Harleston in Suffolk, I think it was 1939 before I really saw the deeds, as they were kept at the bank. Looking through them then, I was struck by a famous name among the previous owners, or perhaps he put up a mortgage for one of the owners. On this piece of paper that held my lowly name was also the name of one of the most famous men in British history. It could be a coincidence that someone else had the same name, but unlikely. I know this little farm was once part of the estate of Harold II of the Battle of Hastings. I would like to add this other name, but will confirm it first and add it later.

1066, or this other noteable man of a much later date would not solve my problems , nor decide my future.

I knew Father wanted me to take the farm over, and I had intimated it to Eva. He was now seventy. Actually, I did not mind whether I had that farm or any other, but I hated to disappoint him. Meanwhile, the Bannisters decided to carry on for another year. Had they given up then, I don't think Eva would have agreed to marry me. She was twenty-three and liked her free life. As it was, we all had another year to make more definite plans.

My family all accepted the fact that the sons would all be started in a farm, although Father never actually said that. There was, however, one very important duty as a father that he seemed to have overlooked. He never by sign, word or action showed much interest in his daughters. He had no plans for them, nor spoke of any. Fanny had been keeping house for her brothers off and on since 1907, which was a dead-end job. None of the three sisters had married. They felt they had no future and, if I took the farm, it looked as if they would lose their home. I did not want to disappoint Father, but had to agree with my sisters' point of view.

This attitude of men towards their wives and daughters, and women in general was not simply Victorian. It stemmed from centuries back and was still practised right into this century.

Returning to my father, he was ahead of his time in business and was a pioneer in some methods of farming. As head of the family and in the home, while you shared his roof, you were his subjects. In religion, he was a non-conformist, and yet in life he conformed to religion. He was honest and upright in all his dealings and never swore, drank or smoked. I am sure he would not quote the Bible to suit himself, but every biblical statement had to be carried out literally as he saw it. "Women, obey your husbands!" It did not matter about being considerate towards your wife. The curse that was put on Eve for tempting Adam, he felt should very much be kept alive. Man was superior. Man's word was law. Women had no power to think or decide.

So it was in about the Spring of 1929, I explained in detail the positions and opinions of my family to Eva. Up to this time, she was under the impression that all my people were eager for us to make White House Farm our home. She saw differently at the next visit when my sisters explained how they felt.

Eva said that she respected their feelings and would never be a party to any suggestion that would rob them of their home, and would certainly not contemplate living at White House Farm under those circumstances.

This settled our course. We must look for another farm for next Michaelmas. The choice was mine. I could either keep the farm and lose my girl, or leave the farm and keep my girl. I had the unhappy niggling feeling I had let my father down, but it seemed the best thing for all concerned. So it was we carried on with our usual routine and we viewed a few farms as they were offered for hire.

Aunt Jane in London and Aunt Lizzie in Bedfordshire, Father's two sisters, were still alive. He paid them the annual visit as he had done for years; and in addition to this little break, he had taken to having a second holiday during the summer. This one he did with his horse and trap. He would be away for a week or ten days: apart from the company of Peggy, the horse, he preferred to take his holidays alone. So he used to set off on a round tour of all his sons, spending a night or two with each. He also took in his native village of Cretingham. On this grand tour, he was never more than twenty miles from home. Even then, when he and old Peggy returned, they had covered well over one hundred miles.

Lucky & Alice Snr

All through the summer of 1929, only one thing filled my mind. It was to find a farm for Eva and I to work as partners - one that would show some prospects of stability. Everything else was secondary, and my ordinary duties were done mechanically. But anything with connections to the new venture was exciting. I had a nucleus herd of seven sows and a boar for the pig side of it, and about three hundred hens and pullets for the poultry branch. Not much, but a start. We had no idea where the seeds of our career would be planted. We were just waiting and watching.

As the weeks passed and the summer wore away, Eva became more anxious. Really, she had no ambition to settle as a housewife. Her one and only concern was for her animals as October 11th, the day Tiptofts tenancy was to end, drew nearer. Farming relatives, intimate friends and acquaintances liberally offered their advice. "Sell out," they said. "You'll lose every penny if you stay in farming."
"But I must have somewhere to take my animals," she said. "Surely if we cut everything down to bare necessities we can get a bread and cheese living."
"No," shouted one of her uncles. "There isn't even a bread and cheese living to be got out of farming." This man proved his own words by going bankrupt a few years later, and this uncle was only one of hundreds who were doing the same.

Speaking from experience, and I think it was general, the years of 1929 to 1933 were the worst years for farming and had not been equalled for over sixty years. It was into those miserable prospects that Eva and I were eager to get; she for one reason only: her exceptional love of animals, and her own in particular. My own reasons were that I loved the farm life. I wanted to get my head into the collar and pull my own weight, and farming was the only thing I knew. Eva was willing to risk all her own savings and the legacy received from her father for the sake of her animals. I was keen to gamble my all, down to the money I had carefully saved from the sale of rats' tails, sparrow heads and moleskins for the sake of an ideal, hoping one day to farm one thousand acres.

I dotted down the cost of a project to suit us both on the back of old envelopes and odd pieces of paper and figured out the possible income to be expected. One day, Eva told me that her mother wondered if I knew enough about the financial side to take a farm. "You can tell her," I reported, "I should do. I have used enough old envelopes to paper my bedroom."

Amidst this mental turmoil, the work at White House farm had to be carried on. It was July, and that left only about twelve weeks to find a farm.

Suddenly three farms presented themselves as in need of a tenant, and they all lay within two miles of White House Farm. The problem shifted from looking for a farm to choosing which one. Working in that same field from whence I sagged back on the plough handles and gazed upon five churches, I could now see all the three farms - Which one would it be?

Haughley Castle? I could not see the house. It lay directly behind the church. The grand old oak trees were plainly visible growing on her two hundred and thirty acres.

Tot Hill Farm? She stood high and stark against the skyline. A few old elms stood around the house and buildings... a rather classy looking farmhouse, seven cottages and, I believe, two hundred and sixty acres.

Dagworth Hall? No, you could not see her. She lay in a basin. From whatever angle you approached, she never showed herself until you were there. I could clearly see the fields as they rose up behind her to one of the highest points in Suffolk: they could be seen for miles around, but the house stood in the misty meadows surrounded by her two hundred and eight acres.

A few years before, I had looked upon the churches dreamily. They represented the past. I was now looking towards these three farms keenly. One of them was going to decide my future. Whichever one we took on would prove a hard battle. Would we conquer or go under? I would have to make some subtle enquiries amongst the locals to find out how generous they had been in the past with their productive output and how they were likely to respond to my treatment. Their merits or otherwise would have to be carefully weighed up against one another.

As I write, I am looking back thirty-nine years. I can see myself, twenty-five and a half and Eva, twenty-five; inexperienced, contemplating hiring a farm of over two hundred acres with enough capital between us to manage only one hundred and fifty. To the experienced, our prospects were nil. For us, we had just youth, determination and hope.

Still looking back, I see those farms as three bitter, sinister sisters. They had known the time when they were courted, nurtured, worshipped, petted and loved. No one needed them or wanted them now. At least one of them could boast of having entertained a king. She was once the playground for earls, knights, wealthy business men; then later, as she aged, less wealthy farmers paid to use her.

She had become no more than a prostitute, and by 1929 she had sunk lower; no-one wanted her any more. This particular farm in the guise of a used and worn-out woman looked upon Eva and I as representing an innocent, dull-witted youth who might be coaxed into keeping her until something better turned up.

She held out her bony arms. We hovered, just out of reach. Her name was Dagworth Hall. Her present owners had ceased to be attracted by her, so they had put her on the market. There was no enthusiasm in the bidding. The owners could not shake her off and they tried to rent her out for a small sum to get her out of their sight for a time. It was then that she saw us. "No," we said, "she will take all we have and then chuck us out penniless. We know of another woman just as eager to have us. At least she is better looking. If we came away with nothing, we should be able to say we lived while we were with her, and she raised our ego."

Yes, we decided we would go and look her over. Her name was Tot Hill Farm. She was so good looking, many men would not mind paying to live with her. But we knew that really we should view her from the angle of husbandry, not as a husband.

She stood upright, firm and well-corseted. Her two hundred and sixty acres of skirts spread out around her. They reached out over to the other side of the A45 road, so all who used this road from Cambridge, Newmarket and Bury St. Edmunds to Stowmarket, Ipswich and Felixstowe would see her and be caught up in her apparel as they passed by.

She proudly exhibited the front of her house and gardens as a shapely bosom for all to see. Compared with Dagworth Hall, she was beautiful. But we had heard whispered rumours about her. She was not sincere; her beauty was only skin deep, and she had not even much depth of skin. A lot of the land was poor and shallow. The crops came up beautifully green in the spring, only to die away in the heat of the summer. We knew we must look away from beauty and seek homeliness.

Then, there was Haughley Castle Farm: the house still stands, surrounded by a high bank that was thrown up to make the moat which encircled the castle mound. It was here that Queen Elizabeth I and her court rested as she was travelling to Framlingham Castle.

This surely had to be our woman. We would be soothed in the bosom of her mounds as we nestled in the tresses of her trees. Perhaps her lethargy would prove contagious. Her homely motherliness might smother us. Older men we spoke to said they would not like to take her on. There were too many trees sucking the goodness from the land. They had never seen very much grow between the shady boughs and hungry roots. We could not afford to live on love and protection alone, so we left her.

Eva was becoming more panicky as the weeks passed with no provision settled for her beloved animals. It looked as if Tot Hill would starve us, Haughley Castle would smother us; and so our thoughts went back to Dagworth Hall.
"Do you think you could get us a bread and cheese living there?" Eva asked. "Of course I can," I replied confidently, "only what about that awful house?" She brightened up. "If we can just manage to live, and I am sure of the welfare of my four-legged friends, the house is the last consideration."

It was a relief to hear the last statement because I could feel I was falling in love with this old woman Dagworth, but I did not want Eva in later years to accuse me of dragging her there against her will.

One day, I talked to an old man who had worked at Dagworth Hall and he was carried away with praise for the farm.

"Yew shudder sin it," he said, "when owd Joe Lankester farmed it. I've sin sixteen grut owd stacks of corn standin' in the stackyard with eaves and sides all trimmed. Thass a marster owd farm to grow beans, and bor, yew gotta git some beans into the hosses afore they can drag a plough up them owd clay hills. But once they are ploughed and the corn drilled, yew can almost sit back and wait for harvest. Them owd hills will watchercall grow wheat. They may not look a much through winter, nor even in May, but git the sun a-shinin' right into 'em as they face south, the crops'll properly go ahid. I've never known 'em to fail."

If Dagworth could be relied on to live up to its reputation, it could at least produce a bit of bread and cheese. But it was a great undertaking. I did not want to leap first and look afterwards.

I gazed across to her from White House Farm, Harleston, to where I could plainly see those clay hill fields. There were First Hill, Middle Hill, Further Hill, Chapel Hill and Further Chapel Hill,

Dagworth Hall in 2011

with two more fields levelling out above them. This group of seven fields covered about eighty acres. In addition to those I could see were another one hundred and twenty-eight acres. I felt weak and small. My capabilities did not seem to match the task.

This old prostitute lay voluptuous and inviting, surrounded by what we in Suffolk call 'high ground.' But I did not see her as an old woman whose glamour and irresistible attraction were now only a memory. I could see her as if she were in the prime of life. Surely to goodness, she could not be fully spent. Perhaps with the right approach and proper handling, there might be a bit left for me.

She had lost her beauty but not her hidden charm. It was what you could not see or fathom that attracted you and held you prisoner... so different from that other woman, Mrs. Tot Hill Farm. She had all her goods in the shop window and they looked marvellous, but when she took you to the store-room, it was bare.

The actual facts about Dagworth Hall at this time was that her owner had been the late Mr. George Woodward who had died, leaving ten or a dozen farms. It appeared that his executors wanted to tidy up the estate by selling off the outlying farms. The offers for this farm had not reached the price they were willing to accept, so they decided to let it.

In this period of acute farming depression, no-one seemed willing to hire it and the executors were anxious to get something settled. I well remember hearing from one of them. In the message he said, 'If you want to hire Dagworth Hall, you must decide quickly because another man is interested and there is nothing at all to stop him from having it.' It worked. I swallowed the dummy bait and said we would take it. I suspect if this other man had existed, there would not have been much chance of Eva and I getting the offer.

There was I, twenty five, five feet eight and one third, ten stones five pounds, and my only experience was working for my father on sixty-nine acres. My chin was much too small for my nose, my manner unmanly and indecisive, I had pink and white complexion and someone asked if I was twenty-one. To take on that farm properly, our combined capital ought to have been double.

Nevertheless, I had ambition, hope and hidden determination. I do not kid myself that these landlords saw it bulging out of my ears. We were chosen solely because we were their last hope.

I signed the lease agreement for both of us. We were committed for success or failure. Eva was delighted on behalf of her animals and I was pleased to have the opportunity of proving what I could do.

The owners had a farm sale at Dagworth Hall to dispense with surplus live and dead stock before we took over as tenants. It was another of those in-between periods, like the months between the death of an old king and the crowning of a new one. It was the end of one era and the beginning of another. Their horses were going to have to make room for our own.

One of the horses sold was a big Suffolk stallion that was bought by a man who also bought a Suffolk mare. Drovers also attended these sales to pick up a living by moving the cattle and the horses for the purchasers. One of the drovers was engaged to get these two horses to their new home. His intention was to ride the mare and lead the stallion. He started off in this manner, but had only covered about one hundred yards of his journey when the stallion gave the mare a friendly nibble. The mare resented this and twisted sharply to give him a kick. The rider was thrown to the ground and received a broken neck. His body was carried on a wooden hurdle and laid in the barn.

I had occasion to return to the farm that evening in connection with the following day's work. It was about ten o'clock. The huge range of buildings lay there quiet and forsaken apart from the corpse and myself. He was covered up, but the covering was not over his feet and he still had his boots on. I must confess, I had a creepy feeling when I left him; a kind of chilly sensation around my behind. I didn't know whether it would be better to run away or keep my face towards him and retreat backwards.

I left this mournful no-man's land, and it did feel like the sun had set on one man's career for ever... in fact, two men's careers - the drover and the late owner of the farm.

Alf & Eva's choice - Above: an aerial view of Dagworth Hall today (now divided into 2 dwellings).
Below: Tothill Farmhouse and Haughley Castle Farm with the castle mound just visible to the left of the house.

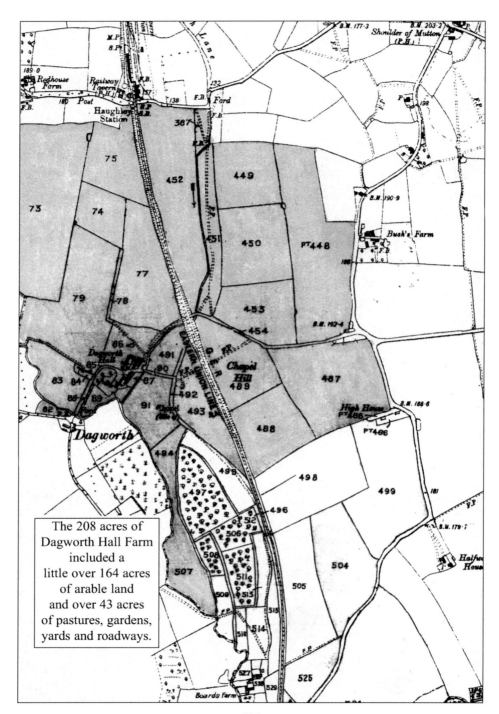

The 208 acres of Dagworth Hall Farm included a little over 164 acres of arable land and over 43 acres of pastures, gardens, yards and roadways.

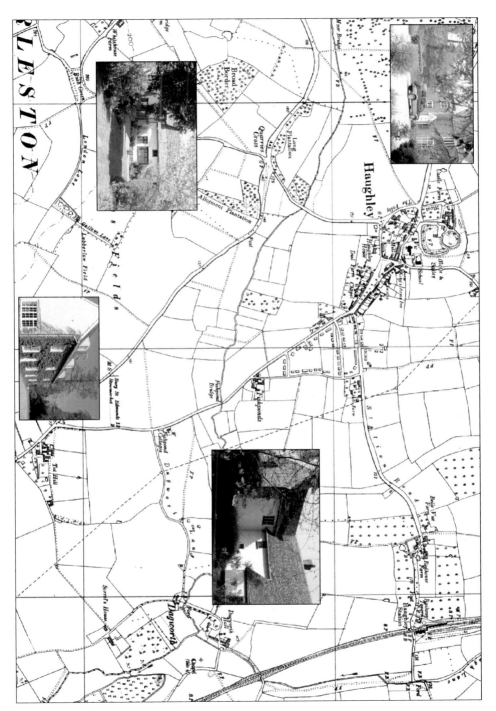

Chapter 19

The morning broke and the sun rose on the day of October 11th 1929. Not only was this the dawning of a new day; it was the dawning of a new life for Eva Bannister and myself. This was the day we would take possession of Dagworth Hall as tenants. It was much more than another chapter in our lives; it was part two of our lives and time to finish leaning on someone else and begin standing on our own two feet.

Of course, after meeting and visiting a girl for six and a half years regularly and jointly hiring a farm, the obvious act would be to marry one another, which I took for granted would happen.

A month or two before we were sure of the farm, I said to Eva, "Won't it be lovely when we find a farm so that we can marry and feel really settled?" "Oh, but I'm not getting married," she said. This was a bit of a blow. But then it was Eva. She did not <u>try</u> to be different from other women: she just <u>was</u> different. She never seemed to do the obvious. "I want to see the farm running to a pattern first," she continued. "But the real reason is that both my sisters married in the winter. I want my wedding to be in June or July."

Well, it is the priviledge of the lady to fix the date, day and time, and it fitted in with our plans as her mother had agreed to live with us. So, the Tiptofts furniture was moved to Dagworth with my future women and I joined them the following summer as one of the family. In the meantime, I went home to Harleston to sleep, but ate and worked at Dagworth. So, the sliding into marriage was a gradual operation. If we missed that wonderful joy of ascending to the skies as heavenly bodies by being suddenly plunged into marriage, we were definitely spared the terrible shock of returning to earth with a bump.

The furniture was packed onto the farm waggons the day before October 11th, ready to move off to Dagworth from Tiptofts early in the morning so that we could get unloaded before dark. Eva's brother Jimmy and Mrs. Bannister's brother Willie kindly offered to help and to spend the first few nights at the new farm to make the transitional period more pleasant.

The mother, a tiny, rather delicate lady with very proper manners and Eva, exceptionally pretty with her naturally curly golden hair, deep dimples in her rosy pink cheeks and mischievous blue eyes, drew up to the house that was to become their home in their Morris Cowley car to arrange the household things as they were unloaded.

Mother and daughter stepped from the car. They stood and gazed at the Dagworth Hall house. The mother, meek and resigned realised it was where her daughter wanted to come and was prepared to stand by her and accept cheerfully whatever came, without complaint. She was a real Christian woman in every way.

Eva stood and stared; her face normally full of laughter was serious. She had burnt her boats. There was no return. She and her mother were looking upon one of the most ugly, inconvenient, ungainly, uninviting, unkempt houses imaginable. I cannot think of one redeeming feature to merit approval, unless it was its past, and even that had been obliterated by time and the position from which the women were viewing the building.

Had they moved a quarter of the way around the dwelling, they would have seen a famous Tudor chimney claiming squatters' rights. It was perhaps the only remaining evidence that the poor tattered and forlorn old woman had seen better days.

But Mrs. Bannister and her daughter were not there for the purpose of seeing this place through the eyes of Henry VII. They were living in the reign of George V, and even he was forgotten as they concentrated on their own lives. They were unmindful that they were subjects of any king at that moment.

Three waggon-loads of furniture stood there.

"Why haven't you started to unload?" Mrs. Bannister gently asked.

"We don't know where to put the things," we all chorused. "There are people still living in the house."

"People in the house!" my future mother-in-law exclaimed.

"Yes," we replied. "They have been working for the owner of the land and have nowhere to go yet."

Another of our gang explained: "You see, two families of the workmen occupied this house. An elderly pair have moved out and the other family hope to go in a few days."

"Well," said our women, "we must move into the rooms that are vacated."

So the waggon with the necessaries was unloaded and the other two backed into the barn to be unloaded when the other family had moved out. The elderly pair that had left could hardly have been civilised. The rooms were absolutely filthy. By comparison, the horse-stables and stockyards were clean.

There was no choice. These rooms would have to be used until the others became available. One bed was fixed up for Jimmy and Willie and another bedroom was prepared for Mother and daughter. Some food was supplied from a kitchen no-one fancied. Uncle Willie, a happy little man, saw the funny side of everything. He and Jimmy joked about the situation to cheer the women, otherwise, I believe, they would have panicked and fled to relations.

Dagworth Hall in Alf's day

The next day I heard how they had all retired to bed, tired out. They were just getting comfortable when, to their dismay, they discovered that the dirty old pair had left their livestock behind.

They were all attacked by human lice. Jimmy vividly related their experiences. He and Uncle Willie endured the condition as long as possible. Apparently, they had the room with the greater number of lice and were so tormented that they lit candles and to keep their spirits up, suggested a competition.

The winner would be the one who caught the greatest number of these disreputable parasites. These two men sat on the bed stark naked, de-lousing their pyjamas and later their bedclothes. I cannot remember who won the award but have a faint recollection of hearing that one caught thirteen and the other nine. The ladies' room was not nearly so bad. They had a total kill of about three.

Dame Dagworth had begun her torturing. I had a premonition she might. She did not realise, young and inexperienced as we were, that we were her last hope. I know the executors of the last owner had the means to support this crusty old bitch, fast developing into a witch, but they did not want her hanging around them.

Their opinion of what she was capable of doing for them must have been very low indeed, otherwise those five keen experienced business men would never have agreed to let a sixteen-roomed farm-house with two cottages, and extensive range of farm buildings and 208 acres of rich land to a couple of kids, with a rent that is now charged for a one-roomed bedsit.

The rent we were asked to pay was one hundred and eighty pounds per annum. Out of that, the landlords paid tithe, fire-insurance, supplied materials for the half-mile drive and paid for all buildings, house and cottage repairs. Just at that particular period in the history of farming, the landlords were spared the hard manual work and the worry, but had practically no return for their investment.

The tenants worked all day, worried all night and just managed to buy a little food to sustain them enough to repeat the performance. The farm-workers did a hard fifty hour week without much worry for twenty-eight shillings, less rent and insurance stamp. The total weekly wages of our four men and a fifteen year-old boy came to six pounds, twelve shillings. Looking through the old farm accounts, I noticed that for several years Eva allowed herself just one pound a week for housekeeping.

I think old Mrs. Dagworth Hall really hated and resented us. You could read her thoughts and almost hear her think of the days when she had amused titled gentlemen. Her body was free for them to indulge in falconry and hunting wild boar and foxes. Wolves were still roaming the country and perhaps could be found here. Her head was the mansion and the windows her eyes. When these sporting men returned, they looked into her eyes and saw the spread of a lavish meal. They possessed horses, carriages and servants and fine women to match.

We loved this old hag. In return, she seemed to say, "I won't destroy you suddenly: I'll just let you linger and then finish you off." We started to live with her happily. She would not listen when we tried to tell her we could see beauty beneath her wrinkles.

She just could not wait to torment. That very first night, she let loose her lice and the victims could not escape. They were confined to lousy quarters.

Eva and her mother could not make a very forceful attack on the little blighters. They had the pail, scrub-brush and soap, but the only means of heating the water was in a saucepan on a rusty old cooking range. Every drop of water had to be fetched from the part where the other family were living. It was a distance of fifty paces (or seventy-five if Mrs. Bannister went). The pump was over the sink. We all felt like unwanted, uninvited visitors in our own house. I had bought two house cows at the sale and the milk had to be taken into the dairy that the other people were using. We would politely knock at the door and ask if we could have some of our own milk or water.

This state of affairs continued for four days. Eva was by then ready to explode, send the house up in smoke or blow up the landlords. She chose the latter and picked on one who lived nearby in Stowmarket. Taking her mother to back her up, she voiced her complaint and said that if something was not done about it, they would not stay in the house.

This executor said, "Why are you living in that end of the house? Why not use Mrs. Cubitt's rooms? She was most particular and clean." "We would like to," Eva replied, "But she is still there." "I am sorry," he sympathised. "There must have been an awful slip-up. They will be out tomorrow." And they were!

Our waggon-loads of furniture were drawn out of the barn and unloaded into the house. With furniture arranged, Eva and her mother settled in the clean rooms and had a sound base from which to tackle the lice in the dirty rooms, which they did very effectively. It is said, 'It's a hard battle where there are no survivors.' Three of these little suckers did survive to appear the following spring and were destroyed. A year later, one more was found hoping, I suppose, to find a mate to preserve its species, but he succumbed to the human victor and his race died out.

These complications were only connected with the domestic side of life. The farm work had to go on if we were to get a harvest the following year. This did not mean problems, but pure hard work. One man was stockman, so this meant that four men including myself and a young boy had to do all the land work. There were about 300 tons of farmyard muck to spread on twenty-four acres for beans, and then ploughed in. There were forty acres to plough before the wheat could be drilled. There were ten acres of cattle beet and swedes to get off the land and protect from the frost. And it all had to be done by man-power and horse-muscle in eight weeks. I had no tractor.

To get the farmyard muck onto the fields, we used four horses and tumbrils and two trace-horses. One boy emptied the carts in heaps on the field; another man and myself took the load to him and the remaining man and myself filled the carts. In this way, we moved over thirty tons a day. We all seemed very happy.

The job I really loved was autumn ploughing. I always worked with the men. At seven in the morning, four of us were in the stable, each harnessing one pair of horses, then moving off to the fields. We had to keep our proper positions - head-horseman, second horseman, third horseman-cum-labourer, and myself last. I always took the lowest place to avoid throwing the others out of position.

There were eight horses, looking like a miniature cavalry regiment, with their manes brushed and their tails braided, moving off with the sun just breaking through the morning mist. Their chain-traces jingled as they walked. I can almost hear them still and seem to get a whiff of cigarette smoke as the second horseman puffs a

Woodbine from his twopenny packet of five which must last him all day. The rest of us were non-smokers apart from the stockman. He smoked St. Julien in his pipe as he fetched the cows home from the meadows, and the scent he left hanging in the morning air made it worthwhile getting up to enjoy it.

We looked to the head-horseman to set the pace all day and every day. He knew just how much the horses could manage, and how long to rest them at the end of each furrow. So, all day long we each moved along with our team, a minute or so after our immediate senior.

It was the custom in Suffolk and Norfolk (and I should imagine this applied to the whole country) that when man took on a farm either as owner or tenant, to bear all the expenses in threshing the outgoing occupier's corn, and the incoming man to keep the straw. Then of course, when you left the farm, the following occupier would do the same for you.

I found I could forget the five executors and look upon Mr. G. Philip Woodward as our landlord. He was the son of the late Mr. George Woodward; the other son was killed in World War I. Any business between landlord and tenant, from then on, was between Mr. Philip Woodward and myself. This Mr. Woodward was owner-occupier of several farms. In his understanding of farming, he did not ask me to thresh his corn until our autumn work was finished.

It was then done in three stages, with intervals of a few weeks to get the corn disposed of. The total amount threshed was 1,480 coombs (a coomb is a sack containing four bushels). This was a total weight of about 140 tons. Besides threshing this corn, the incoming occupier could

be asked at his expense to transport the corn a distance of up to ten miles. This was done by farm waggons drawn by our own horses.

As I have previously described, Dagworth Hall lay in a basin, and to reach the public road meant going up a farm road called 'The Chase' for a distance of about half a mile, with a gradient something like 1 in 8. It took an extremely good cart-horse to pull an empty waggon up the Chase and we had to transport about 100 tons of grain by horse and waggon. We usually used six horses and two waggons. Each waggon had a load of two tons, and each had two horses abreast in the shafts. The teams had a tandem trace-horse. The two teams moved to the bottom of the Chase and stopped. The trace-horse was taken from the second team and put with the trace-horse on the first waggon. An extra man was detailed to stand by the pair with the second load.

Now for the hill and the first load - four powerful horses hitched onto a waggon containing two tons of grain, with Alf Orris the second horseman beside the two leading horses to urge them on. Stephen Crissell, the head horseman, took command of the shaft horses. He put them gently to the collar. "Righto Alf," he shouted. "Take the strain!"

The whole team of four now had an equal share of the strain. They started off gently and then gradually increased the speed to a short-stepped trot. Stephen encouraged the whole outfit. "Get along there Smiler. Bess, stick your toes in, Keep 'em up Alf." And Alf shouted, "Blossom, Prince, get away there!" In this manner they got to the top of the hill.

Stephen left Alf with his two panting waggon horses and took the two trace horses back to fetch the second load and repeat the operation. When at the top of the hill, Stephen and Alf each took one trace-horse and continued the journey with three-in-hand. The extra man returned to the farm thinking, 'There go the first four tons - only another ninety-six tons to follow.'

These hills made the working of Dagworth land very hard indeed when the only power we had was the four-legged type, and often we had to use three horses to do a two-horse job. We did not blame Dame Dagworth for this; it was only part of her features. We took her on with the full knowledge that her cheek-bones were prominent and her complexion pitted with age. You looked upon her countenance and realised she had accomplished much through the centuries, and it had left its mark on her face.

It was her unusual features that made her outstanding and when we had skilfully applied her spring make-up, few could surpass her beauty. Often in the spring and summer evenings, I used to lean on a gate on the west side of the farm, with my back to the setting sun and gaze upon those clay hills. One would see the dark green of the wheat with the striped shades made by the roll. The 'middle hill', when it layed as freshly cut clover resembled the back of an envelope, with marks leading from the four corners to the centre, made by the mower as it turned. The colour of this field changed every day for a week, from the plain purple patch of clover blossoms before being cut, to the envelope back, turning daily from green to brown.

The barley fields lay there in their pale green coverings, often striped by roll or harrow marks. Bean and root crops added variation. I did not see the patchwork effect as might be seen in Devon or Somerset as it was all near enough to distinguish one crop from another.

It can easily be imagined how overwhelmed I felt when I looked during the first spring on my first crops, the result of my management and work, and the promise of a harvest.

But while I looked at this Lady Dagworth with adoration, she was looking at me cruelly and thinking, "You miserable little upstart of a tenant - you're getting far too self-satisfied. I will see that you never match the standard of my ideas."

I had bought a bunch of Irish calves during the autumn to feed through the winter ready for selling in the spring, or to keep to graze the meadows. They had a bad attack of 'the husk' and one died. The stockman, an elderly, experienced man, dosed them up on his own particular brand of remedy: another died. He dosed them again with a tablespoon of turpentine in half a pint of linseed oil. The third one died. I did not blame him. I realised he knew more than I and was doing his best. This particular man had been foreman at Dagworth for many years, and I do not suppose I was really the type of boss he could really look up to.

One morning during the spring, he outpaced his position. and started giving me orders, and orders are things I am not very good at taking. I will take advice and suggestions unlimited, but not orders. "You ought to get Stephen to harrow that you know," he said.
I flew at him. "You ought to keep those calves alive, you know. You mind your business and do your job and I'll do mine."

Our relationship was never quite the same after that. Perhaps he did know best. He should do; his name was Solomon and he had the appearance and manner of wisdom. His hair and moustache were pure white and his eyebrows black. In one mannerism he even excelled the first Solomon - he would click his false teeth when annoyed.

Once, I asked him, "You must have come from a large family - how many were there?"
"My mother had twice twenty-one."
I bought it. "Good gracious, forty-two - what a family!" I left him, then turned back sharply. "She couldn't have done - it would be impossible in a lifetime."
"Ah, but she had twenty-one; then one died and she had another, so twice she had twenty-one." This time, his teeth clicked with happiness.

Although the farm was carried on in my name, we were really partners. Eva had put everything she possessed into it by way of money, live and deadstock from Tiptofts. I put my all into it and also borrowed some money from my father. We had definitely planned to marry in July. The light-hearted courtship we hear of before marriage was ruled out by the hard work and worrying as to whether we would be able to make a go of it.

The three young cattle that died just about wiped out my profit on the whole bunch. I had taken a little herd of seven sows and a boar to Dagworth that I had hopefully built up at Harleston. But vindictive old Ma Dagworth had her eye on them. "I'll prune that little bunch before it grows to any size," she decided. She cursed them with swine fever. I had to have them all slaughtered. That was in May, just eight weeks before the wedding. Still, we had several pigs fattening. They would be ready for sale as bacon hogs at the end of July.

The day of the wedding drew nigh. Hay-making was in full swing. We sold the Irish cattle and were using the money to carry on with. There was no money to buy grazing cattle, so in addition to the arable clovers we cut all the meadows for hay, a total of over fifty acres, thinking we could use the hay in later years for winter feed when we could afford the cattle.

The pastures were nearly all of the marshy type, and mostly enclosed by tall willows and alders. So, with the damp boggy soil, the heavy mists, no sharp breezes, the thick sward of coarse grass, plus a showery period, our task seemed insurmountable. We had no mechanical swathe-turner and, day after day, between the showers, we turned it by hand. By the time our wedding day arrived on July 8th, a little of it was carted, some was on the cock and the rest strewn about.

Old Mrs. Dagworth smiled gleefully from among the willows. "That will give the young fools something else to think about besides romance, and for good measure I'll wave my wicked wand over that yard full of fat pigs."

She did and the hogs went down with swine erysipelas and their skin came out in large red blotches. Some of them died. I wouldn't know if it was usual for pigs to die from this complaint; all I know is that mine did.

That was the picture at Dagworth Hall on our wedding eve. We had booked in at a seaside place for a week's honeymoon.

The wedding - (l. to r) Lucky Jnr., his daughter Sylvia, Alf, Eva, bridesmaid, Mrs. Bannister.

On the wedding morning, I was so concerned about leaving everything that I went down to Dagworth for a final look round in my single state. This was indeed playing with etiquette, fate or superstition as it meant seeing my bride, and a bride should not see her groom until they meet to be joined in holy matrimony.

My mind was so full of the conditions of hay and swine that I overlooked the saying that, 'it is an ill omen to see your bride earlier on your wedding day.' Even if I had stopped to think about it, I would have felt our luck was running at such a low ebb it could not have had any more of an adverse effect.

In the presence of our relatives and friends, we made our marriage vows. When later we left for our honeymoon, we both felt we were going away under the strain of dying pigs rather than the chimes of wedding bells.

Chapter 20

My bride and I returned from our honeymoon to find, under the supervision of the head horseman Stephen Crissell, that most of the hay was carted and stacked. My mother-in-law was there to welcome us home. She made her home with us for the next six years or, it might seem more correct to say, we lived in her home as most of the furniture was hers.

> Editor's note: There are several spellings of the name 'Crissell'. Alf spells it 'Crysal'. The Dagworth Hall sale documents for 1929 spell it 'Crysell'. We have opted for the way the name is more commonly spelt in this part of Suffolk today.

While we were away, the depressing farming outlook was put from our minds, so we returned with renewed vigour and fresh hope to tackle our difficulties together. Eve, my wife - I will refer to her as Eve from now on, not because we lived in any semblance of the Garden of Eden by a long chalk, but it suited her better. She was rarely called Eva by her family; for most of her life, she went under the name George, mainly because she preferred the 'man's world'. She was happier grooming horses than dusting nicknacks.

From honeymoon to harvest was a matter of about four weeks. With hope and joy, we pulled the binder out of the cart-shed, scraped off the bird droppings, cleaned it up, oiled, greased and fitted the canvasses all ready for cutting the corn. Harvest is a happy time, reaping in the results of your year's toil.

This was the year 1930, with a new wife and partner, and our very first harvest. It was the last harvest in which we completely relied on horses - three horses to pull the binder: these changed every three hours for a fresh team, and we kept the reaper going all day for ten to twelve hours.

Carting the waggon loads of sheaves to the stackyard was where Eve really came into her own. She was the 'driver' who took the empty waggons back to the field and returned with the loaded ones. Two horses were required: one in the shafts and the trace-horse.

The trace-horse was there mainly for the purpose of getting the empty waggons up to the field rather than bringing the full ones home - the gradient saw to that.

Eve was a car driver, but much more skill was needed in handling the two-horse outfit. In the first place, the length from the nose of the trace-horse to the back of the load was something over thirty-five feet. To turn out from a ten foot gateway onto a narrow lane without bringing down the gatepost with a rear waggon wheel was a planned art. With a lorry or tractor, one would be in direct control of one's responsibility. With the horse flesh, it was a matter of transmitting your intentions through the brains of the horses and trusting to their reactions through good training. Eve had the gift of a telepathic understanding with animals that not everyone possesses.

We had one very distressing job for a horse, which was driving the stacking elevator. For this, we used the oldest horse. It did not matter how slowly it moved and no great effort was needed, but it had to walk in a circle no more than twelve feet in diameter beneath the elevator to drive it. In my opinion, the horse suffered only from intense boredom. After the second season, we had the mechanism adapted for use with a petrol engine.

The object of the harvest is, of course, to thresh the grain and sell it to pay debts, and still have enough to carry on until another harvest. Proudly we threshed our first stacks and with some importance I presented a sample of wheat to the merchant. Sadly, he looked at it like a doctor dubious about giving a patient some bad news. As if he wanted to shift the responsibility, he said, "If I were you I would try somewhere else."

"No," I said. "I want you to buy it."

I knew he could not bear to disappoint me.

"I've never known the trade so bad in all my life," he said. "All I can afford is nine shillings and sixpence a coomb." That would be equal to six and a third pence per stone, or four pounds five shillings a ton. I sold him 200 coombs and he gave me a cheque for £94.10.0d.

This corn merchant was in his middle fifties, and as he passed me the cheque he remarked, "This is the first time I have paid less than £100 for two hundred sacks of wheat containing two and a quarter hundredweight in each." I made a little more money from the wheat I sold later in the year, but all the barley was sold for an average of five shillings per hundredweight.

Eve and I did not stand out as a single target in need of help or pity. Everyone in farming was experiencing the same at this time. I could not blame the price of corn on old Lady Dagworth - that was farming in general and she had given us a fairly bountiful harvest. 'So,' I thought, 'As she is in a good mood, I think I will try some more pigs. I expect she will be a bit kinder now.'

The buildings had been free from pigs for about three months and I had to make some more money somehow. Oh yes, brother Lucky had kept pigs for twenty-three years, had a good strain, and they had never had any diseases. He sold me ten young sows - we call them 'gilts' before they have been bred. They looked fine and we watched them with great expectations.

But the wizened old woman was watching too. "They won't get away with it," she cackled from behind her creased-up old countenance." We didn't. After about two months, down the pigs went with swine fever and the whole lot were slaughtered. The old witch must have had a germ or two tucked away in the dusty cobwebbed old stone-work of the buildings.

For the second time, our pig prospects perished, so all we could hope to do was to plod along and try to keep our expenses within the income from corn sales. The 'old bird' seemed willing to allow us that much - almost as though she realised it was the only means she had left of keeping her acres of skirts cleaned, repaired and free from weeds; with a faint hope that some day, an aristocrat would appear and claim her.

To that extent, Dagworth Hall was like an old lady's maid who had spent her entire life in a baronial family and would be proudly honoured to give her whole life to them free of charge. She would sacrifice progress and prosperity to keep things the way they had always been, for ever. Dagworth, with memories of her army of grooms, gardeners, butlers, footmen, housemaids and all, might try to stem the tide of progress, but change had inevitably come, in spite of all she might do to try and prevent it.

I remember being told of the year 1870 when my mother, in her native village of Cretingham, was ordered by her school teacher to curtsy as His Grace the Duke of Hamilton and his Duchess passed through in their carriage drawn by four magnificent horses. She never looked back on it as an act of servility. She, poor little soul, nine years old, stepped back on the grass verge in the only outfit she possessed and felt honoured to leave the road clear, and crouch before another human, then talk of it with pride all the rest of her life. This is all wrong - has been proved wrong - and has now changed.

I should be sorry to see the day arrive when there was no respect for anyone, and there is a tendency for this to be amongst us at this present time. I, for one, am proud to respect a man of noble character; but I would respect a person for what he represents in spite of what he is - such as a policeman for enforcing the law, a parson for the good he represents, a soldier for the protection of our country or a doctor for his profession. Such people should not have to demand respect, because respect should be given.

We will return to Dagworth and have a glance at her as she appears today in 1968. She is just a little hamlet with ten houses.

The ford at Dagworth. Dagworth Hall is beyond, through the trees.

There is no official boundary as she is now included in the village of Old Newton. But she is, in the mind of all who know her, still very much Dagworth.

This little hamlet, in spite of rural council boundaries and modern by-laws, is still very much an individual and contains Dagworth Hall, the ugly old farmhouse where I spent so many years of turmoil and joy. She now has modern conveniences and is adapted as two cottages. 'Sorrel House' stands, I gather, where once stood a pub called 'The Sorrel Horse' in the days when Dagworth was a large prosperous village.

Editor's note: Sorrel House is in an unlikely place for a pub. It probably gains its name from the title of the medieval manor in which it sat: 'Dagworth-with-Sorrel'.

Quite close to this house is 'Malt House' - now a beautiful 'olde worlde' residence - but I remember it better as three tumbledown old cottages where, years before, workmen had lived and toiled in the maltings that then adjoined. There is a tiny farm called Hop Farm. Hops were grown here for many years. This leaves four cottages to complete the tiny community living in the basin. Its rim is where the land ceases to rise before dropping away beyond.

Its geographical position makes Dagworth unique. Two roads lead to Dagworth: The Chase leading from Old Newton and Daggar Lane leading from Haughley. These were both designed to terminate at Dagworth Hall. Four footpaths, two from Stowmarket, one from Haughley Railway Station and the fourth from Haughley village, all finish like a spider's legs at one spot. Dagworth is not a place passed en-route to somewhere else. She has always been happy to live unconnected with her neighbours but for all that, she will not be ignored. No-one has ever told her, "We were just passing, so we thought we would call in." You either go to Dagworth for the sole purpose of visiting or keep away. She lies half a mile from all public roads.

You approach Dagworth Hall by the Daggar Lane, a single winding track, with banks on either side and in some places ten to twelve feet high. Just before reaching the Hall, you pass over an unbridged ford which is never dry, being fed by springs throughout the longest droughts.

It is just about here that an atmosphere strikes you - at least it does me, being sensitive in that way. It did while I lived there and each year as I make my pilgrimage, it gets me without fail. I used to feel surrounded by mysteries of past years, long before I learned of any history attached to it.

In the Domesday book compiled in 1086, it is recorded that Dagworth was a large village, its area three miles long and one and a half miles wide. Just previous to 1086 its importance was described as follows... 'Dagworth contains thirty-four cottagers, six farmers and one and a half churches, one mill, forty she-goats, ninety-four hogs, sixteen sheep, thirteen maids bound or slaves.'

At this time, an acre of land could be bought for sixteen silver pennies (£3), a man or slave for fifty-six shillings, a horse for thirty-five shillings, a cow for five shillings and sixpence, a goat for fivepence halfpenny and one swine for one and tenpence halfpenny.

It was around the year 900 when cows were introduced as domestic milk producers; previously milk was taken from goats and sheep for human consumption. These animals were guarded all day by slaves with dogs against wolves; at night they were kept in safe folds.

I do not know what they meant by 1½ churches and have no idea what happened to the half church, but a church - a complete one - once stood in Chapel Hill Field nearly at the top of the Chase. We passed the spot each time we lugged two tons of grain with four horses up the hill. In years of drought, the place where it had stood could be seen by the dark green corn which grew where the boundary ditch had been filled in. I believe historians have other views as to the site of this church.

The land in any village has been there as long as Dagworth land, obviously, but there have been happenings there since before the days of Norman rule. You can sense it as you walk quietly round Dagworth Hall land in the hot summer evenings, by the stream under the long shadows of the willows around the marshy meadows.

The snipe still buzz as they dive down: there you feel so far from the present and so close to the past. As I once rested my horse for a few minutes on a hot afternoon, I would not have been surprised to see a knight in shining armour ride by. This is a place where you feel the past holding you.

In the village of Dagworth during the reign of Edward the Confessor, lived a family by the name of Breme. He was a freedman of King Edward and held 150 acres of arable land, and lived in luxury. Harold, brother-in-law to Edward the Confessor, owned vast stretches of land in this area and when he became king and went to battle against William the Conqueror, it was quite natural that numerous partisans joined him from this area. This man Breme was one of those who fought with Harold at the Battle of Hastings and he, like his king, was killed. They gave their lives on October 14th 1066 to save Saxon England, but by their defeat, the history of England changed and the country fell under Norman rule. William the Conqueror's men took away all possessions from the families of the vanquished and treated them as outcasts. So, as the result of his bravery, Breme's family exchanged their life of comfort for a life of poverty.

Up until the early nineteenth century, a family by the name of Breme was still living in Dagworth and working as labourers on the land their ancestors had once owned. Quoting from the 'History of Stowmarket' compiled by the Rev. A.G.H. Hollingsworth in 1843, he writes under Dagworth: "In 1086, it was called Dag-word or Dagaworda, meaning 'great hall of the day' or perhaps 'Day's great hall.' The great hall was pulled down centuries ago. Spears, coins and keys are often found in its precincts. A church once stood where is now a field. The field is called Chapel Hill and is part of the present Dagworth Hall Farm."

One oak tree stands near to where the church once stood and under its shade I have often rested to take refreshments while working in Chapel Hill Field. It is not unlikely that I was resting in life above the bones of someone who had been resting in death for nigh on a thousand years.

This is Dagworth. When I began my farming career there in 1929, I think she was then as she had been for about one hundred years. Here, generation after generation had farmed these acres a thousand years or more and apart from mechanisation in the last decade or two, these lands are still as they have always been.

I remember looking towards White House Farm, Harleston where my parents were living. I could see the giant redwood that stood near their house. My direction of view was completely reversed. A few years before, I had stood in the fields there and gazed on the clay hills of Dagworth. Had I taken father's little farm I would no doubt have filled my belly with grub more easily earned, but I would have missed the food for thought I gained at Dagworth.

* * * * * * * * * *

Old Dowager Dagworth Hall was a snob. Her glory lay in the past. Although her position had become altered by the changing years, it was kept very much alive in her memory: but memories will neither feed nor clothe one.

When I took on the responsibility of feeding her with good farmyard muck, and covering her aged bent form with beautiful green crops, I did it entirely for my own interest and in hope of personal gain. I had no tender feelings towards her, but my feelings for her grew gradually.

Although I never realised it, Dagworth Hall needed Alfred Burrows more than Alfred Burrows needed Dagworth Hall. In 1929, Dagworth Hall was sick with age. Among the tenant-working type of farmers, those with the means had not the courage to take her. The so-called better type of farmer or the men who considered themselves as such would not look at her, as there were numerous lovely women to be had in the guise of farms who would enhance their status much more.

Even I was not really dependent on her: Mrs. Tot Hill Farm would have welcomed me with open arms without question, and kind Haughley Castle was looking for someone to love; or I could have carried on at White House Farm with my father indefinitely.

But the old girl had to rely on someone coming to her aid. It just happened to be Eve and I, but she tried to put on an act of condescension and liked to think she was doing us a favour, and thought she should keep us in our place. We ignored her rusted and outdated snobbery, overlooked her outbursts of vindictiveness and really began to love her.

We had failed at our second attempt at pig-breeding because of swine-fever. Again the buildings had been free of pigs for three months, so for the third time we tried, again going to a reputable pig-breeder and buying ten young sows. It was now the beginning of 1931 and with spring coming on, we thought the pigs should do well. By March, the new pigs had succumbed to the same curse and went the way of the rest.

This definitely decided us that pigs were out for all time. We knew we must incorporate something into our farming besides corn growing. We had a few cattle and were rearing some calves. These were doing well but it took two years to get them ready for sale. There just had to be something else to bring in a little ready money to pay the men and grow the corn and leave twenty shillings over to run the house.

The only thing was to increase the poultry branch. We had an incubator, so we bought another and used a bedroom for an incubating room. It was grand to see the eggs lying in the drawers and we used to turn them by hand twice a day. We did 250 eggs in a batch and were as excited as kids the morning we opened the drawers to see the yellow fluffy balls of chicks and the wet ones still squiggling out of the shells.

We did this three times and also let some broody hens hatch some on their own, so between us we had incubated well over 800 eggs. I made some brooder houses to put heat in for rearing. The eggs were very fertile; the chicks twittered about and spring was in us all.

Old Mrs. Dagworth frowned when she saw them and seemed to say, "I just won't have these little commercial enterprises running around and making a mess right where the courtyard used to be for my beautiful mansion. I just won't have it!" I wish she could have told us before and saved us the trouble of hatching them. After a few weeks they began to die: it was a misery to see them moping about with drooping wings and backsides all messed up. They had bacillary white diarrhoea.

Out of the 800 eggs we incubated, only one chicken survived. The scourge only persisted for a few more years as the Ministry of Agriculture eradicated it by insisting all breeders have their stock blood-tested once a year.

Just before the chickens finished dying off, I went to bed with the flu and felt quite light-headed. Sometimes the bed seemed to be propped up on six foot stilts; the next minute, they had gone through the floor and I was at ground level.

After a few days, I felt better. The doctor said to my wife, "You could get a few bottles of Guiness - one a day will do him good." Mother called in to see me, saw the empty bottle and said, "I shouldn't have too much of that old stuff if I were you." "Alright," I said. I didn't think it worth giving her the facts. It looked too much like explaining away a weakness that had just taken hold of me.

When I felt well enough to forget myself, I began to wonder what could be done to make some ready cash. An inspiration presented itself. A milk-round. Grass in the evening, milk in the morning and money before midday. Hurrah! One of the quickest turn-overs you can get in farming.

"George!" - Eve was always 'George' in spontaneous moments - "Bring me some old envelopes: I'm going to start a milk-round."

I always worked out possible projects on used envelopes. In fact, I have one in my hand right now with notes about writing on old envelopes.

Eve brought the required paper. "Now," she said. "Tell me all about it." "Well, first of all we must contact the Sanitary Inspector or someone to see if the cowshed will come up to a certain standard and find what we need in the way of a dairy. We have three cows and if the project goes well, we can buy more. We must buy a pony and cart to take the milk and we can supply all the houses as we go to Stowmarket, which is about two miles. We must get all the trade we can away from the other dairymen by selling at a halfpenny a pint cheaper. We shall get some hand-bills printed and take them around Stowmarket a few days before to let people know we are coming." Eve was thrilled. "I shall love that and will help in every way I can," she said.

The Dairy Inspector came before I was fully recovered from the flu. We bought a smart little turn-out that a retired man used to drive. It consisted of a lively black pony called Charlie, well-kept harness and a round-about-governess cart. The churns, delivery cans, measures and so on were bought second-hand. Then, with hand-bills printed, we took them around Stowmarket and we canvassed for trade -

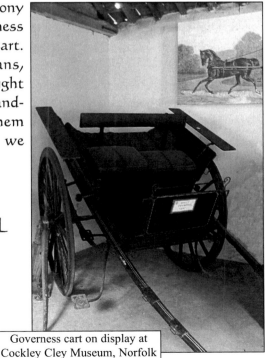

BURROWS,
DAGWORTH HALL
DAIRY,
MILK DELIVERED
TWICE DAILY
AT 2d PER PINT.

Governess cart on display at
Cockley Cley Museum, Norfolk

209

Georgie Hearn, seventeen years old was going to be the roundsman. The morning of the first trip arrived. Eve and I were keyed up to the hilt. This meant more to us than Amy Johnson's flight to Australia meant to the rest of the world. I arranged to go with Georgie several times until the pony got used to the work.

We loaded up this first morning and roped the churn to the cart, which was just as well as the first thing Charlie did was to rear straight up on his back legs like a circus horse. When he returned to earth, he bent his four limbs and gave a great leap and we were away on our new project.

Eve was in the yard to greet us when we returned in our chariot, with the measures swinging and hitting the sides of the empty cans. "How did you get on?" she shouted, before we had time to stop. "Marvellous!" I beamed as I stepped from the improvised milk cart. "We sold three and a half gallons." The afternoon's sale brought the day's total to just over five gallons. It increased during the week to bring our first seven days' takings to £3.10.0d - an average of ten bob a day. It sounds ridiculous, but to us then it was very encouraging. It paid half the week's wage bill for our staff of five.

This milk-round proved to be our salvation, and old Lady Dagworth allowed it to prosper. The cows were more suited to graze these pastures than any other type of animal and it spared us much worry in trying to make hay on the low meadow.

This venture prospered so slowly that we did not feel much benefit from it for the first year. Our second harvest did not produce enough money to meet all our demands. We had value of course in stock and equipment, but could not use that as it represented our working capital. We had outstanding accounts to meet, and being brought up strictly to always pay our way, this played on my mind dreadfully. This is where old Mother Dagworth wanted to see me - on my knees.

The money we needed would not today be the price of a cheap small car. In those days, it was a vast sum. I had reached the end of my tether. I just could not face it any more and definitely hated Dagworth Hall at that moment. She was all around me, jeering. Had it been in my power, I would willingly have destroyed her for all time, and gloated over it.

I was so helpless and had nothing left to fight with. I went indoors and sat leaning on the table. I buried my head in my arms and wept. The wicked embittered old woman had won!

But I still had the support of my wife. I said to her, "We can't go on." We must start again somewhere else. I'll go straight to Mr. Woodward now and tell him we shall have to sell out."

We were by no means an isolated case. Wealthier and more experienced men were going bankrupt all around us. I was still running the same A.J.S. motor-bike: this was our means of getting about, with Eve as pillion-rider. Sadly starting her up, I mounted and rode up the Chase to carry out my mission of presenting my problem to my landlord and tell him I wished to sell out. His uncle, being an auctioneer, would make everything simple and quick to arrange. I rode into the courtyard of White Hall, Old Newton, pulled my bike onto its stand, and with prepared speech and nervous steps, I reached the door and knocked.

White Hall, Old Newton

There was no reply. Twice more I knocked with the same result. I went to the front door and repeated the performance - most unusual - not even the maid was there.

Returning home, I wearily said to Eve, "There was no one at home." We went to bed. In the morning, everything looked brighter and seemed more hopeful. My dead faith came to life. "Perhaps we'll carry on and see how things go," I said.

It was not a case of manna from heaven or sitting and waiting to be fed by ravens, but from that day, as if by a miracle, our big disasters stopped. By long days of hard work, we were able to begin to pay our way and build up towards a more hopeful future.

The government gave the farmers some cash aid on wheat, we obtained a contract to grow sugar beet, the milk-round increased and our herd of three cows increased to fifteen and eventually to thirty.

Lady Dagworth Hall was contented and relaxed to know she had broken my spirit and brought me to my knees. We became friendly and accepted each other in spite of age and youth, past and present.

And I do not suppose that unless Mr. George Philip Woodward reads this, he will ever know I once knocked at his door to announce my failure.

Chapter 21

Compared with the long-known history of Dagworth Hall during her span of nearly one thousand years, my sojourn of nineteen years was but a grain of sand on the seashore.

My stewardship with its hopes, heartaches, joys, sorrows, romance and experiences in those nineteen years will to me be a life long memory. Actually, I did not know what treasured memories Dagworth held for herself until years after I left her. I had not the time to think about such things while I was there. The few snatches of history I had heard, I accepted as stories handed down and perhaps distorted through the generations: surely not facts.

I was certainly not aware that I was living, working and sleeping where once a king of England was entertained. I did not know when I wended my way down Daggar Lane with my bits and pieces to start farming that I was taking the same route as King John of England. His Majesty in 1216, and I a humble subject of King George V in 1929 were both bound for the same spot - he to a great mansion in his day; and I to share an ugly old farmhouse with someone's left-behind lice in my day. But we had one thing in common, and also in common with all who slept there. It was called Dagworth Hall in the Domesday Book and before; it was Dagworth Hall when I was there, and the name is still the same.

During the last year of his reign, King John on one of his travels, left Cambridge on March 10th 1216. The 11th, he spent at Dagworth Hall, the 12th at Framlingham, then on to Ipswich on the 13th, leaving the county for Colchester on 14th March. When on these travels, his court probably consisted of fifty ladies and gentlemen on horseback and fifty attendants.

The Domesday Book's name for this mansion, meaning 'Great Hall of the Day' signifies its size. The fact that King John was entertained there with his court proves its immensity and importance. I found no relics of such bygone days while living there, but 800 years is long enough to obliterate all signs unless a black shadow floating around can be called a relic. This was seen by four people at three different times, each unaware that the others had seen it. But perhaps it would be better to refer to this subject later in my story in the context in which it was seen.

According to King John's character as a monarch, his ghost would be the more welcome guest. I was one of the four who saw 'the black shadow' but it did not in the least make me feel nervous when passing the spot, either by day or night, and when I saw it I had no knowledge of Dagworth history. But as before related, I always had the sensation of being surrounded by the past.

So, on the same ground where once trod royalty, Dukes, Earls, Knights, servants, serfs and slaves, we continued to load up the milk each day for our Stowmarket delivery. The round had grown to about twenty gallons a day.

When the Bannister family left Tiptofts Farm, Eve bought the Morris Cowley car from her mother. Then, after a few months, we could not afford to run it, so we jacked it up in the garage.

By 1932, when the milk-round had reached the twenty gallon mark, we had to put another vehicle on the road as two or three more dairymen were going around selling at our low price of 2d per pint. This made competition so keen we had to sell where we could and our round became very scattered. In the two journeys, we were doing twenty miles a day. This was too much for Charlie the pony, so out came the Morris Cowley. I fitted a false bottom in the rear part for churns, eggs and butter. We had a neat metal frame fitted to the side of the car in which we slipped a name plate bearing the words...
BURROWS, DAGWORTH HALL DAIRY.

Eve was responsible for this outfit and served the outlying customers. For the afternoon delivery, Georgie Hearn went with her, so Charlie only had to go once a day. Before we dared lay out the money to put the car on the road, I bought a cheap side-car and fitted it to my motor-bike. It held just one churn. I cut a hole in the side for the tap of the churn to stick out for filling the hand-can. No doubt, mud, dirt and germs splashed up into this tap as I went along the road and, with no doubt at all, they were washed into the hand-can with every refill. But I heard of no-one dying from germalgia or muditis. I used this method of delivery for about a year and was very relieved when Eve went with the car. It left me free to help on the farm.

Throughout all our farming trials, Eve regularly kept up her duty as organist at Wetherden Baptist Church. Many a time when it was her turn to play at the morning service, she would go straight to chapel off the round with a car-load of dairy utensils. Then, after the service, she would return home and wash the whole lot. For the evening service, we went 'all posh', taking out the false bottom, replacing the seat and removing our trade name.

It is impossible to keep up a regular daily supply of milk from a herd of cows and sometimes we barely had enough for the round. Then, usually in the spring, with the flush of fresh grass and newly-calved cows, there would be an almost unmanageable surplus which had to be made into butter. This meant churning three times a week. Eve and her mother did this, and it was very tiring work. They often made ninety pounds of butter in a week.

The butter was sold on the milk-round. During very hot weather, it was a real worry. We had no refrigerator and with the sun beating down on the open cart and car, by the time we handed it to the customer, it was more like a half-set blancmange than a pound of butter. Although we finished these days with tired bodies, our minds were more at rest as we were now paying our way. There was no opportunity to save money; neither would there be for several years as extra implements had to be bought and the old ones replaced.

1935 - and Father had now reached the age of 76. He was still farming White House Farm, but felt the time had come for his complete retirement. He decided he would still like to live in the house, so asked if I would farm the land. As I lived nearest of all his sons to him, a distance of just two miles, my five brothers all agreed that I was the one to do it. With Dagworth Hall and a few odd pieces of hired land, White House Farm brought my total acreage to about 300. I did take on another farm for a short spell a few years later to help a friend finish his lease, and for this short period, I farmed 450 acres. This was the nearest I ever got to my ambition of farming one thousand acres.

The Burrows men:
Back (l. to r.) Sam, Will, Jim, Alf. Front (l. to r.) Lucky Jnr., Lucky Snr., Jack.

Often problems occurred and difficulties presented themselves as in any other business: otherwise, the farm progressed as would be expected.

Solomon retired a few years back as he found the work too much when the herd increased. His replacement also left and now, a cowman aged twenty was in charge of the herd. Our staff now consisted of eight men: the head horseman was forty-two and the ages of the remaining seven ranged from eighteen to twenty-seven, to make an average age of twenty-two years. I was the 'old man' at thirty-one.

It used to thrill me to watch these young men putting their muscles into the work. They used to whip $2\frac{1}{4}$ hundredweight of wheat on their backs and run across the barn floor with it as if it was a little child of three, laughing and talking all the time - and they would do it all day long if needs be.

It often passed through my mind at that time, what a team they would make at tug-of-war. I longed to challenge any one farm to put up eight men to beat them, but felt it would be presumptuous on my part; although had they won, the glory would have been theirs.

They all seemed so content and I am sure they <u>were</u> happy. There was never any suggestion of coming out on strike for such reasons as having no hand-basin to wash in, or that it was ¾ mile to the nearest toilet when working in the further fields. In any case, they would have been unable to leave the horses. Even if they had the luxury of using our toilet, they would have found they were no better off than bopping in the bottom of a field ditch.

The toilet for the convenience of the inmates of Dagworth Hall was no more than a portion partitioned off from a chicken house. The end of the building which formed our lavatory had sagged so much that the lintel of the door was six inches higher at one end, and the highest part of the doorway (and I am sure my memory serves me well) was under five feet. Light was supplied by a space two or three inches below the door and four or five inches above. The whole building was ended up to a garden wall and this formed one side of the toilet. Some person in the past, for extra light, had pushed out a brick for the purpose, no doubt, of sitting and reading 'The Stowmarket Mercury' as this would have been the only opportunity of so doing.

I'll wager my last bob if there had been a keen south-east wind, the hardiest individual would not sit there longer than necessary. The back was weather-boarded and these had warped so much that you could get your fingers between them. We did store firewood faggots at the back to break the wind. It may have broken it, but it still came through in places. To crown the lot, the seat was rickety: well, it had to be removeable to empty the pail.

I have somewhat drifted away from our noble gang who only faintly grumbled when we pulled or topped sugar-beet covered in frost, and sometimes snow. But actually, at this time, if a man left his job there would be two unemployed only too eager to take it.

They were funny old times - so much near-poverty about that if we had a job that just allowed us to live or a business that just broke even, we felt so grateful; and gratitude is the father of contentment.

For all that, as late as the beginning of 1940, the minimum wage of the farm-worker was thirty-six shillings for a fifty hour week.

217

We always kept a bull to father the calves. They nearly all become aggressive at some time or other, especially a shorthorn bull which we had for over three years. The young cowman could manage him, but when this bull was to be moved around, Bert, his helper seemed to mysteriously be up in the loft, or shut in a shed somewhere else.

I could not claim to be much braver, so used to take the second line of defence behind Reg and hoped I would not be needed. One day, I had to face the bull alone; he was grazing with the cows on the further low meadows. I went to fetch them home for milking and the bull always moved along with the herd. I suppose he sensed I was not the cowman and when I reached a position where there was no fence within seventy yards, he turned and attacked me. Fortunately, I had taken a pitch-fork for self defence. Prodding him about the face and eyes, his head seemed as large as a bus and just about as penetrative. I felt like a dwarf. My legs went weak with fear. Just as I thought I had lost the battle, the bull thought I had won. He turned away and followed the cows home down the lane. I followed on, but on the other side of the fence.

Dagworth Hall farm was a community within itself with Eve and I as king and queen. Our staff represented a parliament and the animals and fowls were our subjects. With thirty cows and their sixty children and grandchildren, the nine working horses and five or six of their children in the form of colts running about the meadows and four or five hundred hens we never had a dull moment.

Each day produced its quota of births, deaths, illnesses and accidents amongst the little nation of animals. We had to arrange educational classes for them. The heifers, after their first calf, had to be taught where their place was in the cowshed and that they must stand still when being milked. The back leg nearest to the milker had to stand back so that he could get at the udder to draw the milk.

The colts had to go through a real schooling before they could be called 'quiet and good workers in all gears.' This was what we tried to get them qualified for when selling them. To achieve this qualification, we had to train the colts to be led, driven with reins, stop or go when told, work in chains beside other horses or in the centre of a team of three, must not rear or kick other horses whilst at work, or at people; must work in shafts, and when the cart or waggon runs forward downhill, they must be relied upon to hold it with their back quarters.

The horseman training these colts should know what he is doing and aiming at. The basic idea to help the colt to learn is to attach it to a good steady mature horse and by constant repetition, each movement develops into a habit.

By breeding our mares with pedigree Suffolk stallions for three generations, their offspring became pedigrees registered and entered in 'The Suffolk Horse Stud Book' which added to their value.

Our little nation was running quite smoothly and the balance of payments satisfactory. We were exporting milk, butter, eggs and apples to Stowmarket; wheat and malting barley within the county; fifty truckloads of sugar-beet we exported to Ipswich and Bury St. Edmunds by rail each year, so we could easily pay for the imports of feeding stuffs, machinery and so on. Our tiny colony of White House Farm, Harleston fitted in with the mother farm quite well.

Although we felt of some importance managing this one unit of agriculture, we as individuals were completely lost among the 300,000 or so farms dotted about the highways and hills of England and Wales.

Everyone has his ups and downs in life, and the expected setbacks were not so crippling financially to us. For example, when I looked out of the bedroom window early one summer morning, I was a bit stunned to see sixty six-week old ducklings lying dead in the orchard. A fox had paid a night visit and had really enjoyed himself mauling, terrifying and killing these defenceless little creatures. If he had killed and satisfied his hunger, it would have been understandable. But to destroy for pure pleasure deserves punishment.

One quiet summer evening just after this I walked down by the stream in the marshy meadows, carrying my gun. I left the stream and crossed the meadow where I had done battle with the bull. I strolled beside a dyke that formed the boundary of a once well-cultivated osier bed. It had been left to grow wild for many years, although I can remember osier cutters going among the weeds and rubbish and collecting many bundles of good osiers.

As I walked beside this jungle in the mystery of the setting sun, I felt as though I was the only human being on a long-forsaken island, like the last survivor of a dying race.

The evening was absolutely still and I was miles away in thought, but returned suddenly when I became aware that the water-reeds were rustling beside me. Then, a beautiful reddish-brown animal broke clear. It was seconds before I realised it was a fox, the first I had actually seen so close. It seemed I was dancing about on the spot trying to get the gun in a firing position. As might be expected, I fired and completely missed.

The fox, baffled and scared, dived back into the reeds; then rather than face the dyke full of water, it broke into the open again. With the remaining live cartridge in my gun, he met a very sudden death. I was literally trembling with excitement, having shot my first fox. It was indeed a lovely creature, but murderers, marauders and thieves can be handsome, and ducklings are pretty too. Even if I had not got the guilty party, I felt I had revenge for the lost ducks.

I hadn't walked through those meadows for the express purpose of searching for a fox. If a reason had to be given, I would reply that there were several reasons. One of them was that I liked the feel of a gun in the crook of my arm, and I had to walk somewhere. Down by the stream was ideal; it was quiet but not too quiet; there was the ripple of the water and always a few snipe sky-diving amongst the usual birds.

As I walked by the willows that grew along the stream, I could think. This was a second good reason for taking this stroll. The branches of the willows spread out: the cattle had kept the underside

trimmed so I walked beneath a natural canopy. It was an atmosphere in which thoughts grew; they would develop in you in the same way as they might if you sat alone in a room, lit only by a wood fire.

You feel selfish not to share these moments with someone, yet in both cases, the instant another person appears, however nice they are, the charm of the situation is destroyed.

Dagworth meadows - just as lovely today

The third reason for this walk was to give my dog his greatest pleasure. So, the three reasons amounted to one enjoyment. Being brought up by my father never to waste time, I found myself always trying to discipline my actions and felt I must be able to account for all my time.

In this case, before setting off, I would say to my wife, "I think I'll take my gun and dog and go down the meadows. I might get a rabbit." This seemed to settle my mind and I thought, hers too; that I was going to do a legitimate and necessary job. It would have sounded silly to say, "I'm going under the willows to think."

These willows, or at least other willows, have been growing by this stream ever since there has been a stream. They have sheltered or shaded lovers, poachers, travellers and workmen for hundreds of years. The willows grow where the stream begins as a trickle of a tributary at Wetherden. The willows, the stream, the low soggy meadows, all go together the four miles to Stowmarket, and continue together as the river Gipping to Ipswich. Then, they go beyond as the Orwell; the willows and grass stay and wave goodbye as the river flows on into the North Sea.

I look back to the nineteen years during which I had the perfect right to use those meadows - I could graze my cattle on them, shoot game and vermin and wander in them whenever I wished. Although I was only a tenant, I now look upon the privilege of those advantages as a heritage: and I feel all who have used and will yet use that land are in direct line from King John who too used Dagworth Hall, if only for one night.

When I hunted my fox and wild rabbits in my day, I was only continuing in the footsteps of the elite of the Middle Ages as is proved by the following...

"Brave knights and noble ladies in all the chivalrous pride of those romantic ages, have often paced with hawk and hounds around the woods and fields of Dagworth and Haughley, and have returned in the evening from the long willow-covered meadows around Stowmarket which abounded in cranes and herons, to these hospitable halls.; but the scene has changed, the living actors lie beneath the

pavements of our churches, the wild birds have gone, nursery or hop-grounds have broken up their lonely retreats, and Dagworth Hall has passed away like a wreath of smoke from the labourer's cottage that now reposes in forgetful care over its foundations."

Rev. A.G.H. Hollingsworth

Many great names were associated with Dagworth over the centuries. The name of one Suffolk knight originated from here in the fourteenth century - Sir John de Dagworth.

In the fifteenth century, the Earl of Shrewsbury, John Talbot, had strong connections with Dagworth. He married one of the heiresses of Dagworth Hall and while her husband was at war in France, she resided there. Unfortunately, the Earl died in battle, shot through the thigh with a harquebus, and his charger was slain beneath him.

His daughter Eleanor was later contracted to King Edward IV by the Lady of Dagworth, but the beauty of Lady Gray led the King to break his engagement. The rejected lady then married John Butler Caron of Sudeley and all Dagworth felt the disappointment and wayward fancies of this vain world.

Chapter 22

We can picture Mrs Dagworth Hall beaming and preening herself before those knights, earls, king and the associates of royalty with their ladies of equal ranks. She was covered by the reflected glory of their personalities; her hall and lands were adequate in everything to entertain the highest in the country.

I have been unable to find any specific reason as to why these blue bloods forsook Dagworth. It may have been because the great mansion began to crumble away, but again these men of noble names may have left for other reasons, to leave the hall in the hands of time to dispense with it.

It is my opinion that the era of those lords and ladies finished not later than the beginning of the sixteenth century. The Suffolk guide-books write of the present Dagworth Hall as having a famous Tudor chimney. This makes the old farmhouse about four hundred years old, which I am sure it is, or at least part of it. Therefore, it appears for the last four hundred years, each succeeding occupier of Dagworth Hall was of less importance than his predecessor.

I assume, as is quite probable, that since the time of Alfred the Great, this place gradually became more important until it reached its peak. Then gradually it deteriorated until it hit bottom with the presence of 'Alfred Burrows the Small' in 1929. It is small wonder that this old woman Dagworth rattled her bones in disgust when she saw me. The thought in no way makes me feel like hiding my head in the sand. My life is just as important to myself as Alfred the Great's was to himself, and I recall a text: "Blessed are the meek for they shall inherit the earth." So I have hope.

Leaving the past centuries and coming forward, we will stop at 1936. That was the year Mother-in-law died. Dagworth had been her home for seven years. She died while staying with her sister at Beccles. Eve never really lost the feeling of letting her mother down. She thought she should have been with her mother at the finish and always felt guilty about it. These morbid thoughts were there when she awoke in the mornings. She used to get long spells of depression when she could not rise above the black feelings.

Eve never let her clouds blot other people's sunshine. She used to sing and laugh all day and everyday, and everyone thought she was gay. Any evening spent at home she would fill in by playing the piano and singing until bedtime. She had to have a crowded life to smother her dark feelings.

The horsman's wife helped in the house two or three times a week. This enabled Eve to carry on with the milk-round, help on the farm and do the things she loved. Four walls would have stifled her. As regular as spring brought spring-cleaning, spring cleaning gave my wife an opportunity to give vent to her feelings: expressing in no uncertain terms her views on the inconvenience of Dagworth Hall. The first few years it frightened me. It was such an outburst. I was alarmed by the crescendo. In the midst of one of these go's, she shouted at me, "Come on, shake that carpet!" But Alfie never took orders! That would be like losing your grip on a mountain - once you start there is no stopping. So I ups and says quite pleasantly, "Is that an order or a request?" She was just as quick with her answer: "It's a request my darling." Never was one carpet shaken so happily by two people. The bigness of her mind gave me no superiority, and neither of us lost our dignity. It was in this spirit we continued throughout our marriage.

I used to pretend to be alarmed at these annual reliefs of pent-up feelings and genuinely sympathised. When it was over, we would laugh together about it. It came out as regular as a calendar, but the setting would vary, as one never knew where the explosion would occur. One year it would be halfway up the back stairs, the next underneath the milk-tray shelves in the dairy. Or it might burst forth when she was stuck, trying to move the great old cast-iron linen mangle.

One occasion I well remember. Every year, Eve dressed and armed herself the same for this onslaught - dust hat, spectacles to see the spiders, wrap-round pinafore, and the usual necessary tools. The brick-oven and ceiling was a space of about two feet. This is where Eve had got to when I came in for dinner. The moment my head entered the door, her face appeared from the top of the oven. The explosion was timed to ignite the minute my foot touched the kitchen floor.

She always started by announcing each year, otherwise a record would have answered her purpose. This particular year I looked up and couldn't see her at first, having come in from the sunlight. Then I saw the rays of light reflecting in her glasses. She turned her head and her eyes flashed even brighter. Her face was scarlet from exertion in that cramped position. Then out came her yearly speech like machine-gun fire. "1940! I ask you. The bloomin' old place ought to have been burnt down years ago. It's a blot on the countryside. I shall be old before my time. Stuck up here with my rotting old glasses, looking like a darned billy owl. My hands are like a damned nutmeg grater, and I'm expected to play at chapel next Sunday. What woman would do it? I ask you. I'm worse off than any of our men's wives. I suppose I'd better leave this perch and come down and get you some dinner." "Can I help you up there?" I offered meekly. "No," she shouted, "I wish I'd never been born, so if I fall and break my neck it won't matter much."

These spasms were only momentary and never upset our mutual understanding and happiness because they were in no way personal. This old kitchen was enough to make any woman go off the deep end. It was not peculiar to Dagworth Hall alone. Ninety per-cent of the farmhouses were the same. This one for example, had the brick-oven with an ashes cavity underneath - a dutch oven built in the wall with cinder place below - a kind of skeleton fireplace in ordinary brickwork where one could have four saucepans and a kettle all going at once, and also have plenty of room to store the next day's kindling to dry. There were three coppers; one was used on washing day, a second used as storage for grain for young chicks, the other kept our potatoes. It would hold four to five hundred-weight.

Then of course there was the cast-iron clothes wringer, about 1890 model. With all this ancient, inconvenient equipment we had a three-burner Valor Perfection Oil Cooker. This was the modern addition where nearly all the baking, cooking and jam-making was done. The floor was made of bricks; uneven, sunk by time, and worn by many generations of hob-nailed boots. It was cleaned with pails and pails of water, and swept away with a heavy broom through a hole in the wall left for the purpose. When the water had drained away, a brick was placed over the outlet hole partly to keep out the wind, and partly to keep out roaming rats. Often these night raiders took advantage of our forgetfulness and once in the house, they were able to run freely, as all the thresholds were worn so much they were able to get under the doors and into the rooms. One surprised rat astounded me once by running over my foot when I went into the kitchen in my socks.

The dairy had the same type of wash-down floor and occasionally a rat would find its way in there. One of these filthy visitors discovered the bowls of milk on the shelf. Eve noticed he had splashed some milk about. I, being resourceful said, "I'll get him tomorrow morning."

We came down fairly early in the morning. I had left my twelve-bore gun and cartridge ready the night before. "Now," I whispered. "Don't make a sound." I stealthily crept towards the dairy door in my socks, and slowly and quietly opened it. He was there drinking the milk and he tried to escape up the wall in the corner. I brought the gun up and fired. In such a confined space the report sounded like a cannon. "Have you got it?" Eve shouted excitedly. She rushed in to look and saw the rat with his guts blown out. Unusually for her, she gave way to feminine weakness and sent up a piercing scream.

It was the early hours of the morning - a gun shot and a woman's scream! I tore out to the cowman before he could turn white. "I haven't shot the Missus, just a rat in the dairy," I assured him and added, "but I'm afraid I've blown a hole clean through the dairy wall." In our way of life, these things were normal events. Farming, as with many other country crafts and occupations, is a way of life. That is why perhaps these simple things dwell so vividly in my memory. The real essence of rural life cannot be bought entirely within the usual rules of employment.

I quite agree and wholeheartedly, that all countrymen are deserving of the same standard of living as the citymen, but why should a man in employment be forced to adhere to a set pattern such as a forty-hour week, and a set number of hours in each day? This is of course unavoidable in most factory and town jobs.

But how refreshing it is to meet the country character, or better still to be one, and to know it is still possible, (at least I hope it is) for one man to say to another, "For £1000 a year I will take full charge of your flock and attend to the lambing, shearing and so on. I will not be watched about, or timid; I want to be judged entirely by results. Perhaps some weeks I shall be working one hundred hours, and some about twenty hours, but I shall be happy just to be able to work on my own initiative."

I sincerely hope that these little pockets of individual freedom will never completely disappear to make every man a tiny unit within one huge organisation, although basically I suppose, we are just that.

It was 1937: Eve and I had now been farming Dagworth for eight years. Our roots had struck in the Dagworth soil soundly enough to bear some fruit. We were confident of the validity of our business and future outlook, saved without a shadow of doubt by our milk-round. It was a sound and fertile farm in spite of my criticisms, and as the prices of corn and sugar-beet advanced slightly, we became very well established.

This was not the case with a great number of farmers; for them it was still touch and go. It only needed a little misfortune to put them in the bankruptcy court. Many were sold out and others sold out under a deed of assignment.

It was this year that the original 'Lucky Burrows Empire' began to disintegrate. Allowing for the fact that half the financial aid came from the Bannister family in hiring Dagworth Hall, we will for this purpose put one hundred acres to the credit of the fruits of my Father's initiative and early ambitions.

Little did my Father think when he was left in the hills of Afghanistan in 1879, with only a fifty- fifty chance of recovering from a fever, that he would live to father eleven children and bring up ten, and that in spite of the fact he left school at the age of nine, and was the son of a nine-shillings-a-week farmworker, he would return to

Suffolk and with his six sons, build up a group of family farms to total 1130 acres, about 400 acres of which were owned.

Shooting party: (l. to r.) Jack, Lucky Jnr., Alfred, Lucky Snr., Jim, Will

As a family, we had farmed our individual farms to total 1130 acres since 1929. The main reason the 'empire' began to crumble was the fact that not one of us had produced a son. Three of my brothers had five daughters between them; Jack remained a bachelor and Jim and myself were childless.

Eve, my wife, liked children but had neither maternal instinct nor desire for babies. She would spend hours attending baby animals and chicks with real maternal tenderness, and loved to help these young lives into the world, but she could not bear the thought of being prevented from doing this by her own offspring.

I was sad about this, especially as there was no other reason why we should not procreate. I took it for granted that children followed marriage and dreamed of the day when I would be followed about by one or two toddlers and plan their lives. Eve was adamant in her opinion on this matter. I did not pursue mine as I felt children should have a welcome awaiting them from both parents. Although my disappointment was very real, we did not argue about it; life is too short.

My wife saw vividly all the disadvantages of bringing up a family. "What good are they, I ask you?" she would say. "You give them twenty of the best years of your life, and when they could comfort you, they despise you. Just when you need someone to ease your burden they want you to start them off in business."

I had to agree with her, but would still have been proud to accept them and felt this sacrifice would have been a pleasure. Over thirty years later when seeing the ingratitude of some children towards their parents, the worries they have brought and their lack of consideration, I have reverently said, "Thank God I haven't any."

The first to give up his farm was brother Jack. He struggled on for twelve years and spent long hours, sleepless nights and all the money that came in to bring a derelict farm back to full production in hopes of better times. The better times came, but three years too late. Jack decided it would be more honourable to sell out while he could pay all his debts. This he did, and returned to Canada.

Bygone implements stand in a field that was once part of Church farm, Hepworth, where brother Jack farmed

About a year later, Jim, who like every other farmer had worked hard for years and was successful in business had, in spite of the bad times, made money. The lease on his farm expired and rather than renew it, he bought a smaller place and moved out. Our acreage then dropped from 1130 to 850. In 1937 Father was made helpless by a stroke; his speech was affected and he had to move around in an invalid chair.

My sisters returned home after keeping house for Jack so were able to nurse Father.

In January 1939, Jim's wife died as a result of an accident in the house. My youngest sister Katie went to live with him as house-keeper.

October 1939, my oldest brother, Lucky, who had farmed for over thirty years, retired and has now at the time of writing, almost completed thirty years in retirement. When Lucky planned to come out of farming, the Second World War had not begun. Had he stayed in business until after the war, he could easily have doubled his wealth.

Father was still being transported about in his bath-chair. He could shuffle along a few steps with the aid of two sticks. Travelling across the kitchen in this manner one day he slipped and fell, hitting his head on the copper. A few days later, on December 13th 1939 he died; a wonderful career ended. At the age of nearly eighty-one he left his tribe without a leader. We all had such respect for him that it almost bordered on fear until his death.

He was buried in the churchyard that surrounds the tiny thatched church of Harleston. His wife, five of his sons, (Jack was in Canada) and three daughters followed him there. His last trip was a weird little journey. After leaving his home, White House Farm, there was no other house on the half-mile route to the church.

The church itself stood in a meadow away from the road with no hard track leading to it. It is still situated in the centre of the four hundred acre farm of Harleston Hall. It was a fitting resting place for one who loved the solitude of the countryside.

Chapter 23

Following the funeral we had the usual gathering of the family, relatives and friends at White House Farm. The atmosphere was heavy and depressing, and being six days before Christmas made it even worse. The three month old war was in the mind and on the tongue of everyone.

Cousin Lucky Lockwood M.C. was with us. He attended all our funerals and most of the weddings. He took our thoughts away from the graves in the churchyard to the shell holes in the battlefields of wars in which he had been present. This did not lift our hearts much: we had heard the same stories many times before. He had taken a very active part in the Boer War and the First World War.

At sixty, he was too old to destroy life so in this war he was trying to save life by lecturing on Air Raid Precautions. On these occasions it seems almost disrespectful to break the sadness, and yet what a relief when some brave person gives voice to a feeble joke. Most of the company indulged in a hoarse, unnatural laugh, while a few pretended to subdue a titter. It is like a dramatic scene at the cinema when one cough is the cue for one and all to join in. We departed to our respective homes and left behind the end of an era.

* * * * * * * * * *

I remember clearly the declaration of the First World War. I was ten. On that day our horses took fright and ran away with the binder. A dark cloud was in the sky.

In 1939, I vividly recall hearing Neville Chamberlain telling us we were at war with Germany for the second time in my life. It was a Sunday morning, September 3rd 1939. I had been helping on the milk-round as I always did on a Sunday morning, and as a matter of fact, I had not missed a Sunday for six years.

This was my last customer. The cottage stood down a lane off the main A45 road. I heard the speech over the radio as I sat on a chair in this, the Whiteheads' cottage. It was the four hundred year old home of Mr. Whitehead , an ex-navy man, Mrs. Whitehead, their two daughters and four sons. One of the sons worked for me. He was a lovely boy and was in the Territorial Army: another son was in the submarines and another joined the navy later. The fourth son was too young for this war.

The Territorial lad was called up right away and was sent to Singapore. He never returned, dying of dysentery. The submarine boy went down with a submarine and never came up. The sailor also gave his life and only the memory of the three sons returned home to their parents. From this little white-washed, thatched-roof cottage called 'Hop Cottage' that nestled amongst the willows, that grew beside the meadows along the same stream that flowed through Dagworth, three brothers gave their lives to save us from fascism.

This was a great contribution from a remote and unknown spot of Great Britain. To take a complete diversion from this patriotic and heroic picture with the background of 'Hop Cottage' we will use the same background, but the scene is out of this world. It is illustrated by a man living in this same cottage over one hundred years previous to the Whiteheads.

Again I take a story from 'The History of Stowmarket' compiled by Rev. Hollingsworth in 1842.

I quote... *"Hop Ground Cottages, Bury Road, Stowmarket. Diary of S... living thirty years in these cottages. Twenty years hence in the meadows now a hop-ground near three ashen trees, on a very bright moonlight night, saw fairies, about a dozen, the biggest about three feet tall, small ones like dolls, their dresses sparkled like spangles, like girls at the shows at Stow fair.*

They were moving silently hand in hand in a ring, and not like solid bodies. I passed on saying, "Lord have mercy on me." I could see them plainly. I got over the stile and looked back, they were still there going round and round. I brought back three women as witnesses but the fairies had gone. I was forty yards from them and did not stop to stare at them. I was quite sober."

So I left the spot where it was alleged fairies had danced, the spot which I knew had given three sons to save our beloved country. To be more correct, when I left that cottage on Sunday morning, all those three boys were alive and full of vigour of youth. The supreme sacrifice came later.

Arriving home, war or peace, we had the usual routine of washing up the dairy utensils, Sunday afternoon rest, and usually accompanying Eve to evening service. In mid-summer there was time to take the dog through the willow-covered meadows and view the dairy herd.

I used these meadows purely commercially but still enjoyed the mystery of them. In the fifteenth century they had been used mainly for sport, when the earls and knights hunted with hawk and hound. Everything points to the fact that when Dagworth ceased to be a manorial estate, she was viewed from a commercial angle by wealthy men who saw profit in her geographical position. Her history may have been an added attraction.

Her soil and the conditions were so ideal for hop-growing that growers could compete with the best crops grown in Farnham or Kent. About one hundred acres were grown in the Dagworth area, which was surrounded by low hills. It is recorded that hops were introduced into this country in 1520, and it is thought that the Flemings brought them when they settled here as clothiers in that period.

Tradition has it, that the first hops ever planted in England were tried in the hamlet of Dagworth, and this could well be correct. I can vouch for the truth about the Dagworth hop grounds being there up to about the mid-nineteenth century, as my old stockman Solomon Cubitt often spoke about hearing his mother say she used to vault over the dykes with a hop pole when she was a girl.

The buildings where I stored the cattle chaff was once the hop store, and below where we mixed the cattle foods were kilns built for hop-drying. The hops had survived through the years by re-seeding themselves and were still growing and climbing up the hedgerows when I lived there. I was talking to an inhabitant of Dagworth in 1967, and he told me they were still growing on his land, having survived for over one hundred years.

Now England was at war again and hardly a spot, however remote, escaped direct contact before the war ended. At the time of the evacuation of Dunkirk we could hear the thud of guns all day. I for one was prepared for the possibility of being over-run by the Germans. I used to calculate that as we were between two main roads, it was possible the Germans would pass us.

I took Churchill's words literally about fighting in the air, on the sea, on the land and on the beaches. In my impetuosity, on going to bed I took my twelve bore with me and with some cartridges I kept it on the landing. This I did for weeks until I was satisfied the forces could manage without my help. But if the enemy had come upstairs, I meant to go down fighting.

Who knows, if the Germans had reached Dagworth and peered down my two rusty barrels, it might have been the turning point of the war. If I was prepared for the battle on the landing, it would certainly have taken more than a German to get my wife out of bed.

Our first air-raid warning sounded. I leapt out of bed and trembling all over began to dress. I thought, this is it, they are now going to broadcast bombs all over our little island. I expected Eve to follow, but there was no movement.
"Aren't you coming down?" I shouted.
"What for?" she answered.
"There's an air-raid on."
"I can't help it."
"Are you getting up?"
"No!" she bellowed.
"You might at least get dressed."
"What for?" she said, "My knickers won't keep a bullet out."

We were both safe anyway; the bombs fell ten miles away. Not all the German bombs fell so far from us. Three dropped on one of our fields when one man was trimming a ditch not fifty yards away. He said, "I just ducked down and the bits went over my head." These bombs were intended for Haughley railway junction and not for Peter the hedger! The main railway line from London to Norwich and Cromer ran through Dagworth Hall farm, splitting it fairly evenly

236

into two. There was a branch for Cambridge and Doncaster at Haughley station which was also the terminus for the Mid-Suffolk Light Railway, and it was worth a bomb or two to the Germans if they could score a hit. Sometimes they did a bit of machine-gun firing along the line, so we had to be prepared to dive for shelter.

Haughley station

Haughley station stood on the boundary of our farm, which was very convenient when loading sugar-beet. Using the horses and tumbrils we could load straight off the fields onto the trucks. It spared double handling. The horses became so used to the trains they hardly flicked an ear when the expresses roared through a few yards from their noses.

During the war, an American piloting a Mustang must have been doing some stunt-flying or the machine may have got out of control. Through our undulating farm, the railway line was in some places running on a bank and at others through a cutting. Just as an engine was emerging from a cutting, the plane dived under the telephone wires, cut the chimney off the engine, scraped through a hedge and exploded on one of the hill fields. One of the pilot's feet was caught in a crutch of the hedge, wrenching off his foot. I was there when the ambulance came for the body. It had to be taken on a stretcher to the road. I well remember seeing the Red Cross men stop to pick the poor young fellow's foot from the hedge. They placed it on the body and as they walked, it fell off. One of the men picked it up again and put it back.

No one was shocked. It was war and they were just doing their job. The government had a better arrangement for the control of man-power during this war. During the 1914-1918 war, men were taken from the farms indiscriminately. It was then that I was taken from school at the age of twelve to do six months on the farm, and again when I was thirteen, finally leaving at fourteen.

During the Second World War, the government had essential jobs for the war effort, listed as reserved occupations. Under this heading came farm-workers as food producers, but these men had to join the Home Guard, A.R.P., Fire Service, Observer Corps attached to the R.A.F. or Special Constabulary. I believe all the Dagworth staff were in the Home Guard. I was already a Special Constable and carried on for my long-service medal.

A second plane crashed on Tot Hill farm, a few yards from our boundary. It had a British crew of five I believe. I, with my confederates had to guard it day and night to keep spectators away until it was taken away; it lay as it had crashed, a twisted pile of metal. Among this maze were the bodies of the crew. Their clothes were burnt off and they looked so white and tiny. Please do not misjudge my comparison, but to me they looked like little bacon pigs just slaughtered.

I could not associate them with the gay, young R.A.F. boys we used to see coming and going on leave, or dancing with pretty female partners. But they were the carefree boys of such a short time before with personalities, intelligence and hopes; they were living sons, husbands or lovers: then in an instant, just charred flesh.

Living in the heart of the relatively flat land of East Anglia, and being a good position for taking off for Germany resulted in our being surrounded by aerodromes. I have counted as many as eighty American planes, all visible at the same time, getting into position for a bombing raid on Germany.

We would see them limping home with one or two engines out of action. These airfields of course attracted the German hedge-hopping light bombers. Some of them used to come streaking over Dagworth and we felt we could almost poke them down with a linen prop.

This cheeky attitude of the enemy really annoyed my tractor driver. He was in the Home Guard, and at one time this organisation was issued with shot guns as there was a shortage of rifles. The cartridges were loaded with a lead ball instead of shot. Leslie, the tractor driver, had a few of these cartridges in his pocket. He looked at those planes in fury. "We can't have those b.......s coming over here like that," he said. "Come on governor, lend us your gun."

Rightly or wrongly I let him have my twelve-bore. We crouched behind a stone wall, his eyes just above the wall scanning the tree tops. He looked exactly like a country squire waiting for driven partridges while I was in attendance as his game-keeper. We waited impatiently, but evidently the covey had passed over before we were in position.

We adapted ourselves to these war conditions as they affected us. As no petrol was allowed for pleasure we had to fit pleasure in with business. Such as taking seed beans to a friend, and also packing my gun to have a day's shoot. That of course meant an evening meal (a wartime one), and a late return home.

If you were stopped on the way home and questioned by the police as to why you were out, and you realised the beans were still in the car, the only way out would be to say that you had been to fetch some! On one such occasion, arriving home late. I could hardly get in the farmyard. It was packed with bren-gun carriers, staff cars and provision lorries. The army was on the move, and using Dagworth Hall farmhouse and buildings for bed and breakfast as had King John in 1216.

I found a niche for the car and threaded my way between the army vehicles to the back door. It was nearly midnight and everything was still and quiet. The army slumbered like sleeping Philistines. I groped my way into the back door; lights were not allowed. I stumbled over something and I switched on my torch to see. It was a man - there were several of them sleeping about the floor on blankets. I expect they were sergeants, but as they had their battle dress off I was unable to tell. Their snores were no more superior than those of a private.

I stepped over them to get to the dining room. This I gathered later was the officers' quarters and they were strewn about the floor. As I wended my way through my own home, I kept apologising for being there. The interlopers were all too sleepy to kick me out or invite me in.

Eventually I reached my bedroom and felt for my sleeping space: my partner was occupying her share. Yes, mine was still vacant. The General or Colonel-in-Chief had not taken over.

The whole outfit moved off the following afternoon, taking in their bellies practically all that day's production of eggs. We did not have many left to pick up and could judge by the little heaps of ashes outside that they had had a boil-up. Whatever happened, the farm routine had to go on. Not even the British Army or the German Air Force could stop that. The cows had to be fetched and driven past the army lorries to be milked. The milk then had to be loaded on the van to supply our 400 registered customers. We had finished using ponies for the milk-round and now had a motor-van. A boy on a bike followed to serve the side-street customers.

I knew one bomb in the wrong place could stop all our operations, but it is definitely true to state that this Second World War took second place to our farming activities, which is pretty obvious as no army can operate without farm produce. At this particular time, the boy using the trade bike on the milk-round was George Tyte. Leaving the farm with three or four gallons of milk, he served the customers en-route. The van would meet him at arranged points for refills. On this hazy morning, he proceeded up Daggar Lane, the same lane that King John came down about 735 years before. As previously mentioned, there were high banks on either side.

Why so many country lanes are like this may be as has been suggested, they were at one time river beds. So many roads all over the country are six feet or more lower than the fields on either side. I cannot fathom it out, for to make them so would have necessitated moving millions of tons of soil and they could not all have been rivers. However, returning to George Tyte on his bike riding up Daggar Lane; (Daggar, of course, is the Suffolk pronunciation of Dagworth) Georgie saw the figure of a soldier standing up there on the bank beside a tree. Not liking to stare, Georgie held his gaze away until he was immediately below him, then he looked straight into the face of a suicide. The young soldier had attached his rifle pull-through to a branch of the tree, made a noose for his neck, and apparently jumped from the bank.

The milk lad fetched the tractor driver working close by, who cut him down, but he was dead of course. Using our car they took the body to the village public house for an inquest. I gathered in a fit of depression, this soldier had wandered away from an army camp and feared to return.

This car that transported the soldier's body, was a 1937 fourteen h.p. Vauxhall and I think the most useful unit in running the farms. With a trailer I used to move ploughs, harrows, forty-staved ladders, calves, corn, milk, and I feel I must describe its finest trip.

One summer I grew eight acres of peas. When ready, we picked them on a Sunday, being wartime. I was not I hope, too badly condemned. This was to catch the Monday market in Covent Garden. We dropped word in Stowmarket and the villages that we needed pickers, and two hundred turned up.

At the end of the day I offered to take the most weary mothers with children back to Stowmarket. I sat in the driver's seat while they loaded up; they piled in. The springs went down and we seemed to be one solid mass of humanity. I completed the two and a half miles to the town. Like a good chauffeur, I opened the door for my passengers and six women with seven children emerged. With myself, fourteen people were inside this car and to this day I cannot understand how it was possible.

Life was hectic, exciting and tiring, farming under these war time conditions. As a special constable, I patrolled three evenings a week up till midnight warning people if they were showing lights. I had to cooperate with the A.R.P. during air-raids, checking identity cards and so on.

These duties had their humorous moments, as when on duty one evening I saw a friend's wife coming along carrying a heavy basket. Although I was in police uniform, I offered to carry her basket. We strolled along, I wheeling my bike with one hand and carrying the basket in the other. Not very policeman-like I admit.

The irony of it was I knew I was carrying black market goods. At least I was not in much doubt that this lady had been to an isolated farm to collect butter and eggs in order to supplement her rations. Nearing the village I suggested that we part as it would be unwise to be seen walking together, so handing back the basket and without putting on my lights, I hopped on my bike.

About thirty yards on, a uniformed shadow stepped into the road. "I say there, where's your light?" This was an A.R.P. man having the audacity to say this to me, a policeman. I was just about to make some excuse or explanation when a colleague strolled up in uniform, and in an officious manner he said to my captor, "It's quite alright Arthur, it's a privilege we policemen have, to ride without lights."

So having been saved from a lighting offence, I thought it better not to mention that I might have been inadvertently aiding the black market. I was never cut out for a policeman, but did not want to disgrace the uniform.

We were extremely fortunate to be living in the country as compared with the people of the big cities. There was always the risk of getting the odd bomb but we had the consolation of knowing we were not a specific target. Also, we were doubly fortunate to be farmers, as food rationing did not affect us too much. We always had ample milk, butter and fruit and by foregoing our meat rations we were allowed to have a pig for the house.

The country was at war, so as would be expected, there was little time or opportunity for recreation or relaxation. With the special constable duties, air-raid alarms, secretarial demands in running the milkround, 400 registered people on the round, and two farms consisting of three hundred acres, I was rarely in bed before midnight. It was manual work during the day and I always helped with the milkround on Sunday mornings, as it gave the boys a chance of having a little more time off before the afternoon milking. In actual fact, arriving at the month of May 1942, I realised I had been going on the Sunday morning round for nine years and had not missed one Sunday.

Previous to the war, as with all young farmers who started in the bad times, I was driven along by the shortage of money, and when the war came along we were driven by the demands of the war. Writing in this vein it would appear I considered myself indispensible. If it was so, I was well and truly taught that the activities of war and industry did not stop when I was unable to work for a spell of twelve weeks and a further eighteen months of reduced activity.

Having been blessed with good health all my life, the start of this enforced rest created a milestone in my life. I needed no diary to remind me of this date: May 14th 1942, as it still stands out vividly in my memory in 1968. As before described, the early years of my life showed me as a rather 'pingly' individual, but after starting school at the age of seven, and at ten finding myself the only little Burrows there with no big sisters to protect me, I began to compete with the boys and become more self-reliant.

Mother's protective wing was not available, and my off feelings were of no interest to the children of my age so my mind and body became healthier.

I never, ever lost completely my sensitivity and uncertainty, that guilty apprehension of being in somebody's way, the feeling I should step back and let some more worthy person go before. And yet, paradoxically, I would lay awake for hours at night bemoaning the fact that some thoughtless or self-important person had elbowed his way into my rightful position. Again, I would spend equally as many wakeful nights wondering if I had been unintentionally unkind to some person, or said the wrong thing.

How I have envied all my life those people who can settle their views with confidence and can occupy any position without a feeling of guilt or self-consciousness.

With a temperament of this nature, I suppose it is understandable that being tensed up for about fourteen years with very little diversion and not enough rest, nature's demands became more powerful than the demands of mind or circumstances.

So on this May day I sneezed all the time and for two weeks it felt like flu. Each time I attempted to use my strength I was beaten back by physical weakness and had to rest. I thanked God my mental powers remained as usual.

Three, four, five weeks passed and my doctor treated me for a nervous breakdown, which I suppose it was, and for which there is very little that can be done by medicine. I am not writing these details for the purpose of indulging in self-pity, but in the hope that should just one person read them, who has had a similar experience, would be cheered by the mutual understanding of another.

My weeks passed by. The effort of going into the garden to gather strawberries would lay me low for hours, feeling my lungs or heart would stop. My wife and 'the boys' kept the milk-round going; the cowman and stockman knew their jobs. I used to pass instructions for arable cultivations to the landmen via Eve, or meet them at the door.

Under these conditions ten weeks passed by. I was depressed especially as I was not actually ill. At the same time there was no indication of returning strength. It had now been going on for twelve weeks.

"What do you advise?" I said to my doctor. "I can't go on like this."

"Well," he considered, "The only advice I can give you is for you to have a complete change; an absolutely different environment. Go away for a month. Don't even take your wife."

It was wartime: where could one go? Tours were out of the question; seasides out of consideration, with every beach barricaded by barbed wire entanglements and anti-landing devices. Hotels and guest houses had been commandeered for troops. What hopes! One could only travel within the country, and then not without identity card, ration card and gas mask. The trains were packed with army, navy and air-force men of many nationalities. To sit or stand with them at the age of thirty-eight, and not to be wearing a uniform or workman's suit, made a person feel conspicuous. Being too weak to stand for long, I could not entertain the idea of travelling far alone.

Perhaps a week or two near Cambridge with relations might help. At least I would be away from the business. We formed some illegitimate excuse to use the petrol so that Eve could drive me there, and I planned to stay for two weeks.

Whilst there, I unexpectedly met a cousin, a sister of cousin Lucky Lockwood, who very kindly said I could go with her to her home in Edinburgh. I could stay a month if I wished. I gratefully and readily accepted her generous offer, this being the means of a real change from Suffolk, with the relief of having the comfort of an understanding companion. In the train, cousin Lizzie Cousins explained to our travelling companions that I could not offer my seat owing to my weakness.

We arrived very late at night at Waverley station in Edinburgh. Lizzie said that her husband Arthur would be there to meet her. Arthur was a veteran of World War 1, but was still doing good work with the Air Ministry and was comparatively young. He had no idea he would be meeting me, and we had not seen each other for fifteen years.

Lizzie marshalled me over the foot-bridge and Arthur ascended in the opposite direction to meet his wife. We saw him coming. Lizzie said, "Here's Arthur." Arthur looked astonished to see his wife with a male companion. If ever I tried to make a good impression something was sure to go wrong. In this case I fixed my face up with a winning smile ready for Arthur, and believe me five yards before we met, I stumbled over a knot in the timber bridge and being too weak to correct my balance, sprawled flat out at the feet of cousin Arthur Cousins.

Cousin Arthur Cousins' wit was always equal to the occasion and he said to his beloved, "What on earth have you got there?" Looking down at the fallen idol, she replied, "This is Alfie."
"Who is Alfie, and where did you find it?" he enquired.
"You remember Alfie, Uncle Lucky's youngest son from Suffolk."
"Whatever is he doing lying about up here?"
"Come on," says Lizzie briskly. "Let's get in the taxi, I'll explain it all by the time we get home."

By the time we reached Portobello near Leith, he knew it all. Lizzie put me to bed where I remained the whole of the following day to recover from the first part of my recovery. The next day I walked around the cul-de-sac outside their house, feeling proud of my accomplishment. Day three, it was halfway down the street and back. Day four, to the bottom of the street and back.

At night my heart seemed to be beating in my waist, and hovering all around it were butterflies just under the skin. I dared not go to sleep in case everything stopped and I never woke again. I felt so far away from Dagworth where all I possessed and valued lay. Dagworth Hall farm would now be in the bustle and throes of harvest, and I was not there.

My boyhood friend, Gerald Williams had promised to visit my staff and offer his advice and judgement. I thought of Eve living and sleeping in that great old ghostly house alone, which she did for six weeks. The war was raging, but fortunately she, like Admiral Lord Nelson, knew not the meaning of fear.

She coped with the demands of each day and kept the whole outfit running. I felt cut off from my wife and all I had worked for. My dog, Pip, the retriever, would forget me and the 400 miles between us might just as well have been 400,000.

After a few more days, I was able to accept whatever came along. I used to go to bed and sleep and thought, 'if I never wake up again what does it matter?' In this attitude I became reconciled, in reconciliation I became calm, in calmness I rested and through rest I began to gain strength. Each day I increased my walks, until a mile was possible, where I had not done three hundred yards in one stretch for four months.

Daily, I took a tram to Princes Street, passing Calton Hill, giving one the feeling of being in Athens. Then I passed Holyroodhouse and St. Andrew's Hall; on my left was Arthur's Seat (not cousin Arthur), 800 feet high, and from which you could see on a clear day mountains seventy miles away. I enjoyed these trips, and began to feel I was at home in Edinburgh. I became attached to Princes Street with her lovely shops on one side and beautiful gardens on the other, even in wartime.

Edinburgh by Leonard Squirrell

I would sit in these gardens for hours, gazing at the castle and living in the past, lost in history. The gardens would bring my mind back to the beauty and miracle of nature. The trains roaring between the gardens and the castle reminded me that there was a link between me and Dagworth, of which I could avail myself at any time. The shops were there to provide my material needs. In what other city could one find such a combination of contrasts, blended so wonderfully that not a single item jarred on another.

I loved my little hamlet of Dagworth, but I fell in love with Edinburgh. It is quite possible to have more than one love and have newly discovered loves without being unfaithful to your first love.

Although Edinburgh and Dagworth were incomparable, they retained a similarity. Neither relied on a current generation for its character. They were above the mere fashions of the day, unlike Monte Carlo, Ascot or fashionable holiday resorts, where people go solely for the reason that people go there. No one is drawn to Edinburgh or Dagworth because, 'it's the thing to do my dear.' Their respective populations of over 500,000 and under 50 give their visitors the impression of being very genuine, and are there because of inner love, not outside influences.

Neither of these places appeared to be man-made, but places used by man for a purpose he had in mind. Therefore, they began as individual land marks and have remained so ever since. If there were maps 3,000 years ago, no doubt Edinburgh would have been marked. We know Dagworth had a name at least a thousand years ago.

I felt I could cling to this city as a child to a foster parent, and was happy to shelter there for a few weeks. I had a feeling of being accepted and have returned four or five times since my first visit. I liked the Scottish people and saw no evidence of meanness that could not be more than equalled by residents south of the border. Spending a month in Edinburgh alone gave me a real opportunity to know it. There were hours spent in the Princes Street Gardens. In addition to the beauty of the flowers, I used to watch the flower of youth in their prime of womanhood and manhood. There were young men in uniforms from every allied country: France, Belgium, Poland, Holland, India and other places, together with every colony well represented. Groups of girls in their respective uniforms of Women's Army Corps, Women's Royal Air Force, and Women's Royal Navy. They all paraded for their own enjoyment through the gardens and were consciously or unconsciously giving much pleasure to all who watched them, including myself.

Although my body was tired, my instinctive faculties for the appreciation of beauty either in flowers or womanly forms were as keen as ever. It is no use any self-righteous male clicking his tongue at my statement. You are only shocked because you have not the guts to be honest. Women were made to attract men, and men were made to be attracted. In this manner were they created. Those too good to be stirred must have missed the original Creator's mould and conformed to some human pattern.

It sounds shocking that I, thirty-eight years old, nearly four hundred miles from my wife, was enjoying watching the shapely legs of the WRNS beneath their fascinating uniforms. Take off your blinkers you critics! I would have enjoyed the scene just as much if my wife had been with me, and what is more, she would have appreciated it too.

I am gratified to state after twenty-six years have elapsed that I can still enjoy the contours of a feminine figure. Amongst all the glamour of war uniforms, the 'wrens' stood out conspicuous by their smartness, the navy-blue enhancing their complexions. The specified haircut of the inch above their white shirts give them distinct lines. From the tips of their toes, to the angle of their hats, they were impeccably turned out. They carried themselves proudly and were indeed a credit to the Senior Service.

I wonder why I was attracted to them so much? Most certainly I had no use for them personally just then. I definitely am not psychic, so it was just coincidence that less than ten years from the time I sat and admired those girls of the WRNS, one of them was to play a very important part in my life. Very important.

My month's stay in Edinburgh came to an end. I left all the glamour, and my cousins, the Cousins, and returned to my old Dagworth early in September in time to help with the tail end of the harvest. The gap made by my departure had definitely started to grow out, like a wound grown over with new skin.

Pip, my dog, gave me a cool welcome; he had attached himself to Eve and was quite happy. My wife did not put on a superficial welcome. We were genuinely happy to be together again. I had been away six weeks and it took time for me to 'get back.' How difficult it must have been for the men of the Forces who were separated from their wives for years, to get to know each other again. These long or short separations do take a bit of readjusting, as I found.

Being out of service for four months, the ranks had closed. I did not feel so necessary, and Dagworth Hall farm had to let me in.

I felt like a new shoot grafted in, and had to wait for growth to be noticed.

The war and my business had lost some of their importance to me as I had been restricted to a small world by the limits of my strength. Yet to myself I felt I had returned from a different world. When I alighted from the train at my home station I almost expected people to turn and look, as they would at the return of a head of state. No one noticed. I wanted to talk about it, but no one wanted to listen. It was like returning from hospital; people always want to tell about their operation but no one is really interested.

We were reminded of the war every day. There would be news of someone we knew killed, wounded or taken prisoner. Odd bombs fell in the district and planes crashed. Looking from my bedroom window at sunrise one summer morning, the sky was clear and everything was quiet. In the peace and glow of the rising sun, I could see three or four parachutists gently descending.

I hurriedly dressed and went to report to my section leader. I had no telephone. The section officer had already gone to pick up the men. They were a German crew who had baled out from their stricken aircraft.

While inspecting my stock late one Sunday evening, numerous explosions could be heard coming from the direction of White House Farm, Harleston. 'Home Guard practice,' I thought. Next morning I learnt that a German plane had begun to unload its incendiary bombs over White House Farm and finished in Haughley village. My poor old mother, now over eighty years old, and two sisters were living in White House when one of the bombs had crashed through the roof and landed on the stairs burning furiously. Fanny, my sister, whipped up a mat, covered it and picked it up. She rushed out and threw it on the lawn, saving their house and home. Though there were about two hundred of these bombs, the thatched cottages, farm buildings and stacks escaped damage.

So through another spring on to summer and July 1943. I was taking up my duties again and certainly did not want to slip back into weakness. I decided, and Eve agreed, I could be spared for a fortnight. A telegram was sent to cousin Lizzie Cousins in Edinburgh... "Can I come for two weeks?" Answer prepaid or otherwise: "Delighted. Please do."

So, I packed my bags and went north. It is never nice, and always sad to leave home, even for a holiday. This time I was not leaving everything behind; seventy-five per cent perhaps. The other twenty-five per cent was calling me to Scotland.

I was not going in search of a welcome, but to receive one. I travelled without a companion. Lizzie and Arthur were just as kind as before. The landmarks were familiar this time and Arthur's Seat had not changed. Sir Walter Scott's monument stood solidly in Princes Street Gardens.

It was impossible for my wife to go with me as we had to have Dagworth Hall house available for washing up all the dairy utensils, and someone had to receive the milk-round takings twice daily. In spite of the inconvenience of the old farm house, Eve loved Dagworth, including the milk-round. She loved all the animals, especially the horses and foals.

Her life was full from the time she rose until bedtime. She finished nearly everyday singing to her own piano accompaniment. Her voice was very rich. She used it at the chapel, and not being content to be organist, she added her voice to lead the congregation. When the war seemed like ending in Allied victory, and we could spend a little money without missing it, Eve felt she could now have her voice trained. She had been wanting to do this for years, and her mother had offered to pay for her lessons, but Eve refused to give the time or accept this offer until the farm was out of debt, and the war came to an end.

Although she was nearly forty years old, she thought it worthwhile for her own enjoyment, against the time when we would have some leisure time, and perhaps she could give pleasure to others. Her life was full. The meaning of her name Eva, was 'life.' Her spirit was turbulent, her actions impetuous. Eve dreaded getting old. She was not born to sit and knit or to do fancy needle-work. Those who knew her could never think of her in retirement. Her dearest friend once said to her, "You must grow old gracefully." "Grow old gracefully!" she exploded. "I hope I shall snap out like a light before I get there."

The hustle and bustle of Dagworth was her joy. She was part of it and would be missed more than I, so I felt justified in going to Scotland alone. This time I was strong enough to walk briskly and pick my feet up, thus avoiding the knobs in the wood on the footbridge at Waverley station and so keep my right end up.

My fortnight finished and I returned home to fill my place again. Unlike the last time, it was still open. I stepped in and carried on. After that, it did not seem convenient to revisit Edinburgh for several years. When I did, petrol was plentiful, so I drove up. No, Eve was not with me, she could not come. But no, I was not alone; I had a companion... an ex-wren!

It was 1944, and the war was getting well into its fifth year. The majority of people were simply accepting it with all its hardships and inconveniences. It was almost a passive acceptance; there was no other choice, therefore it resulted in a weird sort of contentment. Although there was definitely a mental war-strain in everybody, there was even a stronger force than that; it was a decisive comradeship between all classes. As in all wars, there were opportunities in many businesses to make money, as there were few chances of spending it. It accumulated, but it did not create that stupid affluent outlook when you have to 'keep up with the Joneses' or better still, beat them. There was a great diversity of incomes, but the same spirit was shared by all.

Hitler tried everything he knew to break the spirit of Britain. In June 1944, he began sending over the V1 Flying Bombs. We knew them as 'doodlebugs.' They were unmanned. Not being very technically minded I would not know how they were propelled. Their target was evidently mechanically predestined.

We used to hear them chugging over us, sounding like a motor-boat on the Broads. They were rather nerve-racking and gave one the impression that at any time they might come down and explode. Hitler's men would not exactly intentionally direct one towards White House Farm, Harleston where Mother lived and I farmed the land, so something must have gone wrong when one landed on a meadow there. It blew the windows out of the farm cottages, injured one of the wives and did £1,000 worth of damage to the farm buildings. I had a cart horse grazing on the meadow, and he had numerous pieces of wire sticking in his skin like a pin cushion. He had to be put down. Ten cattle were with him and they had just been valued for stock taking. Twelve months later when valued, they were worth less. The shock had stunted them and in fact they became smaller.

It was this same year that brother Sam died at the age of fifty-four. He was the first of the six brothers to go. This reduced our family acreage by one hundred and twenty. Brother William had now retired from farming as his health was not too good and as he had no sons to carry on, it seemed the wisest course to take.

I was the one remaining Burrows in farming. Eve and I planned to look for a more modern and compact farm after the war. It seemed the most reasonable thing to aim at. We dreamed of the day when we could go where electricity was available. We were both forty years old. It was 1944, and neither of us had ever used any lighting apart from oil lamps and candles. To think we had to dress up like eskimos on a bleak winter night to travel forty yards outside to relieve our bowels! When we reached the lavatory, what was it? Well, I've described it before, with the wind blowing underneath the door, through the missing brick, and out at the back of the privy through the warped weather-boards. It was enough to make the stoutest stomach develop voluntary constipation!

We had never known the luxury of a bath with hot and cold water. We had an over-sized galvanized bath up in the back bedroom. We heated water in the copper, struggled up the back stairs with it, had a bath then brought it down again.

A second bedroom was a sort of assembly room for jerries, chamber-pots or whatever you like to call them, and slop-pail. To face facts, like plum season, or if you 'had something that was going about,' there just wasn't the time to light the candle, dress, go downstairs, unbolt the back door, light the stable lantern and run forty yards. To make it in time, would surely qualify one for an Olympic Gold medal.

In such circumstances, the only thing to do was to run for the jerries in the pot room, even at the risk of leaving a 'Chamber full of horrors.' When you are up against three different calls of nature suddenly, and all at the same time with inadequate receptacles, it takes a versatile man to handle the situation, as was my experience only once.

Now a jerry is so constructed that you can only do one job at a time, so if you are doing two jobs, you need two pots. This is how I was occupied on this occasion when suddenly I had a bilious attack, and I brought the third pot into play. Had I performed this act on the stage at the London Palladium I am sure my fortune would have been made overnight, and my fame never forgotten.

We felt we would like to get to a place where there was mains water, to wash our troubles away, hot and cold over the bath and a hand basin and sink. To come down in the morning, switch on the light, plug in the kettle and have a cup of tea in ten minutes would be a real luxury. We would put our dreams into plans, and our plans into reality. It would take time to find a farm in the right spot; a farm we could buy and have as we wanted it. In the meantime, we knew we must carry on until the war ended.

Perhaps we could then have our holidays together. The only shared holiday we'd had was our honeymoon, under a cloud of dying pigs and farming depression and just four days in Somerset. That was when Mother-in-law was alive. These were the only holidays we had shared together in fifteen years.

The war eventually ended. What a relief for everybody to know that the fighting and destruction had ended. With the acute shortages created by the war, it would take years to get the materials to build up again.

A lot of the neglected work on the farms such as hedge-cutting and cleaning out ditches for drainage, was done through an arrangement with the government by using German prisoners of war. We had as many as eighty at one time on Dagworth Hall Farm doing these jobs.

We now felt justified in going out more, visiting friends and going to town without fear of air-raids. With more friends coming to visit us, we seemed to be landed with a number of late nights. On average, we went to bed only twice a week before midnight.

There were of course the evenings when just the two of us sat quietly together. As for instance one Sunday evening in mid-summer. Eve had done her duties as organist at the Wetherden Baptist Chapel and we sat having our supper in the Dagworth farmhouse. It was about 9.30pm and the sun was sinking low. Our dining room had one window facing more or less north and another facing the opposite direction. There we sat, one at each end of the table looking dreamily out of opposite windows. A dark shadow passed the window through which I was looking. It had the movements of a huge bird like a heron, but it was not a bird. We do not have blackbirds of that size in England. It half covered the window. It was not attached to the ground as I could see light all around it.

Perhaps it was an optical illusion. My eyes may have been focused on some distant point and saw a passing jackdaw out of proportion. So to neutralize extremes, I casually remarked to Eve, "A huge black bird just flew slowly past the window." "That's strange," she said thoughtfully. "At the very same instant a black object passed by the window from where I was looking. It looked more like flowing black robes. I wouldn't have commented on it if you had said nothing, thinking that perhaps it was my eyes."

This was just as we saw it. Perhaps there was nothing, and yet we independently saw something. I, being very keen on ghosts, tried to enlarge on it, but Eve being very practical and no believer in the supernatural dismissed the whole experience as nothing, and I felt disappointed.

Often, if one or both of us were out, Cecil Crissell, the horse-man would shut the chickens up for us. Some were in night-arks in the orchard. He was about to stop and close the door of one of these arks when he saw a woman standing there with her garments blowing in the wind. He took it to be Eve; it was the gloomy light of twilight. In telling me the following day, Cecil said, "I thought, I'll just finish shutting this door, then I will have a word with Mrs. Burrows, but when I looked up no one was there. I was so convinced that it was her I took the liberty of going to the window and looked in. There she sat playing the piano. So I don't know who the other woman was." Cecil had no knowledge at all of our dark shadows.

On another occasion, a man and his wife were sitting with us in the dining room. We were chatting together when suddenly Gwyneth stopped and looked towards the window remarking, "Something black just passed the window." She of course knew nothing of our pet ghost, so we told her. She, like Eve had no time for apparitions. She did not believe in them.

I wanted to believe in ghosts and needed real proof. No one would cooperate so I am still doubtful. In the case of our 'black shadow' I have recorded the observations of four people exactly as it had happened. Each one of us saw for ourselves, without the knowledge that anyone else had seen, so we were not influenced by a mental suggestion.

Chapter 24

Our primitive way of living just did not make sense and Eve and I realised it only too well. But we were caught in a web of circumstance. It was not our property; we hired the farm, so we could not modernise it. In any case, electricity and water were not available, and considering the low rent we payed, it would have been most unreasonable to approach our landlord on the subject.

Here we were, living in the middle of the twentieth century and practising eighteenth century domestic standards. Yet, paradoxically, we were (I humbly claim) farming over three hundred acres and employing eight regular men. The war was over and I felt the time had come for us to consider our comforts.

By the summer of 1945 Eve had spring-cleaned Dagworth Farmhouse sixteen times. Sixteen times she had gone off the deep end and expounded the demerits of a farmhouse whose structure had not changed for something like three hundred years. I ask you!

She had taken the view - at least, that's what she preached - "We might as well buy a small modern farm, have modern conveniences in the house and modern farm buildings. There is no point in slaving away here: I shall be old before my time. We have no family to work for, so surely we don't need 300 acres to get the two of us a living."

We went to see people who lived in a compact house with all the modern conveniences that were available at that time. The house seemed crowded out with them. We had gone to get the feel of the modern way of living, but Eve came away depressed. She relieved herself of her feelings on the way home: mostly concerning the inconvenience of all those conveniences.

"Never again," she emphatically announced, "will I ask for a modern house. Fancy being cooped up all day in that confined space with a lot of furniture. You might as well live in a furniture store. I would suffocate. I don't want to be a canary in a cage."

We both agreed it was no use escaping the slavery of an old-fashioned farmhouse to find ourselves slaves to the conventions of modern society. It would have to be something in between - a place of freedom aided by a moderate amount of modernity.

Having now settled in our minds what to look for, the greater problem was relieving ourselves of the fetters of Dagworth Hall and White House Farm. Dagworth Hall was no problem. The landlord was more than anxious to add it to his farming unit and would be grateful to us if we left the farm.

More people were becoming interested in agricultural land now and the outlook had changed since we had hired the farm sixteen years before.

My problem was White House Farm, Harleston. This farm my father had bought in my name in 1920 and in each of his subsequent wills, he confirmed his gift of the farm to me. Yet my conscience would not allow me to look upon it as my farm.

It was the home of my mother and my two unmarried sisters. Mother could not be uprooted at the age of eighty-three, But to be able to find another farm near enough to continue farming White House was limiting our chances of finding the farm we wanted.

The owner of the adjoining estate was most eager to to buy the farm but I had to consider my mother and sisters. The would-be buyer offered to buy it on the condition that Mother could finish her days there, and my sisters would be allowed a further six months possession of the house.

Going to a brother whose counsel I valued, I asked what I should do. He said, "Sell it and give your sisters one third of the money."

Brother Jim took a dim view of these arrangements. He said he would pay me half what I had been offered if I gave the

Katie, Lily (Sam's wife), Jim, Toby the dog, Alice (Jnr.)

260

other half to the sisters. Jim, being a widower, would live there, farm it and the women would have the security of a home.

Although my inheritance was dwindling, I accepted his offer. My conscience was clear and we were free to look for a spot to call our own. So, my legal connection with White House, lasting a quarter of a century, ended. For all this, I experienced no nostalgia, no regrets by ending my association with this little farm that was once part of a vast area owned by King Harold of England.

Reading through the title deeds of White House Farm, Harleston before handing them over, I saw such names as The Right Honourable Frances Catherine Lady Nelson, The Right Honourable Horatio Earl Nelson and The Honourable Rev. John Horatio Nelson. These names were all connected with the nineteenth century, and I must confess it stirred me to see them. Later, in the twentieth century, White House Farm was sold away from the Finborough Hall estate, home of the Pettiward family for many years. This led to names without titles appearing on the deeds of White House Farm.

In 1920, Lucky Burrows bought it in the name of his youngest son Alfred: other names of my family followed when I ceased to be connected. How this and surrounding lands managed to get the 'Nelson Touch' was, I gather, as follows...

After Viscount Horatio Nelson was killed at the Battle of Trafalgar, his honours were bestowed on his brother the Rev. William Nelson. I now lay myself open to correction, but with the help of my sisters, Nan - a niece, an archivist and a solicitor, I have come to the conclusion that Lady Frances Catherine Nelson was daughter or grandaughter of the Rev. Earl William Nelson. Lady Frances

Pictured here with brother Jack is the niece mentioned in the text. This is Nan Drew who was adopted by the Burrows family.

married Robert John Pettiward in 1855, who was heir to the lands in question. The male Nelsons mentioned appeared to be trustees for the estate owner.

Having learnt the folly of over-taxing brain and brawn just for an ideal or an ambition that would benefit no-one, I was now content to look for a farm big enough to occupy my time and bring in a living, and small enough to cause no worry. Had I had a son, my outlook would have been quite different.

Previously, I had great ambitions and still admired ambitious people. My ambition had now taken a turn in a different direction. Having seen the futility of aiming to farm one thousand acres, I now sought comfort and contentment. Eve and I were looking for a house where modern conveniences could be used entirely for comfort, not for competition; a home to invite friends who shared our outlook.

I wanted buildings where our animals could live just as happily as we hoped to. We knew to find a farm that would come up to all our expectations would be very unlikely. There were such farms about, but those who owned them usually kept them. So, I knew I would probably have to settle for the next best and try and make it fit our demands.

About a year before the war, an exceptionally good farm of over 300 acres was on the market for sale for the sum of £4,000. I had ample stock and equipment to farm it, but not enough money to buy. A business friend almost pleaded with me to accept his offer of lending me the money. I was brought up under the strict doctrine of 'never to borrow money'; yet it was quite in order to borrow from within your family, and it was not considered too sinful if it was never paid back.

Under this code of respectability, it was a great honour to hire land for an agreed rent, but a sin to borrow money for an agreed interest. If I had had the courage to break away from the bondage of my family's teaching and accepted my friend's offer, twenty years later the value of that farm with the potential profits within those years would have been well above £100,000. Had I taken this chance, it would no doubt have led to further speculations.

It could have been very gratifying and I definitely see no sin in possessing wealth. People with few possessions are fond of quoting, 'Money is the root of all evil.' If I read my Bible correctly, I think it should be, 'The love of money is the root of all evil.' For myself, I am convinced that enough is sufficient, and true wealth is to be found in the heart and mind.

When a person is looking for something new or different, how quickly the old loses its interest. Now Eve and I were searching for a new farm, Dagworth Hall was losing the keen interest we had for her. We knew there were no long term prospects for us there: it had become a year to year existence and we wanted to get transplanted as soon as possible, to allow our roots to take hold.

For forty-two years, I had lived up narrow lanes. To approach each of the three farmhouses I had lived in, the track was too narrow to pass another vehicle. I had no wish for the fourth time to be at the end of a lane.

I found my farm - its position ideal. The house and buildings stood seventy yards back down a drive leading from an exceptionally good secondary road. But the house was poor - the thatch was bad. It had been used as two cottages, was four hundred years old and inconvenient. The farm buildings were third rate and the eighty available acres was about half what I had hoped.

Eve thought the place impossible. I saw it had potential and was sure it could be made to suit us both. We were like two men looking through iron bars - 'one saw the mud, the other saw the stars.' My wife saw it as it was; I could see it as it would be.

The position was right, mains electricity was available and mains water was coming. The telephone could be connected and the house could be made into a really picturesque dwelling, and moderately convenient. The farm buildings stood well for modernisation and there was always the possibility that more land might be added.

We bought the place and allowed ourselves two years to accomplish our aims. It was hard going. The war only one year past meant that all building and repair materials were by licence under government control. Craftsmen and tradesmen were scarce, not yet being readjusted from war service. German prisoners of war were still in camps and we used them for cleaning out field-ditches and putting wire fencing around the meadows.

Two more spring-cleanings at Dagworth Hall; 1947 and 1948 (I ask you!), then it would be modern conveniences and our very own farm. This new farm was about the same size as White House Farm, so briefly we were back again to the same acreage.

It was indeed a challenge to attempt to transform this place into the farm we dreamed of. I found it thrilling and inspiring, but was disappointed when I realised that Eve had not taken up the challenge with me. I was alone in the eagerness of my enthusiasm.

I felt like a child running with another for a prize; then realised I was running alone, and the prize lost some of its flavour. There was no other way but to carry on. I felt sure the end product would be something we would both enjoy. It was pretty obvious that ten years on, Eve would not have the ability or desire to cope with a place like Dagworth Hall. She was dead-set against anywhere ultra-modern, so this farm, as something in between, ought to be the answer.

As I discussed the alterations with the workmen, I wished my partner would show some excitement in the development of our future home. She was not opposed to it, nor voiced any opposition, but took it all in with an attitude of passive resignation. This was so unlike her usual buoyant and excitable nature that it dulled my ardour too. I think the explanation of her attitude would gradually reveal itself to me over the next few years.

The new farm was in a village called Elmswell, ten miles from Bury St. Edmunds. It was a lively industrial village boasting of a Bacon Factory employing, at a guess, some three hundred workers, an egg-packing station with one hundred employees, a sizeable Agricultural Engineering Works and stores, two Corn Merchants, a printing works and various small enterprises. With a population of between one and two thousand, it could grow into a small town in the not too distant future.

To make our little farm even more insignificant, its name was 'Bennett's Farm'. "We can't have that," Eve said. "We'll change it."

I suggested 'Northfields' as it joined the northern boundary of the village. "No," she said. "It sounds so cold. I wish we could call it Dagworth as Dagworth provided the money for us to buy it. But that wouldn't do - there would be no discrimination between the two farms. I know - we'll call it 'Dagwood', then we shall always have a little bit of Dagworth with us." So, 'Dagwood' it has been for over twenty years.

Dagwood in the 1950s

The last two years at Dagworth Hall were very busy years. One farm was being worked to leave; the other being altered to take a larger number of stock than ever before. We were still running the milk-round, although on a reduced scale. Eve was still having her voice trained and was singing as a soloist in neighbouring parishes.

Dagworth Hall had given us much cause for worry and toil, and yet there was a sadness in leaving her. Actually, I did not feel it so much: my mind was on the future and on having an easier time. Eve was very much more aware of the change and felt as one would when losing a dear and helpless relative, her loss appearing greater than the relief from arduous duties.

She had morbid moments, speaking as if she had no future. Coming from one so high-spirited, it was hard to understand. "Should anything happen to me," she said on one occasion, "don't reproach yourself in any way. You have been a marvellous husband." - Her words, not my opinion.

I did not know what to say or think. "With every tick of the clock, my life is going," she once said. Then the morbid thoughts would pass away and she would return to her usual self. At times, she seemed to see no future, then the funny side of life would present itself and all mental depressions were crowded out once more.

Mother, Jim and the sisters were settled in at White House Farm. At the age of eighty-four, Mother was not very well. She'd had a stroke which she was convinced was brought on by the incendiary bomb on the stairs or the V1 flying bomb that landed in the meadow. Fanny had nursed Father to his end and was now looking after poor old Mother. The other sisters did their share too, of course.

On January 8th 1947, two days after her eighty-fifth birthday, Mother died. In due course, she was laid to rest with Father in Harleston churchyard. It was one of the big freeze-up years and began snowing on the day of the funeral. If the funeral had been the following day, it would have been impossible to get through the snow drifts to the church.

Sister Fanny's life seemed to be one of service to the family. She had kept house for four brothers in turn until they married, nursed her father, then Mother, and was second mother to us all in her earlier years. She was not compelled to do all this for the family. Had she married or taken a career, her place would have been taken by someone else. But I suppose she felt duty bound to do it.

It was Fanny's turn to be nursed next. She was troubled with arthritis and it became worse over the years. Her two sisters waited on her in the pathetic painfulness of her condition.

Eve and I were carried along by time to our last year at Dagworth Hall. I was aiming to make the finish of Dagworth the birth of a new life at Dagwood. But try as she might, my partner could not shake off the feeling that the finish of Dagworth was the end of all interests in life and the running down of a life's song. I know she fought to raise some enthusiasm for my sake, but was unable to disguise the fact that her morbid premonitions were uppermost.

The time drew near for moving. We arranged an auction sale to dispose of unwanted stuff. Threshing our last harvest off the Dagworth land, we then harvested twenty acres of sugar-beet. Finally, we took thirty lorry, tractor, trailer, horse-cart and waggon loads of cattle, corn, coal, firewood, furniture... and so on.

With all this activity, we were too mentally and physically tired to trouble about either premonitions or budding hopes. We had allowed the building firm two years for carrying out the alterations, additions and improvements. With unsuitable labour and material shortage, the day we arrived with our furniture, we found about ten so-called tradesmen working on the house and buildings. Believe it or not, two men were painting the front door as we struggled past them with our domestic possessions.

The master builder presented his accounts more promptly than he had applied his tools. He completed the job and I completed the payment; after which, he went bankrupt. All the wiring for electricity in house and farm buildings I put into the hands of a self-employed man for a contracted sum. As he progressed with the work, he asked for several subs. from the agreed amount. He completed the job, I completed the payment and then he went bankrupt.

A young energetic man with initiative and straight from the forces took on all the plumbing. We moved in on October 11th and he managed to get the hot and cold going and the bathroom rigged up just in time for us to have a proper bath for Christmas - for the first time in our lives. He finished his job in glory, if belated; I paid him. Not to be outdone by the two other mastermen, he joined them in bankruptcy!

One man from the village told me later that he and his mate used to joke about it as they passed the farm on their way to work. They reckoned if those tradesmen did not soon move, I should have to sell the farm to pay them. As they went by each day, one man used to say to his old mate, "He's still solvent - the roan mare is on the meadow." It was a fact that all our renovations cost as much as we paid for the farm and then half as much again.

As we settled in, we planned the garden, planted trees and shrubs and looked upon our family as the twenty cows and their thirty followers. We farmed the land in the routine of the average farmer, but these morbid (I suppose we could call them) premonitions would crop up from time to time in Eve's mind. "Promise me," she said, "should anything happen to me, you will sort out my things. I would hate anyone else going through my bits and pieces." I seemed to be living and working in a grim dream. I never knew what was coming next; it was so strange that a woman apparently healthy and happy at the age of just forty-four should speak so.

At breakfast one morning, she spoke as if continuing a broken conversation. "I hope you will wait two years before you marry again. I want you to marry, so long as you don't forget me. Don't take the first woman that comes along. Meet a lot of all kinds and make your choice. You don't have to marry someone from the Baptist denomination." The last sentence was no slight whatsoever on the members of this particular sect. She was trying to indicate that just because from the age of nine years she and her family had attended one chapel did not make it her entire world.

Eve, you see, was never a chapel-goer too good to mix with publicans and sinners. She mixed with all sorts. She sang to all congregations and at all kinds of functions. We felt no guilt in calling in at a village public house to sup whatever appealed to the palate. In this way, we discovered landladies serving beer with faith and belief in God equal to many with bowed heads in pews. For all that, she was never ashamed to admit that she was a regular chapel-goer.

Of course, to attend chapel services as I have done for over half a century is no guarantee that all worldly thoughts are left outside. For example, one of my brothers-in-law used to come into chapel late and sit beside me. We sat with bowed heads as the minister prayed one Sunday morning. Presently, while the minister still prayed, I felt a nudge. "Done barley seeding yet?" he whispered.
I hoped the back of my head looked righteous as I framed, "No."
The parson continued to pray; then there was another nudge.
"Your mare foaled yet?" I managed to shoot a "yes" out of the corner of my mouth before our conversation was interrupted by the next hymn. It might have been better for us two to have stayed outside and exchanged our family report.

1949 found us three months away from Dagworth Hall. Eve seemed more or less happy, but her duties seemed to be accomplished more from habit than by inspiration. Thoughtfully, she resumed her last conversation of premonition as though there had been no intermediate break. "When you marry again, get someone young.

You are not too old to raise a family. You could even settle for a wife as young as twenty-five." She continued., "When I've gone, be sure to get to know as many women as possible so you are in a position to make a good choice. I shall not look upon it as disrespectful in any way. Enjoy yourself and have a good time."

I felt as if I was waiting for something to happen. My future seemed clouded. Was Eve fated to have an accident or to be suddenly taken ill? It was like hearing thunder in the distance and wondering whether it would pass by or break overhead. This unnatural gloom had been hovering over us for something like two years.

About two weeks before Easter I had to take to my bed with flu. With a high temperature and an aching head, one can imagine anything, so I wondered, 'is this it?' My wife nursed me and attended to my wants and also looked after our four or five hundred hens. As is usual in spring, the winds were strong and bitterly cold. When she crossed from the buildings to the house, her fur hat blew off. She said she felt like cursing the wind and, as if in defiance, let her hat lay where it was for someone else to pick up.

I had never known Eve give in to an illness, but she came upstairs and sat on my bed. "I shall have to give in," she said. "I know when I am beaten. I shall have to go into the other bedroom and lie down."

The next morning, Eve was worse and I was practically helpless to attend to her. We knew help was essential. "I will ring Mary," I said. Mary was Eve's lifelong friend since school days.

Mary came and in her capable manner looked after us both. The doctor follwed and said it was double pneumonia. It was now Friday and one week from Good Friday. My wife became worse. Mary stayed with her all night. On Saturday morning, the doctor returned and ordered an ambulance to take her to hospital. Mary had the manner of a born nurse in emergency and prepared Eve for the journey, saying to me, "I will go with her and then come back and take you home with me. I can nurse you better there."

I stood at the window in my pyjamas and watched them go. I was alone in the house.

By Tuesday, I was well enough to go with Mary to the hospital to see Eve. She was very ill. On Wednesday, I drove myself to the hospital. The curtains were drawn around the bed. There were no available private rooms but the Sister informed me that one would become vacant that day, after which Eve would be moved into it. I sat by her bedside. Then, in a manner as casual and bright as if she was telling me she was going on holiday, she said, "I am going to die." Most people answer such statements the way I did... "Oh no you're not. You'll soon be well again." "No," she said. "I know I'm going to die because I've been through the Valley of the Shadow."

She the spoke of other things. Eve had accepted an invitation to sing in Haughley Congregational Chapel on Good Friday. This I'd had to cancel on her behalf.

I visited my wife on Thursday in her little private room. A nurse showed me in. Eve was not in bed. "My dear, what are you doing?" the nurse exclaimed and motioned me outside. When I returned, Eve was in bed and breathing with the aid of oxygen.

A nurse stood by, feeling her pulse. The look on her face led met to utter, "My wife hasn't..." Looking at me painfully, she replied, "I'm terribly sorry Mr. Burrows, I'm afraid she has." Then briskly she said, "Look here, you had better drink this brandy." This was the Thursday before Good Friday. Just a week earlier, Eve had been feeding the hens; now she was dead.

Although she may not have been conscious of my presence, I was grateful to have been with her at the end. Our eighteen and a half years of married life was over and I can honestly say that in spite of Eve's excitable and turbulent spirit, we never had one quarrel. She was buried the day following Easter Monday. Her life was relatively short, but she used her talent and left her mark on our little world. With an unselfish outlook, she wished me to start a new life without reproach or regrets of the past.

Dagwood Farmhouse today

Behind Dagwood -
a reminder of the
days of Alf Burrows

Looking down towards Haughley
in high summer. Dagworth is
along a narrow lane to the right.

The Scotch Tea-Rooms (Norwich), where Alf
met Josephine are long gone, but for a few years
in the fifties, they could be found in a part of
this elegant building in White Lion Street.

Chapter 25

Easter, 1949 left no happiness for me. I was facing the finality of the death of a dear partner. The cold north-west winds ceased, as if they had finished their job of sweeping the countryside clear of the rotten and broken herbage left about by the winter's snow and frost. The sun broke out warm and the earth responded to begin another generation of plants. It was the fore-runner of a rare and beautiful English summer. But I could not appreciate or enjoy life, growth or the song of the birds; I could clearly remember the dead stalks of last year's life.

As I watched the withered grass waving in the soft, quiet breeze, the whole world appeared to me as desolate, forsaken and pointless. The evenings were light and I felt restless indoors. I found it cold within; unwelcome anywhere, in the way one does in the upheaval of spring-cleaning in the home. It was that in-between time for me.

The words on Eva's gravestone behind Wetherden Chapel begin...
"Eva the perfect pal and much loved wife of Alfred Burrows."

One could elaborate on the numerous miserable in-betweens of one's life... School behind, work before, youth discarded, manhood accepted, virginity and innocence replaced by knowledge and experience. A life of single independence is sacrificed for the joy of sharing in marriage. Perhaps someone gives up the security of employment for the risk of having a business of his own.

All these have their in-betweens, and it is worth giving a few minutes thought to, as it is within these changes of our lives that we experience depression, irritability, concern, sometimes the joy of expectancy, and more often sadness.

Not only are we sad in losing dear ones by death; we are sad at losing our childhood and everything else as we move forward in life. It is simply the price of promotion. We cannot hope to gain in any way without some loss.

Mostly, the changes in life are accepted or are planned within an ambition, but there are occasions through circumstance absolutely beyond our control, when we are forced into a different way of life and feel everything is lost. It is at these times that the way is open for bigger opportunities, although we do not realise it at the time. We are brought to see life from a different angle, which is often a good thing.

I felt the loss of my wife very much, but I am grateful to say I was never bitter towards any person or unseen power because of it. If self-pity began to rise I would tell myself that millions have had the same experience and there would be millions more.

When I saw the glow of happiness on someone's face, whilst in the midst of my gloom, I felt in no way jealous of them but thought without a doubt they have had or will have, their dark hours too. It would be interesting to hear of the first thoughts of the average person when losing a partner. Although nineteen years have passed since Eve died, I well remember one of my first thoughts, ridiculous as it was. Looking down at my shirt I was thinking, 'she washed this one, I wonder who will wash the next?'

Then I remember after a few weeks, the realisation swept over me that I was free to marry another woman if I wished. The ties of love or law no longer existed. I viewed my life and the future in a dazed manner as would a blind person, on receiving sight, view their hands. 'Are they REALLY my hands? Is THAT what they look like?' It was as if I was a pet bird kept within a cage for eighteen years. I had been well looked after and there was nothing I desired or needed. Then suddenly the cage door was thrown open. I hopped outside and the door closed behind me. I was told, you have your freedom; the world is yours. What did I do? I just turned round. Whereas, I had for eighteen years looked through the bars, I now sat outside looking in and longed to be back with my old familiar water pot and seed container.

It was no use. The door was shut and everything locked within. I must turn around again and leave the dead past behind me forever.

I stayed with Mary and her husband Allan for several weeks. They had a land girl living in the house; she was about twenty-one. Allan's sister, who had recently lost her mother, was also living there. She, like myself, was doing a kind of convalescence from grief, or taking as one might say, a rehabilitation course. Mary also had a daily help.

There was a wonderful atmosphere in this household. Appropriately enough, the name of the residence was 'Home Farm'. It was there that Mary brought me after seeing Eve settled in hospital, and there I was when my wife died.

I owe it to the memory of Mary Smith of Gislingham, to record here the greatness of her kind and tender heart, her devotion to her friend to the end, and afterwards her considerate nature and capable mind.

All these qualities were revealed in one act, for when Eve died Mary said, "Oh, she must be brought here. She can't lay at Dagwood Farm all alone and you could not return there yet. She will be with us until the funeral."

When I left Home Farm to return to Dagwood, I said to Mary, "How can I ever repay your kindness?" Her answer has dwelt in my memory. "I need no payment. Just pass it on."

I was very fortunate in having such friends as Mary and Allan. Going to my farm during the day, and to Home Farm for the evening and night filled in the time and left less time to brood.

In this atmosphere, a new life began to open out. It is perhaps unusual for a man when he is bereaved in middle-age to carry on in the same rut. He would find it necessary to have a house-keeper, and quite likely think that as they were to share the same house, they may as well share the same name, and jog along comfortably to the end. I had my instructions to look around and get to know different types of women, and to keep away from the idea that the first one I looked at must lead to the altar!

The advice given, and that statement made by Eve, irrespective of what prompted her to do so, began to become clearly embedded in my mind. They became very real to me, and I felt drawn along by them. No, it is wrong for me to say I was driven. The truth was that I was guided by Eve's concern during her life for my welfare after her death.

As time went on I realised how lucky I was to be able to converse with the opposite sex, to take a lady-friend to a show or meal without having the slightest apprehension of guilt or feeling of unfaithfulness towards my first love. I was, in actual fact, following her wishes.

I think I mentioned before how much at ease I have always been with the opposite sex as companions. I have always found it refreshing to see the funny side of life, however ridiculous. It makes such a pleasant diversion from always trying to be clever. My second mother-in-law often quoted, "If you haven't a sense of humour, you haven't any sense."

The time when Phyllis and I got our underclothes mixed up did not make sense, (Phyllis was the land-girl), but it made for a bit of humour! I was mystified to discover that I was wearing the land-girl's vest. As I took off the singlet one night I noticed the initials P.H. The next morning I remarked to Mary that it was the first time I knew my underclothes were marked thus. She explained, "Why Alf, P.H. stands for Phyllis Hill. You've been wearing her undies," and continued, "Phyllis always wears boys' vests for landwork. They've got mixed up in the wash." So I was cleared of being a 'pansy.'

Mary said to me one day, "How are you going to manage when you go home?"

"I'll look for a house-keeper I suppose," I replied.

Mary of course, had it all worked out in a practical manner to the genuine benefit of all. Allan's sister Bertha, who had not long lost her Mother, was nearing sixty. Phyllis was twenty-one and Mary was exactly halfway between the two, so Allan and I had a nice range of womanhood to talk to. "I am sure my sister-in-law Bertha would come and look after you if you asked her," Mary continued. It was a very good idea, so I agreed. "But," Mary said, "Don't expect Bertha to stay with you indefinitely. You will have to look for someone else after a time."

Bertha and I settled on a date to return to Dagwood Farm, Elmswell. She was a staunch member of The Church of England and a good house-keeper so we managed very well.

In the meantime, we stayed another week or two at Home Farm. To show my appreciation for kindness shown, I used to assist with any job if the need arose. Phyllis was in charge of the dairy herd and a bull was kept to father the calves. As the land-girl turned the cows out after milking one day, she noticed one in season and drew my attention to it. I said, "I will tell Allan when he comes back and then help him get the bull out." "Oh," she said, "I can help you with the bull."

As I had a cow herd, the land-girl and I both understood the operation must be arranged if the cow was to produce a calf the following year. We drove the cow into a yard adjoining the bull's pen. I opened his door and had to quickly stand aside as he was eager to get with his spouse.

Phyllis and I co-operated in an impartial manner with the bull and the cow, as would a doctor and nurse at the birth of a child. The only difference being that we were assisting in the conception, and they at the confinement.

Having finished his duty, the bull was reluctant to leave the cow. However, with shouts, a stick and a prod from a pitch-fork, we got him on the run. He leapt into his shed and I banged the door behind him. Suddenly he changed his mind and forced the door open before I could fasten it, right in my face, knocking out my two false teeth. These fell among the straw and cattle droppings. We had difficulty in finding them as they were similar in colour to the straw. However, seeing the gold wire shining, I fished them out of the straw, rinsed them in the cattle drinking tough and returned them to my mouth before returning the bull to his shed.

The land-girl and I were pleased with our achievement and I proudly told Mary, who threw up her hands in horror. "I don't know what Allan will say. He and the man always attend to this sort of work." She continued, "He would never let Phyllis do anything like that." Allan did not say anything; Mary forgot it. The cow was satisfied and the bull was happy, so I still think we did a good job.

1949 was a lovely hot summer. Friends did not make it obvious they were asking me out, but I just found myself in their company. Bertha was in no way nervous of being in the house alone after dark, so I was not restricted to time. In this way the summer passed by. The odd days of shooting broke up the work routine, and with the fortnightly visits to market, the winter too was soon over. Although

I had not retrieved complete happiness, life was becoming more interesting, and I had got through the stage when I used to literally say, "Thank God time does not stand still."

It is strange how difficult it seems to get rid of unwanted time and in contrast how swiftly our treasured hours pass. You hardly have time to digest them before they become a memory. I do not think it would be fair to describe myself as impracticable or an absent-minded dreamer, and yet I could get lost in day-dreams and even get carried away by romantic thoughts. I make no apology for being this way, in fact I am grateful, as it tends to round off the corners in a hard and practical world, and softens the harshness of our outlook.

In an unplanned acceptance, I had a consciousness of there being a woman somewhere I wanted to marry, and I felt no uncertainty of being mistaken when I met her. Also, I had no need to put on a reserved attitude of coolness to guard against getting caught at the altar in a momentary flush of infatuation, as I knew something deeper than this was needed in a wife.

I was just as eager not to miss the right one as I was to not catch the wrong one. As the second year came along I often found myself taking weekends in London. Then, a friend asked me one evening, "What about a few days in Lancashire Alf?" "Yes, alright, I'll come," I answered. "Well," he said, "the truth is, there is a man up north who owes me five or six thousand pounds, but I have no proof that he owes me this sum. You see, I did business with him in good faith and he never paid." "I know where to contact him in Preston," he continued. "If you are with me and I can get him to admit his debt, you will be a witness." The plan worked and the case was heard in the High Court, with my humble self present as witness, though I was not called upon to bear witness for which I was very grateful. My friend recovered some of the money.

While we were up there for the purpose of contacting this man, my friend and I spent an evening or two in Blackpool. "Let's have our fortunes told," we said. I remember this because it was so uncanny. The fortune teller gave me a true account of my life, and told me I was a farmer, with other correct details. When she forecast my future, I wondered if she would be proved correct. "You will meet a girl in late

September or early October this year," she said. "The girl will be twenty-five years old, the predominating letter in her name will be M and you will marry her within a few months of meeting." We thanked her, paid the fees and continued on our way.

My friend called at a farm somewhere near Oldham on business. I noticed a 1937 Jaguar SS car standing in one of the farm buildings. As we were leaving, I remarked to my friend, "I liked the look of his car; I wonder if he would sell it." "We'll ask him."

1937 Jaguar SS

Yes, he would sell it. Petrol being so scarce during the war, it was hardly used and had not been used at all for the last year or two. I said that if he would get it taxed and so on, I would buy it and call for it within the next day or two on the way home.

We picked the car up. My pal advised me to drive it steadily - after all it was thirteen years old and it had been standing about so long anything might happen to it.

"I don't know the route home," I said, "but I think I can find my way." "Don't worry about that," my friend said, "just follow me."

Where it was possible he drove at well over eighty miles per hour, but I kept him in sight. At our first stop he told me not to push her too hard. "Well," I argued, "I've either got to do nearly ninety, or find my own way home. As it will soon be dark I think it easier to hang on to your tail." We arrived home in one piece, or in other words, our respective pieces.

This particular friend had no design on ending my life, although four or five years previously while walking a field for hares, he was the gun on my right, and his barrels, pointing dangerously, missed me by only a few feet. Firearms should be treated with great care and respect. These accidents are just warnings and luckily no harm was done.

I was enjoying my little bit of farming again at Elmswell in 1950. The farm was too small to show much profit, so to enlarge my scope, I, with two other farmers, hired a stretch of marshes near Yarmouth for summer grazing. It was interesting and enjoyable doing the fifty-mile journey to inspect the cattle. Two of us were widowers. Sometimes we stayed the night at a small hotel near the marshes to be ready for picking out cattle in the morning for market.

If the profits in this venture were small, we all agreed they were large enough to cover our expenses of several visits into Great Yarmouth, and after all, the sea air was free.

It was understandable I suppose, that after consulting the fortune-teller in Blackpool, although I did not believe in this clairvoyance, I used to think it would be strange if I did meet a girl of twenty-five with a prominent M in her name. Being friendly with a young lady named Mary made me wonder. She was very kind, perhaps her manner was acquired through her profession. She was a nursing sister, but I still think Mary was naturally kind. I used to meet her off duty and take her to her home, or for a car ride. This went on for several months. She was certainly seriously friendly in a happy way, but I found it hard to imagine she had serious thoughts beyond friendship.

Of course, I was temporarily infatuated and flattered - who wouldn't be. Mary was slightly less than half my age, and I was easily old enough to be her father. By age, it was possible for my house-keeper to have been her grandmother! I did not feel inclined to tell Bertha of this friendship for fear of getting some sound advice.

Such secrecy led me into a bit of scheming on one occasion. This nursing sister informed me that she and some of the staff had been invited to a colleague's wedding. The girl was marrying a naval officer and they would emerge from church under an archway of crossed swords and one thing and another. The gist of the conversation was, I could consider myself one of the guests if I would transport three or four off-duty nurses to the church several miles into the country.

Far be it from me to disappoint so many worthy women: I said I would gladly be anybody's guest if they would honour me by being my passengers.

I was quite aware that I had also accepted a day's shooting on the same day. Perhaps I could manage to leave Bertha thinking I was out shooting, when in fact I would be at a wedding with Mary and her friends. But then, I could not adorn myself for a wedding and tell Bertha I was going shooting! On the other hand, I could not turn up at church in tweed jacket, breeches and gumboots.

It was stupid of me to try and deceive Bertha, yet if I did not, I should meet with her silent disapproval and could not risk upsetting a good house-keeper. So I compromised. The outer part of my wedding apparel I placed in the car the night before. On the day of the wedding, I dressed up for the occasion, then put on a boiler-suit which covered everything including starched collar and cuffs. With my tweed jacket and gumboots my house-keeper took me for a sportsman, I hope!

Marching down the path with my cartridge bag on my shoulder, and gun under my arm Bertha called out, "Good bye, I hope you get plenty of sport." "Thank you Bertha, I'll do my best." I slung the gun and ammunition in the boot of the car and left. There have been many marriages described as 'shot-gun weddings' but this was the only time I knew, when a shotgun had actually been taken to a wedding.

In a quiet road I exchanged my disguise for the appropriate clothing and used the first telephone kiosk to inform my shooting host how disappointed I was not to be able to come, and offered my apologies.

Mingling with the guests I was careful to keep my countenance from the cameras. Returning home I deposited the girls at the sister's quarters and further on replaced my camouflage. A welcome greeted me, "Have you had a nice day?"
I may have mumbled, "Yes thank you. I saw lots of birds but did not get a shot." I could have added, "The company itself was ample reward."

It became apparent that Mary was not the girl the clairvoyant had seen in her crystal ball, palm or wherever they see the future. The M was in her name all right, but her age was twenty-two instead of twenty-five and we had met in the wrong month. Please do not think I was carried away by these magic powers of an ordinary woman, and the way forthcoming events had been foretold. I am not trying to convince myself or anyone else on this matter. This is a true story and I am merely stating facts.

It was the sincere wish of my late wife that I should meet various types of women, which I did, unless I knew they were the very undesirable types. Some proved very interesting, some were entertaining, some simply amusing and a few absolutely boring.

The slaughter of so many young men started by Hitler, had ended five years back and had left behind many war-widows. Personally I did not meet any who were bent on securing a second husband at any price, although I was legitimately in the market. But I was fortunate to be friendly with a lady who had become a widow through the war. She was very intelligent indeed, and I found her most attractive.

We had many interesting conversations, and she never in any way jarred on my sensitivity. She had a ready sense of humour and was always well dressed and fashionable to the moment. In addition to these qualities, she had a very shapely pair of legs. I did not look upon those legs as an addition of course, but as a necessary part of the whole assembly. Viewing the complete structure, the entire area above the waistline compared very favourably with the lower regions. This young widow made a trip to London worthwhile. After seeing what the motor industry was doing at their show at Earls Court, and then learning what the cows were doing at the Dairy Show, the show

'Carousel' with pleasant company was like finishing a good dinner with a dainty sweet.

Widow and widower seemed to be enjoying an understanding friendship. It's something that never really gets anywhere, and yet never ends. There was no sense of possessiveness in either way, so no jealousy was created. She loved the city life and all it offered, and I loved the country of which I was a part. Neither of us would have been happy to permanently change our environment, so would not have made suitable permanent partners.

We were not together in the crystal ball either. This lady's age was wrong, she was perhaps in her middle thirties, so therefore born in the wrong decade. There was no M in her name!

I was not spending all my time escorting ladies about, just an odd evening sometimes, and part of a day occasionally. The farming occupied most of my time, including the marsh cattle-grazing near Yarmouth during the summer. My cattle project was not a big one, and at the peak of the season the numbers would only be about one hundred head. My two friends, whom we will call Edwin and Henry, did the cattle job on a much larger scale. This widower settled on a future partner and he used to bring his intended with him to inspect the cattle.

They all tried to be helpful in getting me 'fixed up' too. Even when I was not with them, I gathered they still had me in mind when they saw what appeared to be a suitable match. This especially applied to Edwin. He knew nothing about the women, but if he saw one who looked interesting he would say, "She'd do alright for old Alf."

Perhaps it gave him a second-hand thrill, similar to reading a love story. Edwin travelled all over England cattle buying; he also went to Scotland and Wales and even over to Ireland. Often I would accompany him on these journeys which sometimes lasted three or four days. Bertha, my house-keeper, was quite happy and content to stay alone at the farm and look after the dog, cats and fowls.

Usually my pal found cattle and sheep to meet his requirements, but there did not seem to be a woman in the British Isles to meet mine. September was drawing to a close, the time when,

284

according to the Blackpool fortune-teller, I would meet my fate. Actually, she predicted late September or early October.

The morning of September 30th 1950 came, but no twenty-five year old damsel had appeared on the scene, and I was spending the day on the farm so there was not much chance of the prophecy being fulfilled. Edwin had gone to Norwich, cattle buying, which he usually did on a Saturday. Often, during the evening he called in for a chat, or we would go out for a drink.

On this particular Saturday, he drove into my yard, sounded the horn, and waited in the car. I went out and he opened the car door. "Hop in," he whispered. Edwin always whispered when he had important news, even if he was in the middle of a hundred-acre field. I hopped in, and shut the door. "I say Alfie," he still whispered, although he and I were the only persons on the farm apart from Bertha and she was indoors. She was behind closed doors and we were outside shut in the car.

Having now felt he had all my attention, my cattle-dealing friend whispered the whole mysterious sentence. "I say Alfie, I've found you a gal." I looked over into the back seat. "Where is she?" I asked. "In Norwich. Well, she was at lunch time."
"How do you know she wants a chap?"
"I've been talking to her," he said. "I've seen her two or three Saturdays. She always has her lunch in the same restaurant as I do. I talked to her today." Edwin could make conversation with anyone. "What's she like?" I queried.
"She's a bit of alright. A rare nice gal." He knew nothing about her. "You wait 'till you see her. You'll say the same."
"How old is she?"
"About thirty." That was his guess and the age he thought would rouse my interest. Edwin could always make a story fit his desired end. So to make possibilities appear more possible, he added, "And I can tell you another thing. This gal said she would like to marry a farmer!"
"Anyway, if all you say is true, I cannot imagine anyone like that wanting to marry a widower of forty-five."

This old rascal of a match-maker forgot to whisper, and his voice could have been heard well outside the car. "Ah! But I told her I knew a nice bachelor of forty was farming, and if she would be at the restaurant the following Saturday, I would bring him along." "So you see," he continued, "I've done my best for you and made all the arrangements, so do you ruddy well come!"

I had heard some of Edwin's talks and illustrations before. He was the sort who could sell refrigerators to Eskimos. Still, it looked like being an adventure so I said, "Oh yes, I'll come." I did not have to prepare for a disappointment because I did not expect to be thrilled.

It would no doubt lead to the same result as when I answered an advertisement in our local paper a few months previously. According to this advertisement, a lady wished to meet a farmer. Her qualifications were outstanding. She could rear calves, feed pigs, thoroughly understood poultry, was a good gardener and apparently a perfect house-keeper.

What an asset, I thought, such a woman could be to a farm. I would be relieved of all responsibilities; life would be a dream. To contact this remarkable female a number in Surrey was given. Toying with the idea of taking a chance at ringing this number just for a bit of fun, I tore out the advert and put it in my wallet. A few weeks later, wandering around the Kensington area in London alone, I remembered this wonderful woman, who was searching for a farmer. I thought, I'll give her a ring and then drive into Surrey and call on her.

I got through on the telephone to the number stated and the voice that answered made me hold the receiver away from my ear. It sounded more like the frothing bark of a boar but it turned out to be human, so I related my mission and was told to 'hang on' for the desired maiden. The voice that answered was worse than before; it sounded like the braying of a donkey, and it had an awful foreign accent. I felt I had contacted a female Beast of Belsen. I hung up and fled.

My coming appointment at Norwich on Saturday could not be any worse, so I meant to keep my promise and go with Edwin as he had arranged it all for my sake.

The cattle-market first, and then to the Scotch Restaurant for lunch where I was supposed to meet an ideal woman of thirty; and she wanting to meet a prosperous bachelor of forty. Which one, I wondered, was going to get the greatest shock, she or I.

I hadn't the faintest notion of who or what I was going to meet apart from Edwin's description of 'a rare nice gal of about thirty.' When we entered the restaurant, there was no one there to resemble the description in any way, in spite of the fact that I did not know whether to expect someone short, fat, tall or thin.

We sat down at a table and ordered our lunch. Ten to twenty minutes passed, when I received a violent thump under the table from my pal, and he whispered, "Here she comes."

I looked up cornerwise, hoping I should not be noticed looking. Two women had entered with a little boy of about four years old. The older lady looked bright and under sixty and was short. The younger was tall, slim but not thin - her well-fitting suit of a fine material did not straighten out her curves. On the contrary, it revealed them. It was impossible to take in everything at a glance, but I knew her face was interesting and I wanted to look longer. Her hair was soft, dark brown and heavy; she walked with smooth decision and took a seat. There was an air of quietness about her.

The little party of three were not far from Edwin and I, but for all that we might have been either side of the English Channel. In unconscious consciousness they pursued their meal with bitty conversation. We finished our meal, leant back and importantly offered each other cigarettes. Being aware that the older woman had lit a cigarette meant that the two women and little boy had come to the end of their appetites.

As my friend was the instigator of what was in most of our minds, it was up to him to bring it out, and this he could be relied upon to do. So he half turned and, accompanied by the scrapes and squeaks of the chair, he told the other little party what the weather was like. They did not divulge that they already knew, but pretended to give the matter serious thought then fully agreed.

In politeness we had now turned our backs away from each other. No introductions could follow as neither party knew the other!

Fortunately each camp possessed a good conversationalist, and anyone gifted in this art knows the key to another's life is to ask questions. "And have you two gentlemen been to the cattle market? I assume you are farmers," said the senior lady.

This of course opened our hearts and mouths and made a sound excuse to use our eyes too. While the conversation proceeded, I conjectured, no doubt we all did. The older woman was perhaps the tall young lady's mother. They were not at all alike, so maybe she was her mother-in-law. The little chappie was distinctly like the young lady, and of the same strain there was no doubt.

Having exposed a certain amount of our manner of living, it was now Edwin's turn to look beneath the surface of the other party. "I gather," my pal began, "that judging by your shopping bags and parcels you have had a busy morning." We then heard a bit about the homely domestic side of life. "It would give us pleasure to take you home," he offered. "It is very kind of you, but we live twenty miles beyond Norwich on the north-east coast of Norfolk. It's rather a long way for you." We both chorused that the distance was nothing. "Thank you so much," the spokeswoman accepted. "My name is Clements - Mrs. Clements; this is my daughter Josephine, and grandson Christopher. Josephine is in the civil service at the City Hall and lodges here at Norwich during the week. Christopher is the son of my other daughter who is moving house today. Christopher has two brothers, Graham and Philip."

We met an hour or two later and loaded up my old Jaguar before heading for the unknown shores of Norfolk beyond the Broads. This is where the marsh and water fowls live, the land of the herons locally known as harnsers.

Josephine sat by my side in the front seat. We all talked to each other about things in general and our own lives in particular. Mrs. Clements' husband had died suddenly nearly a year back. He had been farming Manor Farm, Eccles on Sea with an uncle who was eighty. Unfortunately the younger man died first, and the old uncle had disposed of the farm away from the family.

Leaving young Christopher with his mother at Stalham, we drove on to the home of Mrs. Clements and definitely seemed very much at ease with each other. This was understandable as we were all country folk with interests in farming, although Josephine was descended from three generations of school-masters and mistresses, on her mother's side.

We were accepted into the household as part of the family, as indeed I felt I was. We were having tea from the same table. Five hours before, we had been having lunch at separate tables, and had never spoken to one another. Three hours before that, I had been on my farm in Mid Suffolk sixty miles away, unaware these people even existed apart from the information about 'a rare nice gal in Norwich of about thirty.'

I knew this cattle-dealer and grazier was master of his job, but did not put much faith in his judgement as a matrimonial agent. To my surprise, his skill in this field proved equal to his selection of a winner in the cattle meadows. At least that was the conclusion I arrived at by my first impression of Josephine.

When I had waited in the restaurant to view Edwin's opinion of 'a rare nice gal', I must confess the type I expected to encounter was a giggly, fluffy blonde trying to follow youthful fashion, and looking for free drinks.

Josephine

Contrary to expectations, I was struck by what I saw. A face of peaceful serenity, eyes with a depth of expression, a direct gaze that indicated unobtrusive determination. One could clearly see by her attitude that if spoken to, she was too good-mannered to ignore any attempt of friendship be it from duke or dustman.

The presence of Miss Clements at 'The Scotch Restaurant" in Norwich at one o'clock on October 7th 1950, had no connection at all with her meeting my friend Edwin, or of him telling her he was bringing a prosperous bachelor farmer of forty along, as a potential partner.

Josephine was at this particular place at this precise time purely for the purpose of partaking of the repast. It was her weekly habit to meet her mother here after leaving work at the City Hall. It was the routine, and if a Persian prince or Polish peasant should have chosen to eat at the same place, it called for no change of plan.

The Scotch Tea Rooms
18 WHITE LION STREET
NORWICH
Between Orford Place and Back of the Inns

Daintily served Luncheons and Teas

Home-made Cakes

Telephone 21907

I have heard vague quotations of women being deceitful above all things. This is not generally correct. The truth is, women are not usually what they appear to be, and for men to understand the opposite sex perfectly, he must accept the fact they are not meant to be understood. If they were, there would be nothing left to look for. This does not make the female deceitful, but rather emphasises the inflexibility of the man's mind.

So be not deceived by the demureness of Josephine. Behind that direct gaze was an unexhausted world of imagination, and her desire for adventure was not quenched by the necessary habits of life. It might appear that both Josephine and I were not very particular to what company we kept, or who we met, if we were willing to meet strangers under such circumstances. I could have argued, "I don't want to meet a strange woman. She might be a bad lot." She might have taken the view, "I've no wish to meet an unknown farmer. If he is a bachelor at forty he's probably not worth having or he would be married, or on the other hand he might be a gay old boy and not sincere."

However, Miss Clements and myself put no obstacle in the way to avoid the meeting, taking the view, "Oh well, you never know what people are like until you meet them." In this spirit we met. She showed no surprise to learn that instead of being a prosperous bachelor farmer of forty, I was a working farmer of forty-six and a widower. I was definitely surprised to find this 'rare nice gal of thirty' appeared very much better than portrayed, so therefore after seeing her I was not so astonished to learn her age was twenty-five years and two weeks.

My friend Edwin, in consideration had tried to bring our ages closer, but the fact remained the gap was wide, twenty-one years and seven months.

It was a very pleasant evening indeed and the time passed quickly in the company of mother, daughter and son Ted, aged twenty, who had just completed his National Service in the Royal Air Force.

Leaving Eccles On Sea after midnight, and not being sure of the route to Norwich, we completed the sixty miles home by two o'clock the next morning. Before leaving, we made it plain we should be having lunch at the same place the following Saturday and would feel honoured to take the ladies home again. They did not turn the offer down and we all turned up at the Scotch Restaurant to repeat the procedure.

We did it a third time. I came, I saw, and liked what I saw. Could I conquer? I could try. I would not give much for my chances! Josephine Yvonne created an atmosphere of quiet peacefulness; her voice was rich and soothing. Her mother, having been a school teacher had taught her children to be well-mannered, and to speak well. Should they put on any 'airs and graces' she had quickly subdued them, and they were trained to be themselves.

At the age of nineteen, Josephine had joined the Women's Royal Naval Service. I would love to have seen her features, figure and five foot nine and three-quarter inches adorned in the uniform I had admired so much eight years previously, as I sat and gazed in appreciation as the girls had paraded through Princes Street Gardens in Edinburgh.

How I would have loved to have seen Josephine on parade in Reading during her naval career. She, with her company had used every device to achieve perfection when her idol Admiral Lord Mountbatten had been coming to inspect their ship.

At the last minute the girls were told that the Admiral was unable to attend, and a substitute, a high-ranking Army man, would be taking his place. It was a disappointment Josephine never forgot. But it never took away from her the satisfaction of the experience whilst serving with the WRNS which gave her the chance of seeing the greater part of the British Isles. Now, at the time of our meeting, she was in the Civil Service at the City Hall, Norwich in the Motor Tax department.

The second meeting was an interesting and happy continuation of the first. The third meeting indicated I was keenly interested and eager to cultivate the friendship, and I was more than grateful to be welcomed within the family. My friend Edwin felt he had fulfilled his mission, so after arriving home on three successive Sunday mornings at two o'clock, he told me he was getting tired of these jaunts saying, "I've done my bit. Now you must manage this little job on your own."

I carried on with the 'little job' and increased the meetings with a regular mid-week visit to Norwich. I was, of course, keenly interested in my newly-found young girlfriend. She was different from the general run of young people, or people of any age in fact. She did nothing for competition. The things she did, she wanted to. Nothing would induce her to engage in any activity or social gathering because, 'it is the thing to do my dear.' In her mind, those who attached any importance to the word 'status' were as empty and meaningless as the word itself.

One of her interests was the stage: she would rather be on it than be a mere spectator. As a contrast, Josephine was a member of a cycling club, not as a status symbol, but for the love of the countryside. As I knew her better, I learned she preferred the company of older men. The proof of this was her acceptance of my companionship.

I was rather slow in realising the depth of sincerity in one so young as Josephine. It was the true worth of humanity she valued, not the value of possessions. She appreciated the value of material things as a necessary means for comfort and contentment, but surplus possessions were to her more of a liability than an asset. "Look around," my first wife had advised. "Meet as many women as possible of various types. You could even consider someone as young as twenty-five."

I had now looked around and met one twenty-five years old. "Don't think she must be of the strict Baptist faith," Eve had said. Josephine was Church of England. One does not go around looking for someone to match a pattern, or carry a mould about, thinking that when someone fits into, she is the one. You meet a person casually, and she grows on you. Her appearance attracts you; you can see her personality in her manner and her character in her features. The subjects of her conversations are in keeping with your own ideas. You find her presence soothing and would like to spend the rest of your life with her.

This is the way I felt towards Josephine after knowing her for only a few weeks. When two people are together frequently and for three or four hours at a time, many details of their lives are revealed. At the same time I met this girl from Eccles on Sea, she was in the early stages of a broken engagement, having decided that a broken engagement was better than a lifetime of unhappiness. By bits and pieces, and not by any boasting on Josephine's part, I gathered she'd had six proposals of marriage before I came on the scene.

When our acquaintance had been going on for about eight weeks, I had no doubt

Josephine & Alf

about making mine the seventh. Should I get turned down I would not count the disappointment a disgrace. Mrs. Clements informed me her daughter was fussy about cleanliness. She was methodical in all things, and one of her greatest pleasures at the weekends was to wash her 'smalls' and 'bigs' too! Strangely enough this led to my proposal. Actually I never made a proposal of marriage, or asked for her hand in a gallant way, but made a subtle offer that could easily have been ignored without hurt, or it could be accepted in the spirit in which it was intended.

When Mrs Clements disclosed the joy experienced in laundering garments, Josephine swept away the toil of the operation by saying, "I just love to stand and watch them blow on the line." This was my opportunity. "How would you like to see YOUR linen blowing on MY line?" I offered.

I was staggered to learn that Jo was quite willing to mix her linen with mine in the wash and hang them all on the line at Dagwood Farm, Elmswell, Suffolk. On Christmas Eve, exactly eleven weeks from our first meeting, we clinched the deal with an engagement ring.

The prophecy of the Blackpool clairvoyant seemed about to be fulfilled. She had said, "You will meet a young lady in later September or early October, who will be twenty-five years old. You will marry her a short time after that. The predominating letter in her name will be M." If we accept the M as being the strongest sounding letter in Clements, the forecast was correct in every detail.

We married in April 1951. My bride and I toured my beloved Scotland as a honeymoon, to John O'Groats and home via Edinburgh. I was not alone this time. With my ex-WRNS wife, we walked together where the wartime Wrens used to stroll.

For two weeks the old S S Jaguar almost felt like our home. She gallantly brought us down the drive to Dagwood Farm, having taken us two thousand miles, and blown over one hundred gallons of petrol through her exhaust pipe.

Needless to add, the next day OUR linen was blowing on OUR line!

Finale

Alf Burrows wrote this story in 1968, less than a year before he died. Several copies of the manuscript have been circulated around the family since that time. After marrying Josephine, Alf continued to farm at Elmswell, taking on more land and buying another farm, Botany Bay Farm. In later years, Alf & Josephine moved further up the road to a house known as The Pastures. Members from all sides of the family were regular visitors. This picture shows Alf with two of Josephine's nephews. Everyone seems to have remembered him with great fondness.

Josephine in 1990

Alf died from a heart attack on 2nd March 1969, whilst cutting a hedge. His grave can be found in the little graveyard at Harleston. Josephine, who survived him by 25 years is buried with him.

Those of the Burrows family whose last resting place was also there include Alf's parents, Lucky and Alice; also sisters Fanny, Alice and Kate, and brother Jim.

Mary, the only sister to die young, has a grave in Wickham Skeith churchyard.

A stone marks the grave of Sam Burrows, his wife Lily and their daughter Kathleen in Bedingfield churchyard. Will, his wife Doreen and their daughter Dorothy have a stone to mark their passing in Walsham-le-Willows graveyard.

Jack died in the 1970s in British Columbia, but we have no further details. The eldest of Alf's brothers, Lucky Jnr. is buried at Bentley along with his wife Lily, though there is no stone to mark their grave.

Their grandson, the last to bear the Lucky Burrows name, is contentedly retired at Bentley. This is, therefore, the end of the story of 'Lucky is the name.'